PRESENTED TO:

Elise Claire Duffy

FROM:

Self

DATE:

_2/1/22_

ENDORSEMENTS

Do you hunger to see how today's moves of Holy Spirit are truly built on the past moves of God? Do you desire to take a peek into the future and see into part of God's vast plan for mankind and the Bride of Christ? Are you tired of negative eschatology based out of fear rather than based out of faith in the completed work of the cross? Then look no further! Dr. Bill Hamon has done us all a great favor. He has delivered to all those seekers of truth and revelation a powerful treatise on God's purposes with the Bride of Christ. This book is practical and relatable. This book is historical and revelatory. This book could save the Church from veering from one ditch to the next. God's hand is upon Bishop Hamon to bring us his most complete work to date. It is an honor to commend to you this dynamic compilation that took 67 years of ministry experience to bring about! I thank the Lord for Bill Hamon. I thank the Lord he is casting a shadow of the Lord Jesus Christ for us all to be impacted by. You will love *The Final Reformation & Great Awakening*!

JAMES W. GOLL
Encounters Network
Author of *Prayer Storm, Compassion Acts, The Seer, The Lost Art of Intercession, The Coming Prophetic Revolution, Praying for Israel's Destiny, The Prophetic Intercessor*, and many more

There are few authorities in the prophetic ministry who could offer such a global, historical, and balanced perspective of the times and seasons of God and His dealings with the Church and mankind.

The Final Reformation & Great Awakening will become a classic. Bill, you did it again—it's a masterpiece.

DR. MYLES E. MUNROE (1st Edition)
BFM International Nassau, Bahamas
Building a Kingdom Community Through Kingdom Keys

Genesis 28:3 (NIV): *"May God Almighty bless you and make you fruitful and increase your numbers until you become a community."*

Another outstanding book by Bishop Hamon to help us understand God's present and coming plans for the Church. In the many years that I have been equipping leaders and churches, I have found that there is one clear factor that divides the successful from those who are not. Those who understand God's plan to restore the Church are able to successfully and positively move ahead. Those who do not comprehend this usually end up protecting status quo and eventually stagnate. The progressive revelation from this book provides powerful impetus for moving ahead.

RONALD W. SAWKA D. MIN.
Director, Christian International Asia
Japan, Korea, Malaysia, Taiwan, Indonesia, Russia, Burma

There are certain books that define an age in the Church. Few people are capable of cognitively assembling the information that is necessary to define an age. Dr. Bill Hamon is one of those who not only understands the Church historically, but sees prophetically into the future of how God's assembled saints will affect the earth. There has never been a better book written that takes you into the capsule of history to understand the last two reformation seasons of the Church, and then places you in a capsule to understand the future of the Church. *The Final Reformation & Great Awakening* shows you the past reformations and a new era of reformation to come. This book will be the guiding textbook on how to take dominion in the future. This is a must read for anyone who wants to understand the DNA of the Lord Jesus Christ that is flowing through their blood and how He gathers us to rule in the season to come.

Chuck D. Pierce
President, Global Spheres Inc.
President, Glory of Zion International
Harvest Watchman, Global Harvest Ministries

Dr. Hamon has received profound revelation from God's throne regarding the events that are unfolding in the end times. You will discover, as I did, that this book is a captivating read, answering many complicated questions pertaining to previous moves of God and the future of the Church! He removes critical questions about how church history interacts with us today and brings to life God's intentions for His Body!

I not only believe that this is important information for every believer to read, it's Kingdom illumination designed to release the saints in their end-time calling to align with the Kingdom! I enthusiastically and wholeheartedly recommend this book to everyone who desires transformation!

Bishop, you're a gift to the Body of Christ and once again you've pioneered a fresh move of God that will lead us into *The Final Reformation & Great Awakening!*

Vance D. Russell
Apostle of Arise Ministries International
Founder of Kingdom Prayer Network
Author of *Victory at the Gates*

I always take notice when Bill Hamon prophesies or writes a book on God's prophetic times and purpose. Bill's 67 years of ministry and writing on the restoration and destiny of the Church, along with his prophet anointing, qualifies him to be an authority on revealing the time of God's The Final Reformation & Great Awakening!

DR. ORAL ROBERTS (1st Edition)
Oral Roberts University

Apostle Bill Hamon makes a passionate and extensive presentation about the times and seasons of God's complete plan for humanity. Personally, I consider this book to be a must for all the ecclesiastic leaders and Christians of this century who wish to be a part of the third and last great worldwide Church Reformation.

APOSTLE GUILLERMO MALDONADO
El Rey Jesus

Finally, a book that offers more than a negative spiraling down of social and moral conditions! Dr. Bill Hamon gives us a view from 67 years of apostolic wisdom and prophetic ministry, using God's perspective and calendar. This book has potential to bring revelation, timing, and mobilization to the Body of Christ. This is a must read for everyone.

DR. SHARON STONE
Christian International Europe

This all-encompassing overview by Bishop Bill Hamon is the result of a lifetime of searching the heart and mind of God concerning the purposes for His creation and, more specifically, for His Church. Bishop is a highly respected pioneer on the matter who, in addition to more than 67 years of ministry, has the anointing to speak to our generation and call the Church into its destiny as we enter what he refers to as the Third and Final Reformation. May we truly hear that which the Spirit is saying through His servant!

ED SILVOSO
Author of Transformation and Anointed for Business
Founder and president of Harvest Evangelism
and International Transformation Network

It is rare that a vessel is chosen to pioneer more than one advance in the Body of Christ, but Bishop Bill Hamon is that rare exception. I listen closely whenever he speaks because he combines a mastery of church history and a prophetic perception of where we are going. This gives him a commanding height with which to proclaim the things that have been and are about to be. Read this as if it were history about to happen!

LANCE WALLNAU
Director, Lance Learning Group

This is a groundbreaking book. Bishop Bill Hamon has the unique, God-given ability as a prophet to the Church to write what God is saying to the Church that literally shifts our thinking into new seasons. His book *The Day of the Saints* was used by God to give us a biblical understanding where we are today in the purposes of the Lord. *The Final Reformation & Great Awakening* thrusts us into the prophetic destiny of our generation in a way no other book has achieved to date.

DR. CINDY JACOBS
Generals International

Bishop Bill Hamon has invested the last seventy years of his life understanding God's purpose for His Church—how it was birthed, its times of falling away, its restoration and glorious culmination of the ages as it brings God's Kingdom to earth. There is no one who has a better grasp on the significance of church history and how it points to the future fulfillment of every prophetic purpose for mankind. This book presents a masterful understanding of the times and seasons of God and how we can partner with Him to see the Third and Final Church Reformation and the last Great Awakening sweep the earth. This masterpiece will mobilize a passionate Church to bring Kingdom transformation everywhere we go.

JANE HAMON
Co-Apostle of Vision Church @ Christian International
Author of *Dreams and Visions, The Cyrus Decree, The Deborah Company, Discernment* and *Declarations for Breakthrough*

The Final

REFORMATION
&GREAT
AWAKENING

DESTINY IMAGE BOOKS BY BILL HAMON

The Eternal Church

Who Am I and Why Am I Here?

The Day of the Saints

Prophets, Pitfalls, and Principles

Prophets and the Prophetic Movement

Prophets and Personal Prophecy

Apostles, Prophets, and the Coming Moves of God

Seventy Reasons for Speaking in Tongues

Prophets and Personal Prophecy (Spanish)

The Final

REFORMATION
& GREAT
AWAKENING

*Take Your Place in Fulfilling the
End-Times Prophecies that Will Usher
in Jesus' Second Coming*

DR. BILL HAMON

DESTINY IMAGE® PUBLISHERS, INC.

P.O. Box 310, Shippensburg, PA 17257-0310

"Promoting Inspired Lives."

This book and all other Destiny Image and Destiny Image Fiction books are available at Christian bookstores and distributors worldwide.

Cover design by Eileen Rockwell
Interior design by Terry Clifton

For more information on foreign distributors, call 717-532-3040.

Reach us on the Internet: www.destinyimage.com.

Previously published as *Prophetic Scriptures Yet to be Fulfilled*, Destiny Image, 2010

ISBN 13 TP: 978-0-7684-5183-2

ISBN 13 eBook: 978-0-7684-5184-9

ISBN 13 HC: 978-0-7684-5186-3

ISBN 13 LP: 978-0-7684-5185-6

For Worldwide Distribution, Printed in the U.S.A.

1 2 3 4 5 6 7 8 / 25 24 23 22 21

The CHURCH is NOW in
The Third and Final Reformation
& The Beginning of the Great Awakening
DR. BILL HAMON

DEDICATION

This book is dedicated to my children, grandchildren, and great-grandchildren and all those who are part of the generation that will fulfill God's purpose for the Third and Final Church Reformation. I dedicate this to my wife and Christian International leadership who have so efficiently kept the worldwide ministry of CI fulfilling its ministry and destiny while I have taken the time off to write this important revelation for the Body of Christ. The Third Reformation is very important and exciting to Christ Jesus, for it will bring about the restoration of all things that have been prophesied by the prophets and apostles and that must be fulfilled before Jesus can be eternally joined to His newly immortalized Bride and take their mutual dominion over new earth.

CONTENTS

BOOKS OF THE BIBLE

Abbreviations Used in This Book

OLD TESTAMENT	
Genesis, *Gen.*	Ecclesiastes, *Eccles.*
Exodus, *Exod.*	Song of Solomon, *Song of Sol.*
Leviticus, *Lev.*	Isaiah, *Isa.*
Numbers, *Num.*	Jeremiah, *Jer.*
Deuteronomy, *Deut.*	Lamentations, *Lam.*
Joshua, *Josh.*	Ezekiel, *Ezek.*
Judges, *Judg.*	Daniel, *Dan.*
Ruth, *Ruth*	Hosea, *Hos.*
1 Samuel, *1 Sam.*	Joel, *Joel*
2 Samuel, *2 Sam.*	Amos, *Amos*
1 Kings, *1 Kings*	Obadiah, *Obad.*
2 Kings, *2 Kings*	Jonah, *Jon.*
1 Chronicles, *1 Chron.*	Micah, *Mic.*
2 Chronicles, *2 Chron.*	Nahum, *Nah.*
Ezra, *Ezra*	Habakkuk, *Hab.*
Nehemiah, *Neh.*	Zephaniah, *Zeph.*
Esther, *Esther*	Haggai, *Hag.*
Job, *Job*	Zechariah, *Zech.*

Psalms, *Ps.*	Malachi, *Mal.*
Proverbs, *Prov.*	

NEW TESTAMENT

Matthew, *Matt.*	1 Timothy, *1 Tim.*
Mark, *Mark*	2 Timothy, *2 Tim.*
Luke, *Luke*	Titus, *Titus*
John, *John*	Philemon, *Philem.*
Acts, *Acts*	Hebrews, *Heb.*
Romans, *Rom.*	James, *James*
1 Corinthians, *1 Cor.*	1 Peter, *1 Pet.*
2 Corinthians, *2 Cor.*	2 Peter, *2 Pet.*
Galatians, *Gal.*	1 John, *1 John*
Ephesians, *Eph.*	2 John, *2 John*
Philippians, *Phil.*	3 John, *3 John*
Colossians, *Col.*	Jude, *Jude*
1 Thessalonians, *1 Thess.*	Revelation, *Rev.*
2 Thessalonians, *2 Thess.*	

FOREWORD

God has all things in His hands, including past, present, and future. Those of us who are attempting to serve Him need to be fully aware of all three. Of the numerous books I have personally read, none does a better job than this one of bringing the past, the present, and the future together in a simple and understandable way. No one has to have a college degree to grasp what Bishop Bill Hamon is saying, even though what he says goes far beyond what most ordinary people who have accumulated graduate degrees could produce themselves.

I say this because Bishop Hamon is an unusual type of church historian. He has done his homework, and he thoroughly knows church history, but his interest goes far beyond what I heard one person characterize most history books as being confined to: "dates and dead people." I have not heard this term used before, but I would label *The Final Reformation & Great Awakening* as "prophetic history." This may sound at first like an oxymoron because *prophecy* usually refers to the future while *history* refers to the past. In this case, however, it is not an oxymoron because what we have here is a person with the recognized gift and office of prophet writing past history in such a way that it brings life to the present and to the future as well.

Hamon's decades of painstaking research and of penetrating observation of the movements of God throughout history have awarded him the enviable ability to paint the big picture. He does this with masterful, broad brushstrokes depicting the First Reformation and the Second Reformation of the Church. Then he shows us how the details of where we are now and where we are moving in the future fit into the big picture. This is extremely important if we want to be hands-on participants in the current powerful movement of God rather than ending up as mere spectators. The current movement of God is clearly the Third Reformation, and we are invited to participate in it according to the gifts and the callings that God has given to each one of us. As you read this book, you will discover where you fit!

I feel personally honored to have been invited to write the foreword for this major literary work. Not only will it circulate widely, but I believe it will stay in print for a long time. Only time will tell, but to me it has the feel of a classic. I personally identify with what is written here because I have also gone through many of Bill Hamon's experiences, transitions, and paradigm shifts. Yes, I remember when our escapist eschatology led us to believe that our singular task was to get souls saved before the world collapsed in disaster, the Church was raptured to Heaven, and the antichrist took over.

Now Bishop Hamon and I both believe and teach that our mandate from God is much larger than we had thought. The Gospel of the Kingdom goes beyond saving souls and multiplying churches to a new level that is nothing less than social reformation. Our goal is to see the values of the Kingdom penetrate every aspect of our society here on earth. The Great Commission tells us to make disciples of whole nations, not just of individual men and women, important as saving souls always will be. If such a thing seems strange to you, please move ahead and read the rest of this book about the Third Reformation. I would be surprised if Bill Hamon doesn't convince you that you should also be a reformer!

In the few years that we have left, I want to be shoulder to shoulder with Apostle Bill up there on the front lines. Retirement isn't in the Bible, and it isn't in our thinking. God has ordered us to take back the dominion over His creation that satan stole from Adam and Eve in the Garden. The advance of the Third Reformation will not be led from rocking chairs, but by those who have put on the full armor of God and entered the battle with fire in their eyes and the sword of the Spirit in their hands. Satan will be defeated, and I want to be there when *"the kingdoms of this world have become the kingdoms of our Lord and of His Christ, and He shall reign forever and ever!"* (Rev. 11:15). I know that you want to be there as well, and reading this book will help you find the place where you fit and where you can make the greatest contribution toward the final thrust of the Kingdom of God!

C. PETER WAGNER
Presiding Apostle
International Coalition of Apostles

FOREWORD

Holy Spirit is about to pour out new wine. He wants you and me to be part of the process. Are you ready?

When wineskins are emptied of wine, they dry out and harden. Unless refreshed and softened, they cannot handle the fermentation process of new wine—the pressure and expansion destroys them. That's why Jesus said winemakers don't *"put new wine into old wineskins; otherwise the wineskins burst, and the wine pours out and the wineskins are ruined; but they put new wine into fresh wineskins, and both are preserved"* (Matt. 9:17 New American Standard Bible).

The spiritual correlation is simple: leaders often harden into the shape of Holy Spirit's last movement, making them too inflexible to receive His new outpouring. It's so easy for us to get "set in our ways," comfortable in the methods and ways of past movements. These comfort zones create routines and "boxes," which usually resist change. Hey, "if it ain't broke, don't fix it." Sadly, when Holy Spirit shows up with another outpouring, bringing new revelation and fresh ideas, many leaders are simply too inflexible and comfortable to make the shift—the box often wins.

Then there are the Bill Hamons of the world. This pioneering leader and apostolic father epitomizes the fresh wineskin Jesus spoke of. Bishop, as he is often called, has actually led the Body of Christ through several seasons of restoration and outpouring. Yet, at 87 years of age, he's gearing up for another!

Bishop Bill Hamon is the most Caleb-like person I know. Caleb, the great warrior and compatriot of Joshua, was 85 years old when he told Joshua, *"I am still as strong today as I was on the day Moses sent me; as my strength was then, so my strength is now, for war and for going out and coming in. Now then, give me this hill country about which the Lord spoke on that day, for you heard on that day that Anakim* [giants] *were there, with great fortified cities; perhaps the Lord will be with me, and I will drive them out just as the Lord has spoken"* (Josh. 14:11-12 New American Standard Bible). Bishop is 87 years young, strong, healthy, brilliant, full of fire and vision, flexible and ready to go to war. As was said of Caleb, he simply "has a different spirit" than most (see Num. 14:24). There is no prophetic voice I trust more.

No one, and I mean that literally, is more qualified to write this book than Bill Hamon. The phrase "he's seen it all" is applicable to him—but not only in reference to the past. Yes, after 68 years of ministry, Bishop's experience is incredibly broad; equally as unique, however, is his prophetic ability to see into the future. His book *The Eternal Church*, the content of which spanned yesterday, today, and tomorrow, has brought understanding and perspective to hundreds of thousands. This insightful work will as well.

Not only is Bishop Hamon a modern-day Caleb, he is also a "son of Issachar." First Chronicles 12:32 tells us the sons of Issachar understood the times, with a knowledge of what Israel should do. "Understood" in this passage is the Hebrew word *biyn*, for which we have no English equivalent. The word means both *wisdom*, understanding gained over time, and *revelation*, spontaneous knowledge or information given by Holy Spirit:

- Revelation brings *timing*; wisdom produces *coordination and planning*.
- Revelation reveals *what*; wisdom knows *how*.
- Revelation *stirs up*; wisdom *stabilizes*.
- Revelation sees the new; wisdom marries it to the old.

We could go on, but it isn't necessary. Clearly, both elements of the Issachar gifting are essential. And Bishop Bill Hamon skillfully marries the two as he writes of the coming awakening and reformation.

Don't get stuck in yesterday. Navigate the transitions, span the seasons and outpourings of Holy Spirit. New wine is about to flow and Holy Spirit wants you to be a vessel He can fill and be poured out from. *The Final Reformation and Great Awakening* will help you accomplish this.

Do yourself a favor—read this book.

DUTCH SHEETS
Author and speaker

INTRODUCTION

THE FINAL REFORMATION
& GREAT AWAKENING

Over the past several decades, all over the world, God has been preparing His people for the greatest move of God and the most powerful outpouring of the Holy Spirit the earth has ever seen. We are going to see more souls saved, more miracles manifested, more saints activated to demonstrate Kingdom power and a mature Church arise that has the capacity to impact nations more than any other time in history. Many apostles, prophets, and even theologians agree that we have entered a new era in Christiandom, a new day of power, which I have termed the **Third and Final Reformation**, when all remaining end-time prophecies are fulfilled and God's eternal purposes are accomplished. Simultaneously, we are also on the verge of a worldwide Great Awakening which will sweep the globe, releasing the tangible presence and power of God and usher in the last days harvest. As the final Reformation and this last Great Awakening converge, the stage will be set and God's purposes will be finalized for the return of our King, Jesus.

One of the main purposes of this book is to bring understanding of the times and purposes of God so that all who read may participate and receive the overcomers' reward of ruling and reigning with Christ. For the past 60 years of my 68 years of ministry, my special revelation and anointing has been the restoration of the Church (Acts 3:21). I began teaching on the restoration of the Church in 1959. I wrote *The Eternal Church* in 1981.[1] It covers the Church in its origination, deterioration, restoration, and destination. It is more than a church history book. In the words of my friend, C. Peter Wagner, who did the foreword for the original printing of this book, it is "prophetic history...writing past history in such a way that it brings life to the present and to the future as well."

In *The Eternal Church* I discuss God's desire and purpose for the Church. I cover the origination of the Church, which in this book we will refer to as the First Church Reformation. Primarily, this first reformation constituted the *formation* of the Church; in terms of *reformation,* it was the time when God changed the whole criteria for determining who God's chosen people on planet Earth were. The Church is not a second choice after Israel rejected their Messiah. The Church was conceived in the mind of God from eternity past. It was planned and ordained to be in Christ from the foundation of the world (Eph. 1:4). The Church was in the mind of God when He planned the human race and His Son to become one of that race (1 Pet. 1:20). Jesus loved and wanted the Church so much that He became a mortal human in order to die on the cross and purchase His Church with His own lifeblood (Eph. 5:25; Acts 20:28). Jesus authorized the Church by His resurrection from the dead and then birthed it into the world by His Holy Spirit (Rom. 1:4; Acts 2:4). Jesus has a purpose for His Church to accomplish on earth during its mortality and an eternal purpose to accomplish after the Church is resurrected-translated into immortality (Eph. 3:10,20). The full understanding of God's purpose for the Church was revealed in the First Church Reformation period.

In *The Eternal Church* I then dedicated 170 pages to cover all the restoration movements during the period of the **Second Reformation of the Church** (1517–2007). A restoration movement is when God decrees for the Holy Spirit to bring revelation to some apostles and prophets of what God wants restored back into the Church from what was lost during the 1000-year ark Age of the Church. There have been nine major restoration movements and three minor ones during the Second Reformation. Some of these included the restoration of the truths of being saved by grace through faith, baptism through water immersion, holiness, divine healing and baptism of the Holy Spirit and speaking in tongues. Acts 3:21 and Ephesians 4:11-16 declares that all Christian truths and ministries must be restored and operating, including the Church reaching maturity before Jesus returns.

It was during this period of the Second Reformation that we find several spiritual awakenings, two known specifically as the **First and Second Great Awakenings**. These were more than local church revivals in which souls were saved, but were instead, sovereign moves of God which awakened the Church to its divine purpose to change a region or a nation. Men such as Jonathan Edwards, George Whitfield, John and Charles Wesley, Charles Finney and Jeremiah Lamphier spearheaded these awakenings which were marked by conviction of sin and repentance, fervent prayer, tremendous spiritual hunger and passion for God that resulted in millions of souls coming into the kingdom. But these awakenings didn't stop at the church doors but were also instrumental in bringing societal change, confronting injustice such as with the treatment of native Americans and the slave community. It was from these awakenings that the Abolitionist Movement arose which eventually saw the end to slavery. These awakenings also became the catalyst for the great missionary movement, sending the Gospel around the world. The Great Awakenings were an essential part of the Second Reformation, taking a restored truth, adding the flame of passion which then released the fire of cultural transformation throughout the land.

This book will introduce you to the **Third and Final Reformation** which began in 2008. God planned three reformations to accomplish His purposes for the Church to fulfill during its time of mortality here on earth. The First Reformation accomplished the birthing of the Church, establishing it in proper doctrine and practice, demonstrating these Kingdom truths and then taking it into all the world. Then, as Jesus and some of the apostles predicted, the Church went into a great falling away from the truths and ministries that were in the first centuries of the New Testament Church. The Second Reformation was to accomplish the restoration of all those truths and ministries back into the Church to be fully experienced and practiced.

This Third and Final Reformation is to accomplish the fulfillment of all end-time prophecies that must be fulfilled before Jesus can return. When ministers talk or write about the Third Day, the Great Awakening, and other names regarding what is to come, they are talking about what is scheduled to happen during the Third and Final Reformation. The Third Reformation saints must take all the restored truths and ministries and demonstrate the Kingdom of God to every nation with signs, wonders, and miracles to give them witness that Jehovah Jesus is the only true God and Savior for mankind and thereby reap the great harvest. The end purpose for the Third Reformation is to fulfill and establish God's original and eternal purpose for mankind and planet Earth, which will be finalized by the return of Jesus Christ.

During this Third Reformation period God will once again add the spark of passion of a last-days Third Great Awakening. It will be the beginning of God's decree in Numbers 14:21 and Habakkuk 2:14 that the knowledge of the glory of the Lord shall fill the earth as the waters cover the sea. During the pandemic of 2020, I was on Zoom with a total of about 150 prophets from around the world over a period of months. We were all sensing and witnessing the same thing, that we are on the verge of the greatest move of God ever recorded in the history of the Church. Every saint who is ready and willing shall be enabled to demonstrate the glory of the Lord. The Great Awakening will release a Holy Spirit invasion within certain cities, regions, and nations, bringing godly conviction to individuals and the reverential fear of God over the area. It will be a time when we see the values of the Kingdom of God penetrate every aspect of society in the earth bringing major cultural transformation. It will cause every nation by their response to become either a goat or sheep nation. This makes the preparation for when Jesus returns to *"sit on the throne of His glory"* and separate the sheep nations to His right hand and the goat nations to His left (Matthew 25:31-34,41,46). The Who, when, where and how all this will be revealed and accomplished is found in the later chapters of this book. This time will be greater than anything I have ever read about or experienced in my 68 years of ministry.

This book will deal with God's eternal purpose for all of God's creation—natural and spiritual, in Heaven and on earth (Eph. 3:11). It will reveal the part the Church plays in the redemption of all things. The Third Reformation is to bring about the restoration, completion, and fulfillment of all mortal things until man transitions into the immortal age (Acts 3:21). The saints in every walk of life will become Kingdom of God demonstrators and enforcers (John 14:12; Matt. 10:7-8). They will be transformed into Christ's maturity and ministry enabling them to bring transformation to cities, states, and nations. The Church, the saints of the Most High God, will then rule and reign with Christ forever in God's new heavens and new earth (Rev. 5:10). This book will reveal where the Church is right now in its progressive purpose, what it requires to be a part of the Third Reformation of the Church, and the rewards for those who overcome and fulfill all things with Christ Jesus (2 Cor. 3:18; Rom. 8:18).

I may be 86 years old at the publishing of this book, but I believe the greatest days of the Church are still ahead. I have a fire in my eyes, a passion in my heart, and a sword in my hand as we enter this last-days battle to see *"the kingdoms of this world have become the kingdoms of our Lord and of His Christ, and He shall reign forever and ever"* (Rev. 11:15). I hope you will join me in advancing God's reformation purposes in the most exciting time the earth has ever seen.

NOTE

1. Bill Hamon, *The Eternal Church* (Santa Rosa Beach, FL: Christian International, 1981).

GOD'S TIMES AND PURPOSES

The purpose of this book is to reveal to the church world God's times and seasons for our present time (1 Thess. 5:1-6; Eph. 5:16-17). The major revelation and presentation will be the fact that the Third Reformation of the Church was launched in 2008 (Eph. 3:3-5). We will reveal God's third major purpose for Christ's Church. Jesus purchased the Church for Himself (Acts 20:28; 2 Cor. 5:17), not only to be His corporate Body, but to be like a bride who becomes a co-laborer and one with the man she marries. Jesus has a destiny and ministry yet to fulfill. He brought forth His Church to be one with Him in all that He shall ever be and do both now and throughout eternity.

God's third purpose for Christ and His Church will be fulfilled in the Third Church Reformation. The Third Reformation has much to fulfill and accomplish, just as the First and Second Reformations fulfilled their purpose. This book will reveal what the

First and Second Reformations fulfilled in God's purpose and what must yet be fulfilled in the Third Church Reformation.

GOD'S TIMING AND PURPOSE DETERMINE HAPPENINGS

Things happening and being fulfilled on earth are mainly the result of God's timing and purpose. For hundreds of years Jews looked for their Messiah to appear. Many Jewish women hoped they would be the mother of the man-child who would be the promised Messiah.

Through the centuries, devout priests who knew the Scriptures concerning a coming Messiah no doubt fasted and prayed earnestly for Christ to appear in their time. They especially prayed this way when they were being oppressed. They cried out for their great deliverer to come and bring deliverance from their enemies and restoration of their land. God gave them kings like David, Hezekiah, and Josiah who brought reformation and prosperity to the nation. But all their praying, fasting, pleading, and even prophesying about a Messiah coming did not make it happen in their day.

GOD'S FULLNESS OF THE TIMES

Nothing could motivate God to send the Messiah until everything was in divine order and the time was right: *"But when the fullness of the time had come, God sent forth His Son, born of a woman, born under the law"*—Christ, the Messiah (Gal. 4:4). Jesus could not descend to earth until the fullness of the times had come, and He could not ascend back to Heaven until He had fulfilled all the Messianic prophecies (Acts 3:18). It had been prophesied that the Messiah would be in the grave three days, and when that time was fulfilled, Jesus arose and ascended back to Heaven. Jesus is now seated at the right hand of the Father in Heaven (Eph. 1:20), but He cannot come back to earth until the *times* of the restoration of the Church are fulfilled and all enemies are made His footstool (Acts 3:21; Heb. 1:13). Eternal God established earth to have day and night, months, years, times, and seasons. God made it that way so that He could have certain times and seasons for His predestined purposes to be accomplished on earth.

The Scriptures declare that there is a *season* and a *time* for everything that happens on earth: a time to be born, a time to die, a season to plant and a season to harvest, a time to weep and a time to laugh, a time of war and a time of peace, and more (Eccles. 3:1-17).

Even God's purposes are brought forth at special times and seasons, *"for there is a time for every purpose and for every work. ...And a wise man's heart discerns both time and judgment, because for every matter there is a time and judgment"* (Eccles. 3:17; 8:5-6).

God gave Israel certain days to keep holy such as the Sabbath. He set times for Israel to celebrate certain feasts such as Passover and Pentecost. However, when reference is made to the *"fullness of the time"* it is not speaking of a certain day, month, and year (Gal. 4:4). It speaks of all things coming together, of reaching maturity or fullness, of certain conditions being established and everything put in order that is needed for that event to properly take place. The time and conditions must be rightly aligned so that God's purpose for the event can be properly implemented and fully accomplished.

FULLNESS OF THE TIMES AND PURPOSES IN CHRIST

Apostle Paul revealed that God the Father made known to him the mystery of His will, according to His good pleasure that He *purposed* in Himself, that in the dispensation of the *fullness of the time* He might gather together in one all things in Christ, both those who are in Heaven and those who are on earth. God has predestined that when the *fullness of the time* has reached maturity and fulfillment, then all things that have been restored and properly aligned with God in Heaven and on earth shall be unified and consummated in Christ Jesus (Eph. 1:10; Acts 3:21).

JESUS' EXPLANATION OF FULLNESS OF TIME

In Mark 1:15, Jesus declared that the *time* is *fulfilled* and the Kingdom of God is at hand. Jesus explained that God's timing is like the process of seed planting and harvest time. The seed sprouts and begins its progressive growth to maturity, and then when that *time* arrives, the crop is immediately harvested: "When the time comes that the grain has ripened, the farmer begins harvesting because the time for harvest has come" (Mark 4:29, paraphrase).

I was raised on a farm where we grew cotton, peanuts, and corn. When we planted corn with the purpose of reaping a harvest, we did not set a certain day of the month that we would harvest. It was dependent upon progressive growth and maturing of the ears of corn on the corn stalks. Jesus is saying that His second coming is not an arbitrary date that has been set from the beginning, but it is based on progressive growth until everything reaches full maturity, restoration, and fulfillment.

TIME OF CHRIST'S SECOND COMING

Ever since Jesus, Paul, and John spoke and wrote about Christ's second coming, Christians have looked for His coming in their lifetime. This is especially true during times of persecution, wars, catastrophic happenings, and personal suffering. Christians have cried out, "Even so, come, Lord Jesus." Even preachers throughout the centuries have set hundreds of dates when Christ would return.

But Jesus said no one knows the day and the hour of His coming. That's because there is not an arbitrary day and hour set, but it is based on certain things happening first. (The Eternal God, who knows the beginning and end of all things, knows the moment it will finally happen.)

Apostle Peter spoke by revelation and declared that Jesus cannot return from Heaven at just any time. For He is held in Heaven *until* the restoration of all things that has been prophesied by the prophets (Acts 3:21). The *"all things"* include the full restoration of the Church and all that was lost by the fall of lucifer and the sin of Adam. Jesus came to seek and to save *that* which was lost, and God so loved the world that He gave His only begotten Son, not only to redeem mankind but to restore the earth and this world back to their original creation and purpose (1 Tim. 1:15; Rom. 8:19-22; Luke 19:10).

TIMES OF VISITATION

However, there are times and seasons that we need to know. We have now entered one of God's predestined times and seasons. Apostle Paul declared that we are all *"sons of light and sons of the day."* Therefore, we should know the times and the seasons of God (1 Thess. 5:1-6).

Jesus prophetically saw the future destruction of Jerusalem resulting in the temple being leveled and more than a million Jews being killed. He wept over the city and conveyed to the Jews that if they had only known that this was the long-awaited *day* of their Messiah they could have avoided this great destruction. But Jesus prophesied that now it is all going to happen *"because you did not know the time of your visitation"* (Luke 19:41-44). This prophecy of the destruction of Jerusalem and the temple was fulfilled about 40 years later in A.D. 70.[1] There is nothing more important for Christians than to know the day of our visitation. Knowing and properly responding to God's times and purposes can drastically affect our success and destiny.

Prophets Discern the Times

Prophet Daniel was taken with the Jewish captives to Babylon. They took copies of all the writings of Moses and the prophets. He was studying the prophecies of the prophet Jeremiah. He discovered that Jeremiah prophesied that the Jews would be in captivity for 70 years and then would be restored to their homeland (Jer. 25:11; 2 Chron. 36:21-22; Dan. 9:2).

He came to know the timing of God by prophetic revelation of a Scripture (Dan. 9:2). He then studied it out to make sure it was a valid revelation. Daniel knew that God always uses a human instrument to participate in bringing a prophecy into fulfillment. The ninth chapter describes the steps Daniel took to activate the prophecy into fulfillment—confessing the sins of his people, prayer, and supplication with fasting for God to fulfill His Word and start the process of restoring the Jews back to their own nation. One lone prophet of God in a foreign land received a revelation and took appropriate action, which resulted in the restoration of God's people and the rebuilding of their temple of worship.

Daniel received the revelation in the first year of King Darius (538 B.C.), but the prophecy in Isaiah 44:28 and 45:1-13 declared that the king who would make it possible for the Jews to return to their homeland would be named Cyrus. Two years later, Cyrus was made king (536 B.C.) and gave the decree that allowed all Israelis who so desired to return to their homeland and rebuild the city of Jerusalem and the temple of their God. Evidently,

Daniel had to keep praying for two years before he saw the answer to his prayers and the fulfillment of Jeremiah's prophecy.

PROPHETIC TIMING AND TERMINOLOGY

In my trilogy of books on prophets and personal prophecy, there is a chapter on prophetic terminology. From several stories in the Bible, we discover what God means by certain terms relative to time.[2]

When God says *now* this or that is going to happen, He means it is prophetically decreed, but it may not literally happen until many years later. Samuel prophesied to Saul after he failed to obey his personal prophecy that *now* his kingdom would be taken from him and given to another, one who would be faithful to fulfill God's Word the right way at the right time and place: *"But now your kingdom shall not continue. The Lord has sought for Himself a man after His own heart"* (1 Sam. 13:13-14).

It was 38 years later before Saul discontinued being king and another 7 years before David, the man after God's own heart, was made king over all Israel. The prophetic decree was made for *now*, but it was a total of 45 years before it actually happened. In our way of thinking of time, if God said to us *now* you are going to be and do certain things, we would think He meant *immediately, within 24 hours.* Another example is God's use of the word *today.* A few years later, Saul again failed to fulfill every detail of God's instructive prophecy to him: *"So Samuel said to him, 'The Lord has torn the kingdom of Israel from you today, and has given it to a neighbor of yours, who is better than you'"* (1 Sam. 15:28). God said *today* the Kingdom has been taken from you, but it was some 30 years before it literally took place.

PRINCIPLES OF PROPHETIC FULFILLMENT

The prophet Isaiah prophesied in his day, *"For unto us a Child is born, unto us a Son is given; and the government will be upon His shoulder. And His name will be called Wonderful, Counselor, Mighty God, Everlasting Father, Prince of Peace"* (Isa. 9:6). It was some 700 years before the Child Jesus was born on earth and God's Son was given to become redemption for mankind. Although the prophetic decree was made in Heaven and prophesied and written by the prophet Isaiah in his day and time, it was not literally fulfilled until hundreds of years later.

If a prophecy of the prophets or a prophetic statement of Jesus does not give a date or number of years for its fulfillment, then we cannot assume it has to happen in a certain period of time. Though there may be terminology in the prophecy saying *now, shortly come to pass, soon,* or even *this generation,* a limited time period cannot be set in which all the prophecies must come to pass.

For instance, there is a religious Christian group who has established their whole Christian eschatology and belief on such prophetic terms. They declare that because Jesus said that *"This generation will by no means pass away till all these things take place"* (Matt. 24:34) and *"things which must shortly take place"* (Rev. 1:1), every prophetic statement made in Matthew 24, First Corinthians 15, First Thessalonians 4:17-18, and the entirety of the Book of Revelation was fulfilled in the first generation or century of the Church. This includes the first resurrection, the literal second coming of Christ, and the creation of the new heaven and new earth; in fact, everything mentioned in the Book of Revelation has already been fulfilled based on their interpretation and application of certain Scriptures. Those who build a whole doctrinal belief based on prophetic statements do not fully understand the nature of prophecy, prophetic terminology, or the principles of biblical hermeneutics. Mankind tries to use human logic, thinking, and understanding to interpret Scripture, but God declares that His thoughts and way of doing things are not based on man's way of thinking and expressing: *"For My thoughts are not your thoughts, nor are your ways My ways,' says the Lord. 'For as the heavens are higher than the earth, so are My ways higher than your ways, and My thoughts than your thoughts'"* (Isa. 55:8-9).

As an example, take the word *generation*. In man's way of thinking, that would be the generation alive at the time of the statement or a period of time of 40 to 100 years. Let us look at a biblical prophetic application of a *generation*. In Psalm 22, David made some prophetic statements about the suffering, praise, and posterity of the coming Messiah. Then after describing all the Messiah would do and accomplish, he made a prophetic statement: *"A seed shall serve him; it shall be accounted to the Lord for a generation"* (Ps. 22:30 KJV). Apostle Paul declared that the promise to Abraham was to his *seed*, by which he revealed that prophetically God was not just speaking of Isaac but of Christ Jesus. He then stated that we the Church are the promised seed of Abraham by being the seed of Christ by being born of His Holy Spirit (Gal. 3:14-29).

THE CHURCH AGE COUNTED FOR ONE GENERATION

Matthew 1:17 says there are 14 generations from Abraham to David and 14 generations from David to the Babylonian captivity, and so there are 14 listed. Then he states that there are 14 generations from Babylonian captivity until Christ, but when you list all the names, there are only 13 generations. That is not a mistake because the one Body of Christ is the 14th generation. The Church is that seed that the Lord counts as one generation. Apostle Peter declared that the Church is a *chosen generation* and a holy nation (1 Pet. 2:9). The Church is now God's holy nation and chosen generation. These Scriptures show that God counts the Church from its birth until it is immortalized as "one generation" that spans all the time from Christ's crucifixion to His literal second coming. So when Jesus said, "this generation," He could have been speaking from His prophetic thinking of the one generation of the Body of Christ, His Church.

We can see the folly of trying to base a whole belief system on prophetic phrases, especially when that belief system does away with some fundamental truths of the true Christian faith, such as the physical resurrection of Christ, bodily resurrection of the dead, and the literal second coming of Christ Jesus.

God's use of *time* terms is quite different from ours. In the last chapter of the Bible, Jesus said three times, "Behold, I am coming *quickly,*" and that statement was made almost 2,000 years ago. Apostle Peter declared, *"that with the Lord one day is as a thousand years, and a thousand years as one day"* (2 Pet. 3:8). Based on the Lord's thinking, He has only been gone for two days. If Jesus comes back again during the third day, His second coming will be quickly and soon. The prophet Hosea prophesied that *"After two days He will revive us* [full restoration]; *on the third day He will raise us up* [resurrection]" (Hos. 6:2).

Jesus also told John not to seal up the prophecies he had just written in the Book of Revelation, for the *"time is at hand"* for their fulfillment (Rev. 22:10). Jesus started His ministry by saying the *time* is fulfilled, and the Kingdom of God is at hand (Mark 1:15). And He ended it by saying the *time* is at hand for the prophecies in the Book of Revelation to be fulfilled, but He gave no certain time periods in which the prophecies would be fulfilled.

THE TIME OF THE THIRD REFORMATION HAS BEEN PROPHETICALLY DECREED

I am saying in this book that the decree was made in Heaven and echoed by the prophets on earth that in 2008 the Third and Final Church Reformation officially began. This reveals that the *time* is fulfilled, the Church is sufficiently restored, and *now* the Kingdom of God will be demonstrated by the Church until Revelation 11:15 is literally fulfilled. No one knows how many years will transpire before this prophetic decree becomes a historical fact. It is based on how obedient the Church will be in fulfilling the prophetic Scriptures.

WHEN WILL IT HAPPEN?

It should happen in a few decades, but it could take a few centuries. Nevertheless, because of certain biblical types that indicate that the Church Age will be about a 2,000-year period, I believe it could happen in the lifetime of my children, grandchildren, or great-grandchildren. One of my motivations for writing this book is to make known this revelation to my children and all of the ministers for whom I am an apostolic overseer and for all who desire to understand the times and season in which we live. Hopefully, many will receive the revelation and vision to co-labor with Christ in fulfilling His purpose for bringing forth the Third Church Reformation.

DON'T ASSUME FUTURE TIME IS THE SAME AS PAST TIME

We should not say it cannot happen by a certain time, for Jesus can escalate things to happen quickly. As an example, from conception to crucifixion to resurrection, Jesus' time on earth was approximately 34 years, consisting of 1,786 weeks or 12,500 days. However, Jesus fulfilled more Messianic prophecies during the last week of His life than He did during all the rest of His time on earth.

Samson, after his seven locks of hair were restored, destroyed more of Israel's enemies in his last day on earth than he did in all of his previous days. The prophets and apostles declared that God would do a quick work in the last days and cut it short: *"For He will finish the work and cut it short in righteousness, because the Lord will make a short work upon the earth"* (Rom. 9:28; see also Matt. 24:22).

We shouldn't say it has never been done before, for God specializes in doing what has never been done before. *Consider*—the flood destroying the inhabitants of earth, or God splitting the Red Sea and 3 million people walking across on dry land, or tearing down thick walls by the shout of His people, or a man walking on water, and on and on. God has done many things on earth that have never been done before or since.

God is about to do things in and through His Church that have never been done before. The Lord is saying at this time, "Behold, I am doing a *new* thing" (Isa. 43:19, paraphrase). Much of our success and destiny is based on rightly discerning God's *times and purposes*. Every Church member needs to know and be convinced that the Church has entered its Third and Final Reformation. Let us now venture forward and discover God's purpose for the First and Second Reformations, which have been fulfilled by past generations. But our generation has been given the responsibility and privilege to fulfill God's *purpose* for the Third and Final Reformation and the ministry of Christ's Church. If we will hear it, receive it, and believe it, then we will be God's prophetic pioneers who fulfill it.

NOTES

1. Hamon, *The Eternal Church*.
2. Bill Hamon, *Prophets and Personal Prophecy* (Shippensburg, PA: Destiny Image, 1987).

Chapter 2

REVELATION AND PREPARATION

The First Church Reformation is the most important event to take place since the creation of man. It brought about redemption for mankind to be reconciled to God. It brought about the fulfillment of God's major purposes for creating mankind. In my book *Who Am I & Why Am I Here?*[1] revelation of eight reasons why God created mankind is given. Four of the eight reasons were fulfilled during the time of the First Reformation. In the book, many pages and numerous Scriptures are used to fully explain each reason. However, just a brief explanation is given here to help the reader better grasp the reality of each of the four reasons fulfilled during the First Reformation.

FIRST REASON: LOVE

First, God purposed for Christ to become a mortal human being, having a body that could be crucified on a cross to reveal the motivational core nature of Eternal God—agape *Love.*

God planned it all from the foundation of the world. God is Love, but He had no way of making that known to His creation with things as they were in eternity. So He devised a way to demonstrate what divine love is (John 3:16). The creation of earth, time, and mortal man implemented the plan. God-Love cannot be demonstrated by the giving of things, only by the giving of oneself. Jesus created man with the potential of suffering, bleeding, and dying so that through His Son, which was the mortal body of God on earth, He could demonstrate that Almighty God is love. God so loved... that He gave. God demonstrated love...by dying for us (Rom. 5:8). Evidently, God knew there was no way for Him to demonstrate His core being and what love is without having a mortal body that could die. So He created earth and made mankind from the earth for the main purpose of demonstrating Himself as love to all of His creation in Heaven and earth. It was a revelation to angels, cherubim, and seraphim, but it was redemption and eternal life for mankind who received and believed.

Some have asked, why didn't God demonstrate His love by dying for the fallen angels? There are two reasons. First, angels are spirit beings and are not redeemable. Second, eternal God cannot die. That's the reason the Scriptures say, *"A* [mortal] *body You have prepared for Me"* (Heb. 10:5). Now all creation has a living revelation and demonstration that God is *Love* (1 John 4:8-10).

SECOND REASON: FATHERHOOD

Second, man and woman were created so that God could Father His own biological Son. Adam was a created son of God (Gen. 2:7). But that did not fully satisfy the Father heart and nature of God. Scripture states several times that Jesus is the only begotten Son of God (John 1:14,18; 3:16-18)—the only Son whom God actually begat. The sperm cell that joined in conception with the egg cell of the virgin

Mary was from Father God (Luke 1:30-32). All of Christianity rests on the reality that Jesus is the biological Son of God. God's fatherhood nature could be fully satisfied only by fathering a biological human child of His own, and before He could do that God had to have a race of biological beings who were like Himself in image and likeness and endowed with the power of procreation. *Jesus* was the name given to that body that died on a cross, was buried, but resurrected back to life and is now seated at the right hand of His Father God in Heaven.

THIRD REASON: THE BRIDE

Third, Father God created man in order to provide a many-membered Bride for His only begotten Son, Jesus Christ. God planned the human race in order to bring forth His Son with a human body. Father God planned from the beginning to turn all rule and reign of Heaven and earth over to His Son. But God did not want Him to have to rule and reign alone. God planned to bring forth a redeemed body of mankind to be joint heirs with Jesus and rule and reign with Him as His Bride. Jesus was not to be one of a kind but the firstborn among many just like Him. Jesus gave Himself in death that He might redeem mankind, then sanctify and mature them until He could present to Himself a glorious Bride without spot or wrinkle to sit down with Him in His Father's throne to rule and reign over all things forever.

FOURTH REASON: A CO-LABORING CHURCH

Fourth, God created man in order to bring forth the Church as the Body of Christ on earth to co-labor with Christ Jesus as joint heirs in carrying out God's eternal purpose.

God planned the Church when He created earth and mankind. In fact, Ephesians 1:4 says that we the Church were chosen in Christ before the foundation of the world. Jesus loved and wanted the Church so much that He came to earth as a man to give His life's blood to purchase the Church for Himself. When the Church was born by the Spirit of God on the Day of Pentecost, Jesus joined Himself to the Church as its Head and the Church became His corporate Body on earth. Ephesians 2:22 declares that the Body of Christ is built together on earth for a dwelling place of God. The body of Jesus was the dwelling place of God and the full expression and instrument of fulfillment of all that God wanted to be and do on earth. The Church is the Body of Christ and the place where Christ lives and headquarters on earth. Christ will fulfill all things in and through His universal corporate Body, the Church. Jesus is one with His Church and will never ever do anything alone again. Everything that Father God has planned for Jesus to be, do, and fulfill will be done in, through, and with His Church. This is an essential truth we must understand in order to fulfill God's purpose for the Third and Final Church Reformation.

GOD'S PURPOSE FOR THE CHURCH

The Church that is the "One Universal Many-Membered Corporate Body of Christ,"[2] the Kingdom of God, and Reformations are the main topics in this book. For the Church is the one who fulfills God's purpose for all three Reformations. Everything Jesus will ever do will be done through His Church. When I make reference to the Church with a capital "C," I am referring to the universal Church, the Body of Christ. When spelled with lowercase we are referring to a local church or some denominational church. The most common word used in the Bible concerning members of the Church is *saints*.[3] The term *saints* is used to describe God's people in the Old and

New Testaments. Because God changed Jacob's name to Israel, all of his descendants became known as the Children of Israel, and in modern times they are referred to as Israelis. When Jesus established the Church, He required both the Israelis and Gentiles to become members of the Church the same way. All have to believe in Jesus Christ as the only way to God (John 14:6) through being cleansed by the blood of Jesus, justified by faith, and born again by the Spirit of God (1 John 1:9; Rom. 5:1; John 3:3-5). Jew and non-Jew become members of the same Body of Christ the same way (Gal. 3:22-29). The Body of Christ is now the dwelling place of God on earth (Eph. 2:22). The saints of God become His main instruments for fulfilling all God wants to accomplish on the earth. That is why the Scriptures that refer to the saints possessing the Kingdom and then being given governmental powers to execute the judgments written *are* speaking of the Church.[4]

All that will be discussed in this book concerning the seven-mountain kingdoms of this world becoming the kingdoms of our God will be accomplished by the Church saints. Saints in every group and activity of mankind will become Kingdom demonstrators and enforcers. The final divine process is taking place now to conform them into Christ's maturity and ministry, so that they may become transformers of cities and nations. There is a Third Great Awakening that will be part of the ministry of the Third and Final Reformation that will establish the Third Tabernacle where God Himself dwells with redeemed mankind and rules on new earth (Rev. 21:3).

God's purpose for the Third Reformation is for it to restore all things that have been prophesied by the prophets (Acts 3:21). The prophets and apostles prophesied about the ultimate end of all things, such as Christ Jesus returning to redeem the bodies of the saints to be the immortal Church. The voice of the Lord spoken by

His prophets will help identify and determine the goat and sheep nations. The Third Reformation ministry will enable the saints to demonstrate the Kingdom of God sufficiently to bring transformation to the kingdoms of this world. When all things are restored that were negatively affected by the fall of lucifer and the sin of man, then Christ Jesus will return to earth as King of kings and Lord of lords. Jesus will gather all His saints from Heaven and earth unto Himself and organize them into His great army of saints who will co-labor with God's heavenly angelic army. Jesus, as their Commander-in-Chief, will lead them forth as they sweep through the first and second heavens binding satan and all his evil angels and demons, casting them into the bottomless pit and sealing them there for a thousand years. The overcomer saints then co-labor with Christ in setting up His Kingdom over all of new earth (Rev. 5:10; 2 Pet. 3:13).

JESUS GAVE PROPHETIC DECREES THAT MUST BE FULFILLED

Jesus gave some prophecies that are not conditional prophecies. They are prophetic decrees that must be fulfilled some time by some people at some place. In my book *Day of the Saints*,[5] I list the prophetic decrees in the Bible concerning the Church, Israel, the nations, planet Earth, all natural creation, the devil, and all wicked people. Here are just a few things concerning the Church. Saints will be ministered to by the fivefold ministers until they reach Christ's maturity and ministry (Eph. 4:11-16). Those overcomer saints will inherit all things and rule and reign with Christ on earth (Rev. 21:7). It is prophetically decreed that the kingdoms of this world will become the kingdoms of our God (Rev. 11:15). Saints are to be the kingdom demonstrators bringing transformation to the nations (Matt. 24:14).

When we read all of these biblical prophetic descriptions of what the final outcome will be, it becomes very hard to fathom. When we realize that we the Church play a vital role as joint heirs with Christ to bring these prophecies to fulfilled reality, it is overwhelming to our natural minds (Rom. 8:17). It has been decreed, so it must be fulfilled. We will cover many things that will help us understand how this can be accomplished. However, at this time, no man on earth has all the answers, power, or strategy for getting the job done, but God will continue bringing more and more revelation through the prophets and apostles to give wisdom and power to fulfill all of God's prophetic decrees (Eph. 3:3-5).

HOW WILL IT BE DONE?

Certainly, it cannot be done by the Church becoming as powerful, popular, and influential as it did during the Dark Age of the Church. During the Dark Age, the Catholic Church and the Pope became as powerful, political, and influential in the affairs of the nation as the king and princes. The Church of the Dark Age was not a force for righteousness and Kingdom principles in the nation, and it did not bring transformation of nations.[6]

There have been great revivals during the last 200 years that have added many members to the Church. The salvation of souls is the primary work of the Church, but it has not brought transformation to the nations (Matt. 28:18-20; 1 Tim. 1:15). There have been many restoration movements that have restored the Church back to the faith and ministry of the New Testament Church, but they have not brought the transformation of nations.[7] The main reason is because of God's timing and purpose. God's purpose for the First Reformation was to birth and establish the Church in all the earth. The purpose for the Second Reformation was to restore all truth and ministries back into the Church that were lost during the Dark

Age of the Church. God's purpose and timing is now for the Third Reformation to complete the restoration of all things and bring transformation to the nations and the kingdoms of this world until Revelation 11:15 becomes a historical fact.

REVELATION AND FULFILLMENT IS PROGRESSIVE

Fulfilling the Second Reformation required many revelations, bringing about many restoration movements during several hundred years. It usually takes one generation to make the preparation and then several following generations to bring it to fulfillment. My personal experience and study of Church history has made this real in my life. For instance, I functioned as a prophet, preached about the prophetic ministry, and trained thousands in the prophetic for 15 years before the Prophetic Movement was birthed in 1988.[8] Likewise, at our Christian International headquarters in Santa Rosa Beach, Florida, we started conducting Prophetic Businessmen seminars in 1989 to train ministers in the marketplace. I described in my book *Day of The Saints* that we are all kings and priests unto God.[9] But to better understand our function inside and outside the local church, the kingly anointing represents the ministers in the marketplace, and the priestly anointing represents the pulpit ministers who, like the priests, function mainly inside the local church. We taught and wrote about every saint having a ministry and that they can be Kingdom ministers in the workplace. When I wrote my book, there were fewer than ten books saying some of the same things, but now there are hundreds. Just a few ministers were preaching it, but now there are thousands. There were only a few organizations dedicated to ministers in the marketplace, and now there are hundreds.

THIRD REFORMATION MINISTERS MULTIPLYING

Since the birthing of the Third Reformation in 2008, there are hundreds of ministers writing and preaching about this new era of Christianity. They are writing about the things that are prophetically destined to take place during the Third Reformation, such as the Church becoming God's delegated authority to bring transformation to nations until every nation becomes a goat or sheep nation. We are speaking of the prophetic scriptures that must be fulfilled in order for Jesus Christ to return and the kingdoms of this world to become the kingdoms of Jesus Christ and His anointed Church. We are now in the first stage of the Third Reformation where pioneering apostles and prophets are preaching and writing the revelation so that those who read and hear can become kingdom demonstrators and Third Reformation reformers.

PERSONAL COMMITMENT AND DIVINE COMMISSION

King David provided most of the gold, silver, bronze, and much of the timber and stones that Solomon would need to build the temple (1 Chron. 28:11-12; 29:1-8). Like David, I have dedicated the rest of my years of ministry to prepare revelation, wisdom, and ministry that the next generations will need to build the Kingdom of God on earth. Abraham received the revelation of the movements to begin and establish a chosen Hebrew race for God. He received the revelation that the place was the Land of Canaan. He even received the overall borders of their inheritance (Gen. 15:18). He made the covenant of circumcision with God (Gen. 17:1-14). He pressed on and believed until he received the promised son, which would be the lineage that would fulfill all the prophetic decrees God gave Abraham

(Gen. 17:15-22). He made all the preparation, but it required several generations before they possessed the Promised Land and made it the nation of Israel. Jesus made preparation for the birthing and building of His Church, but it was the generation He had trained that was used to birth and establish the Church.

In reference to the whole Church Age, the First Reformation apostles and prophets received the revelation of the Church and its purpose. They laid the foundation and revealed the final work of the Church. But the Third Reformation generation is in God's timing and purpose to restore all things and fulfill all that has been prophesied.

The First Reformation saints were martyred by the millions. Their lifeblood was sown in the earth by natural death and martyrdom, so that the last generation of the Third Reformation Church may be reaped in living and not dying by Christ Jesus resurrecting and translating them into the immortal warriors who will subdue all things under the dominion of Christ Jesus.[10] It is not a matter of God favoring one generation over another, but it is all according to His purpose and the time for its fulfillment.

NOTES

1. Bill Hamon, *Who Am I & Why Am I Here?* (Shippensburg, PA: Destiny Image, 2005).

2. Hamon, *The Eternal Church*, 40.

3. Bill Hamon, *The Day of the Saints* (Shippensburg, PA: Destiny Image, 2002), 22.

4. See Daniel 7:18,22,27; Psalm 149:6-9; 1 Corinthians 6:2-3.

5. Hamon, *The Day of the Saints*, 374-380.

6. Hamon, *The Eternal Church*, 96-97.

7. Ibid., 173.

8. Bill Hamon, *Prophets and the Prophetic Movement* (Shippensburg, PA: Destiny Image, 1990), 66.
9. Hamon, *The Day of the Saints*, 205.
10. Hamon, *The Eternal Church*, 87.

Chapter 3

THE FIRST CHURCH REFORMATION: 4 B.C. TO A.D. 313

TIME PERIODS IN THE HISTORY OF MANKIND

Natural historians divide the history of mankind into different ages covering millions of years. Christian historians divide the history of man into eight different time periods called dispensations, covenants, or ages.[1] These are specific periods of time when God works with man according to a set of divine rules and principles that man must follow in order to have fellowship with God and to fulfill His will.

For instance, the time from the creation of man until his fall is called the dispensation of innocence or the Edenic covenant. The time from when God gave Moses the law of God until the coming of Christ is called the dispensation of the Law or the Mosaic covenant.

The time from the first coming of Christ to the second coming of Christ is called the dispensation of grace or the Church Age covenant.

Each covenant/dispensation/age prepares the way for the next. Rather than repeating all three, the word *age* will be used to describe these time periods. The ages are successive; each age makes way for another. Each new age is greater than the previous because it moves into a higher level in the eternal purposes of God. Each age reveals more of God's will, His way, and His desire for humanity. The Age of Law revealed more than the Age of Promise. The Church Age is greater than both the Age of Promise and the Age of Law. The Millennial Age and the ages to come will supersede all previous ages.

THE CHURCH AGE

This book will mainly deal with the Church Age. Our main focus will be the three reformations in the Church. Two have been fulfilled, and the third and final Church reformation was launched in 2008 and will continue until it fulfills its purpose. God's purpose for the First Reformation was to birth the Church and launch it into all the world. The purpose for the Second Reformation was to bring the Church out of its dark age of bondage to dead religion and begin its period of restoration of all Church truths and ministries. God's purpose for the Third Reformation is to activate the Church into all restored truth and demonstrate the Kingdom of God until the prophetic decree of Revelation 11:15 is fulfilled.

DIFFERENCES BETWEEN REVIVAL, AWAKENING, AND REFORMATION

The Holy Spirit has a different purpose to accomplish in each of these divine visitations. During a restoration movement, God sovereignly chooses to restore certain major truths, ministries, and spiritual experiences that have not been active since the early years of the Church. A refreshing/renewal is the time when God sends His refreshing spiritual rain to prepare His people for the next restorational move of God.[2] Revival in evangelical circles often means to have an evangelist hold a series of special meetings for the purpose of winning more souls to the Lord. In the corporate Church it is when the Holy Spirit moves to revive God's people in truths and ministries that have already been restored but have been allowed to become inactive in the Church. An awakening is a time when God awakens mankind to a God-consciousness, repentance, and the reverential fear of God. Righteousness is emphasized for society to change their way of living. Church revivalist historians have recognized three Great Awakenings, one each taking place during the eighteenth, nineteenth, and twentieth centuries. There is another Great Awakening for the twenty-first century.[3]

Revivals, refreshing, and renewals happen every so often in the Church most times just before a restoration movement.

WHAT IS A CHURCH REFORMATION?

A *reformation* is a time when God makes a major shift in the Church to accomplish a specific purpose. There will be many times of refreshing, revivals, and restoration movements during a Church Reformation. There are new orders, new grace, and new vision that give a new directive and goal for the Church to fulfill God's newly revealed purpose for His Church.

A reformation brings a revolutionary change and separates the old from the new. Those who stay with the old order and refuse to accept the new become the main persecutors of those who become participants of the new reformation. It was that way in the first and second reformation, and will end up being the same in the third reformation.

DIVINE MOVEMENTS ESTABLISHING THE FIRST REFORMATION

Conception and Birth of Jesus (4 B.C.)

The preparation for the birthing of the first reformation began when the Archangel Gabriel made the announcement to a young virgin woman named Mary. He declared, *"Behold, you will conceive in your womb and bring forth a Son, and shall call His name Jesus. He will be great, and will be called the Son of the Highest; and the Lord God will give Him the throne of His father David. And He will reign over the house of Jacob forever, and of His kingdom there will be no end"* (Luke 1:31-33). Mary could not grasp how all of this could happen, so Gabriel explained to her, *"The Holy Spirit will come upon you, and the [procreative] power of the Highest will overshadow you; therefore, also, that Holy One who is to be born will be called the Son of God"* (Luke 1:35).

Jesus' Coming Sets Time Before and After

About nine months later, Mary gave birth to Jesus in Bethlehem. This was not only the birthing of the promised Messiah but the means by which God would birth the Church during the First Church Reformation. The birth of Jesus was the most important event that had ever happened on earth. Nevertheless, less than a dozen people knew what had happened. It is doubtful that it made the local news, unless a baby being born in a barn was a novelty to the area. It was the fulfillment of prophecies that had been spoken since the Garden of Eden. Many people think something cannot be a major divine event unless it makes the world news. But that event was destined to change history and time. Our calendar and calculation of time are based on the time of the birth of Jesus. Time before His birth = B.C.; time after His birth = A.D. When the Roman calendar was established in the third century, they later discovered they had actually miscalculated the time of Christ's birth by four years. That is the reason that all Christian historians place the birth of Jesus at 4 B.C. instead of A.D. 0 B.C. The conception and birth of Jesus were the first steps in bringing forth the First Reformation.

The John the Baptist Preparation Movement

The prophets Isaiah and Malachi prophesied that there would be a prophet come forth in the spirit of Elijah who would prepare the way for the Messiah to be manifested on earth (Isa. 40:3; Mal. 3:1; 4:5); God declared in the Old Testament that He would do nothing on earth without first revealing it to His servants the prophets (Amos 3:7). In the New Testament, the apostles are added (Eph. 3:3-5). Now apostles and prophets are given the spirit of revelation to know the times and purposes of God. They also have the sons of Issachar anointing to know the times and seasons and what God's people need to do (1 Chron. 12:32). Isaiah prophesied that there would arise a prophetic voice in the wilderness crying out, *"Prepare the way of the Lord"* (Isa. 40:3-5). John the Baptist arose in the wilderness crying out, *"Prepare the way of the Lord."* Jesus declared that John the Baptist was the prophet Elijah whom Malachi prophesied would appear when it was time for the Messiah to begin His ministry (Matt. 11:9-24). God is faithful to have a few voices crying out that something new is about to happen.

This has set the pattern for every restoration movement or reformation that is to take place during the Church Age. There will always be some prophets and apostles somewhere in the world proclaiming what is about to take place in the Church. Throughout history it has been proven that God has revealed His times and purposes to apostles and prophets to proclaim God's timing and purpose for His Church. Prophets and apostles received revelation that produced all the moves of God that have taken place in Church history, just as prophets and apostles are proclaiming the Third Church Reformation that has now been launched in the Church.

The Manifest Messiah Movement

Jesus went through 30 years of preparation before God anointed Him to be the manifest Messiah of Israel and Redeemer of all mankind. Christ Jesus launched His "Manifest Messiah Movement" by being baptized by John the Baptist in the river Jordan. His calling and ministry received confirming signs: the Holy Spirit descending on Jesus like a dove lighting on Him, and the voice of Father God said, *"You are My beloved Son; in You I am well pleased"* (Luke 3:21-22). This was the beginning of Jesus' public ministry, the launching of a new movement as the Messiah of Israel, the Redeemer of mankind, and the Son of God fulfilled His purpose for coming to earth. Again notice that this all-important event had all of Heaven's attention but not mankind's. The trumpet sounding in Heaven was being heralded throughout the eternal universe, but on earth it did not even register as a news item. Just John and Jesus in the water and a few people on the shores of the Jordan River participated in this historic event. Nevertheless, it was the birthing of the movement to manifest Jesus as the Messiah and God's only begotten Son.

The movement progressed when Jesus passed the temptations of the devil after fasting 40 days in the wilderness (Matt. 4:1-11). Then *"God anointed Jesus of Nazareth with the Holy Spirit and with power, who went about doing good and healing all who were oppressed by the devil, for God was with Him"* (Acts 10:38). Jesus then began to choose His disciples, and within a few months He appointed twelve to be His apostles (Matt. 10:1-4). He began to set in the structure that would assure that the truths of the movement would be carried on after He was gone. He knew that His personal ministry would only last a few years on earth. Therefore, Jesus spent more time with His disciples than He did with the multitudes. Jesus gave His disciples intensified training 24/7 around the clock day and night. We who have been and are leaders of movements must make sure we thoroughly establish those whom God has given to work with us in the truths, spirit, and purpose of the movement. For this reason, when the Prophetic Movement was birthed in 1988, I wrote the three books on the prophetic and developed the 300-page manual used for teaching and activating the saints in prophetic ministry.[4] More than 500,000 Christian saints and leaders have been trained on every continent of the world. God's prophets and prophetic ministry are now accepted by hundreds of thousands in Christendom. But I first had to train a company of prophets and prophetic ministers in being anointed, wise, accurate, and mature prophetic ministers.

Books and teaching manuals had to be produced to introduce the ministry to the Body of Christ and then years of teaching, activating, and maturing were required before the Prophetic Movement was fully established in the present-truth Church.

The purpose of this book is to introduce the reality that the Third and Final Church Reformation was launched in 2008. Jesus' ministry was publicly announced and launched at His water baptism, and then He was hidden away and tested for a period of time. After Jesus passed the time of testing, He began to manifest all the power, miracles, and ministry of the movement. In like manner, during the writing of this book, the Third Reformation is going through its testing time, but when the testing is over it will begin manifesting the miraculous and all the truth and purposes to be fulfilled in this major move of the Holy Spirit.

The Church Birthing Movement

All of Christ's time on earth was moving toward His destiny and purpose. The greatest desire and purpose of Jesus was to purchase His Church and provide everything needed to fulfill its destiny (Eph. 5:25-27). The Scriptures say that Christ Jesus came to save sinners. Jesus not only came to save sinners so that they could escape hell and go to Heaven, but to make them members of His Church (1 Cor. 12:12,27). He was not reconciling them to a place, but God was in Christ reconciling the world unto Himself (2 Cor. 5:18-19). Ephesians 5:25 says that Jesus loved the Church and gave Himself for the Church to be His corporate Body. Acts 20:28 says Jesus purchased the Church with His own blood. Mel Gibson made a movie called *The Passion of Christ,* which gives a living demonstration of the pain, suffering, shame, and agony Jesus went through to provide redemption for you and me. Hebrews 12:2 declares that Jesus endured the cross, despising the shame, for the *joy* that was set before Him. The Church was the joy set before Him. Jesus loves the Church more than He loves life itself, for He gave His life on the cross to redeem the Church to Himself. The death, burial, and resurrection of Christ provided everything needed for the Church to be birthed on the Day of Pentecost (1 Cor. 15:1-10).

When Jesus brought forth the Church by His Holy Spirit, it started a whole new order. It immediately established a new way for mankind to become the people of God. It was not an extension of Judaism or a makeover of the Mosaic Covenant but a completely New Covenant or Testament. That is why the Bible is divided into Old Testament and New Testament. When Jesus brought forth the Church, that was the end of righteousness by the Law for everyone who would believe in Christ Jesus (Rom. 5:12-20; Rom. 8:4; Gal. 3:10-25). God's dwelling place and headquarters was moved from natural Jerusalem to spiritual Jerusalem, the Church, from Mount Sinai to Mount Zion (Heb. 12:22-24). Apostle Peter wrote that the Church is a royal priesthood, a holy nation, His own special people (1 Pet. 2:9). Jesus is the firstborn and the head of the Church of the firstborn.

The First Reformation of the Church was revolutionary, starting a whole new way for mankind to become children of God. It was the most radical and expensive change ever concerning how God and man relate together. It cost Heaven more than what had happened or ever would happen on earth. It required the lifeblood of God's only begotten Son (John 3:16; Acts 20:28; Heb. 11:17). There will not be another radically revolutionary change like this until Christ's second coming, which will be the last redemptive experience of the Third Reformation Church.

The First-Century Apostolic Church Movement

Jesus chose from His disciples 12 men and called them apostles (Luke 6:13). He demonstrated to them the life they were to live and the ministry they were to have in building His Church. Jesus invested Himself in those who would build His Church, which was His greatest passion. Jesus gave the revelation and made the prophetic declaration, *"I will build My church"* (Matt. 16:18). He then purchased the Church with His blood, authorized it by His resurrection (Rom. 1:4), birthed and empowered it by His Holy Spirit, ascended to Heaven, and sat down at the right hand of His Father (Acts 2:4; 1:8; Eph. 1:20). Christ then took all of His ministry for building the Church and gave it to certain members of His new race of mankind, the Church. Jesus Christ divided His complete headship ministry to the Church into five gifts. He called the five gifts apostles, prophets, evangelists, pastors, and teachers (Eph. 4:11). His fivefold ministers were to equip every member of the Body of Christ in their special membership ministry. They were commissioned to function until they brought the Church to the fullness of Christ's maturity and ministry (Eph. 4:12-16). The Church was to be built on the foundation-laying ministry of the apostles and prophets aligned with Jesus, the chief cornerstone (Eph. 1:19-22). The Body of Christ is to be built up by that special ministry that every member has been given, just as in the natural human body every member must perform its particular function in order for the body to be healthy and able to fulfill its purpose.

The New Testament Apostolic Movement played a vital role in establishing the Church on earth as the Body of Christ. It was to be the Body expressing Christ fully to the world as Jesus was the human body that fully expressed God the Father (John 17:18; Heb. 1:1-4). But it would take another movement to take the Church Gospel to the whole world. And it would require yet another revelation movement to take it to every tongue, tribe, and nation.

The First-Century Saints Movement

In chapter 8:1-13 of Acts, it tells of great persecution that arose against the Church that was at Jerusalem, and they were all scattered throughout the regions of Judea and Samaria except the apostles. The apostles stayed in Jerusalem while the saints went to the nations, being the Church and demonstrating the Kingdom of God. This was the launching of the Saints Movement. Acts 8:4 says that the saints who were scattered went everywhere preaching the Word. One of them was Philip, who was one of the seven who had been appointed over the business affairs of the Church. The requirement for being one of the seven was to be full of the Holy Spirit and wisdom with a good reputation, which probably included being a successful business man. When Philip arrived, he began witnessing and preaching the Gospel of Jesus Christ. God began to do what He promised to believers who preach His Word. He confirmed the Word with salvations, healings, and casting out of devils. This set the pattern for the Church that all saints have a ministry and as believers they can heal the sick, cast out devils, demonstrate the Kingdom, preach the Gospel, be the salt of the earth and the light of the world (Mark 16:17; Matt. 5:13-16). The first-century Saints Movement broke the Church out of the box of thinking that only the apostles could preach the Gospel. They discovered that every saint according to the gifts and grace given to them can manifest the Kingdom of God in their sphere of influence. This was the first-century Saints Movement that was part of the First Church Reformation. God also destined that there would be a twenty-first-century Saints Movement at the end of the closing of the Church Age that would launch the Third and Final Church Reformation. *The Day of the Saints* reveals the first-century Saints Movement and gives all the truth and ministries of the twenty-first-century Saints Movement.[5]

The Gentile Church Movement

The apostles for the first ten years of the Church thought Jesus was the Messiah promised only for Israel. They assumed the Gospel of Jesus Christ was only for the Jews. They assumed that for anyone else to receive the benefits of Jesus the Messiah they had to become a proselyte Jew first. To get the Church out of its limited vision, God gave apostle Peter a supernatural vision showing him that no animal was unclean for eating (Acts 10:9-16; 11:4-10). An angel appeared to Cornelius, a non-Jewish captain of a regiment of Italian soldiers, to send for Peter who would show them the way of salvation. When the men came, the Holy Spirit told Peter to go with them. When he arrived, Cornelius' house was filled with people gathered to hear what Peter was going to say. Peter told them about the vision he had received and how it revealed to him that he should call no human being common or unclean. Then Peter said, *"In truth I perceive that God shows no partiality. But in every nation whoever fears God and works righteousness is accepted by Him"* (Acts 10:34-35). He then preached to them the Gospel of the death, burial, and resurrection of Jesus Christ.

When Peter made the statement that whoever believes in Jesus will receive remission of sins, the Italians believed and received it for themselves while Peter was still speaking without him realizing it. But suddenly right in the middle of his message, the Holy Spirit fell on them, and they received the gift of the Holy Spirit and began to speak in unknown tongues just as the apostles and the 120 did on the Day of Pentecost. Peter realized God had forgiven these Gentiles their sins and baptized them with the Holy Spirit without them becoming proselyte Jews first. He then commanded them to be water baptized in the name of the Lord Jesus.

This was the beginning of the Gentile Church Movement that made the Gospel of salvation through Christ available to every tongue, tribe, and nation (Rev. 5:9-10). However, this one experience and revelation of Peter's was not sufficient to deliver the Church from Judaism. God had to bring in a special messenger to really establish it. Saul of Tarsus was saved and became later the apostle Paul. The personal prophecy that Ananias gave Paul declared that God had called him to take the Gospel to the Gentiles (Acts 9:15-17). Paul went to the desert for three years and then back to his hometown of Tarsus (Acts 9:30; Gal. 1:15-18). Some of the saints who had gone everywhere preaching went to Antioch and began to preach to everyone. Many Gentiles began to get saved and filled with the Holy Spirit without first participating in the Abrahamic covenant of circumcision. The Church at Jerusalem heard about it and sent Barnabas down to investigate (Acts 11:19-26). When he saw that the light of the Gospel was going to the Gentiles, he remembered the prophecy that Paul had received that he would be a sent one (an apostle) to the Gentiles. He immediately went all the way to Tarsus to get Paul, for it was his time to be launched into his ministry.

Paul and Barnabas were in Antioch for a year; then the Holy Spirit spoke through the prophets a timely directive word (Acts 11:19-30). They were to lay hands on Paul and Barnabas and apostolically commission them to start traveling to the nations, taking the Gospel to every tongue, tribe, and nation. Paul received a strong revelation that God had changed the whole order of salvation from circumcision and keeping of the law of Moses to simple faith in Christ Jesus. Being a natural Israelite or a Gentile was the same to God, for He had declared both equally sinners in need of the one and only Savior, Jesus Christ (Gal. 2:11-21). The only way to be saved was to believe on the Lord Jesus Christ, be born again, and made to be a child of God by being cleansed from all sin by the blood of Jesus (1 John 1:9).

This revelation and ministry that was brought forth in the Gentile Church Movement was absolutely necessary in order for the First Church Reformation to fulfill its God-ordained purpose. Nevertheless, there had to be one more move of God before the First Church Reformation could be complete enough to fulfill its full purpose. The purpose for the First Church Reformation was to birth the Church into the world and then establish it as God's new people. It was a new order, a new covenant based on a new set of standards for mankind to become children of God and His chosen people. God had moved His dwelling place from the temple made with dead stones in Jerusalem to the temple of the Church that was being built by living stones of born-again people. God transferred His people from Mount Sinai (the Law) to Mount Zion (the Church); from the old city of Jerusalem to the New Jerusalem, the city of God—the Church (Heb. 12:21-24).

For this to be officially established and sanctioned, there had to be one more movement by the apostles and prophets. Jesus gave them the ministry of laying the proper foundation for the Church in doctrine, practice, and ministry.

The Apostolic Council Movement

After 20 years of church function, there were still those associated with the Jerusalem church who were preaching that it was necessary to keep the law of Moses and the Abrahamic covenant of circumcision in order to be a Christian. Some of them came to the church in Antioch and started teaching, *"unless you are circumcised according to the custom of Moses, you cannot be saved"* (Acts 15:1). This was completely contrary to Paul's revelation of salvation through Christ apart from the Law and circumcision. This caused much arguing and debating among the leadership at Antioch with Paul and Barnabas being the main defenders of their Christian faith. The matter was temporarily settled by leaders from both sides going to Jerusalem to present the matter to the church apostles (Acts 15:2-5). Apostle James was the pastor of the church in Jerusalem and many of the 12 apostles still headquartered in Jerusalem. When all the leadership had gathered at Jerusalem, some time was spent with much heated discussion.

Finally, the apostle Peter stood and gave testimony of his vision and angelic visitation and the sovereign move of God at Cornelius' house. Barnabas and Paul gave their testimony of the Holy Spirit sovereignly bestowing all the benefits of Christianity on the Gentiles, apart from the Mosaic law. These testimonies, visions, and supernatural experiences were eye openers and served as a witness and confirming evidence (Acts 15:7-11). But it was not until Senior Pastor-Apostle James received a revelation and application of a

Scripture from the Logos that the issue was settled and written into established foundational doctrine for the New Testament Church. A letter was written, and apostles Paul and Barnabas and prophets Judas and Silas were commissioned to take the letter and read the doctrinal decree to the church at Antioch (Acts 15:12-29).

The actions taken during the Council at Jerusalem established five criteria to determine true Christian practice and doctrine. These are also principles that should be used when determining the validity of a new restoration movement or Church Reformation: 1) the claimed revelation from God; 2) the fruit of the ministry among those who are propagating a new restoration, doctrine, or practice; 3) the supernatural working of God accompanying it; 4) the Logos and Rhema word of God providing application and authority for the doctrine or practice; and 5) the witness of the Holy Spirit and the unified consent of the mature and proven leadership present. The Council at Jerusalem was the official move that spiritually separated Christianity from Judaism. But it would take 20 more years and another major move to make all the world know that the Jewish religion and Christianity were two completely separate entities.

THE DESTRUCTION OF JERUSALEM A.D. 70

During the year A.D. 70, the Roman emperor sent a great army to subdue the open rebellion of the Jews in the Jerusalem area. The fortified city was taken and the temple destroyed. This resulted in making the great distinction between Christianity and Judaism, Christians and Jews. Up to this time, the world viewed Christians as part of the Jewish religion; both seemed to believe in the same invisible God. For 40 years the Church had been viewed as a part of Judaism. But now, after 13 centuries of Israel being a Jewish state, it was destroyed. Their religious headquarters of Jerusalem and the temple were destroyed, and the Jewish people were all killed or dispersed throughout the

Roman Empire. The Jewish historian Josephus records that 1.1 million Jews perished in the city, that another 257,660 were killed in surrounding areas, and 97,000 were taken captive. Those above 17 years of age were sent to work in Egypt, but most were distributed through the Roman provinces to be destroyed by sword and by wild beasts as they were forced to fight as gladiators in the amphitheaters.[6]

PROPHECIES OF JESUS FULFILLED

The thousands of Christians who were in Jerusalem believed the prophecy Jesus gave concerning Jerusalem and what they should do when Jerusalem began to be attacked by an army. Jesus prophesied that they were to flee the city immediately and they would be spared. In his commentary, Adam Clarke writes, "It is very remarkable that not a single Christian perished in the destruction of Jerusalem."[7] There was a window of opportunity opened when some confusion and transition took place in the leadership of Rome. The armies withdrew from surrounding Jerusalem for a short time. When God gave them that divine delay, all who believed in Christ Jesus left immediately and fled to Pella and to other places beyond the river Jordan.

During the destruction of Jerusalem, the temple caught on fire— causing the gold to run into the lower wall and between the blocks of the foundation. The soldiers took the temple apart stone by stone to retrieve the precious metals. There was not one stone left on another, thus fulfilling the prophecy Jesus gave in Matthew 24:2, which more clearly manifested the fact that God's headquarters was no longer in the Law and tabernacle of Moses or in the great temple made of stone and precious metals. It was now in the Church.

The fall of Jerusalem in A.D. 70 was a significant happening in light of the Jewish nation, the Church, and fulfilled prophecies. It definitely forever separated Christianity from Judaism. This was another step in the First Reformation fulfilling its purpose of establishing Christ's Church. The Church was now God's chosen people and holy nation with its citizens being built together for a habitation of God through His Holy Spirit (Eph. 2:22). God's headquarters was now in the building of the Church. God's body for expressing and performing His will on earth is now the corporate Body of Christ, the Church. During the First Reformation, Jesus fulfilled the Law and the prophecies of the prophets concerning the coming of the Messiah of Israel and Redeemer of mankind (Acts 3:18). The old natural Jerusalem was destroyed, and the new heavenly Jerusalem established. The temple that typified the tabernacle of Moses where God said He would dwell and meet with His people was removed, and now the Church is the temple of God where He dwells and meets with His people. The state of Israel is removed and is no longer God's nation on earth, but now the Church is God's holy nation, His royal priesthood, and His own special people (1 Pet. 2:9).

THE BEGINNING OF THE GREAT FALLING AWAY

The Romans assumed that the Christians were just another sect among the Jewish religion, and they were tolerated as such until after the destruction of Jerusalem. At that time, they were exposed as a separate group and made to stand alone with no laws to protect the Christians from their enemies. During the years of the great persecution of Christianity (A.D. 100 to A.D. 313), the Christian religion was forbidden in the Roman Empire, and its followers were outlawed. Christians had no more citizenship rights than the slaves in the southern United States had before the Civil War. Persecution was not continuous, for only certain emperors brought severe persecution during their reign. The persecution did not hinder the Church from growing and being established in all the world. Apostle Paul declared that they took the Gospel to every person under the sun (Col. 1:23).

The Church maintained its original commission, most of the fundamentals of the faith, and supernatural ministry during its time of great persecution. The Church continued manifesting all the attributes of the Spirit and living the life of Christ.

THE LAST MAJOR PERSECUTION

The last, most systematic, and most horrible of all the series of persecutions took place during the reign of Emperor Diocletian and his successors, from A.D. 303 to A.D. 310—seven years of great persecution and tribulation.[8] (The Christians fully believed he was the antichrist spoken of in the Book of Revelation.) A series of edicts ordered that every copy of the Bible should be burned, that all churches throughout the Empire should be torn down, and that all who would not renounce the Christian religion should lose their citizenship and be outside the protection of the law. (Many Roman officials and citizens had become Christians during the prior 50 years of rest from persecution.) In some places, while Christians were assembled, their churches were set on fire and burned with all the worshipers within their walls. It is said that Emperor Diocletian erected a pillar inscribed, "In honor of the eradication of the Christian superstition."[9] Yet within ten years, Christianity became accepted and Christians were allowed to be citizens. Within 70 years, Christianity became the official religion of the emperor, the court, and the Empire.

THE CHURCH TRANSITIONING FROM SPIRITUAL TO STRUCTURAL

In A.D. 313, the Emperor Constantine issued his memorable Edict of Milan. By this law Christianity was sanctioned, its worship was made lawful, and all persecution ceased, not to be renewed while the Roman Empire endured. This came about because of a vision

Constantine received. He saw in the sky, just before the setting sun, a vision of the cross, and above it the words, "In this sign, conquer." He decided to fight under the banner of Christianity, and he won that battle of Milvian Bridge, just outside of Rome on October 28, A.D. 312.[10] Constantine favored Christians in every way. He filled chief offices with them, exempted Christian ministers from taxes and military service, and encouraged and helped in building churches. Constantine made Christianity the religion of his court and issued a general exhortation to all his subjects to embrace Christianity.

Constantine encouraged constituents to become Christians, but 70 years later Emperor Theodosius made it compulsory when he made Christianity the state religion of the Roman Empire. His decree forced all Roman Empire subjects to formally accept Christianity in order to maintain their citizenship, hold office, and carry on business. This was the final blow to the pre-eminence of the spiritual Church, which required personal repentance from the conviction of sin and believing the Gospel in order to become a Christian. Prior to this time, conversion had been voluntary and marked by a genuine change in heart and life. Christ had designed the First Reformation Church to conquer by purely spiritual and supernatural means.

When we come to the Third Reformation of the Church, we will be sharing about God's ultimate purpose of Christ and His Church ruling and reigning over all creation on earth. From this historical event, we can see that our method cannot be by natural means or the way Rome did it, for Theodosius not only demanded adherence to Christianity, but he undertook the forcible suppression of all other religions and prohibited idol worship. Under his decree, heathen temples were torn down, and there was much blood shed among the heathen priests and worshipers. (What a reversal from less than a century before!) The man-made military spirit of Imperial Rome had entered the Church. Christianity appeared to have conquered the whole empire, but by making the Church over into its own image, the Roman Empire had conquered the spiritual Church.

BLESSING AND BONDAGE OF THE TRANSITION

The popularity and political positioning of the structural Church began the deterioration of the spiritual Church as revealed in the Book of Acts. The acceptance and political dominance of Christianity enhanced the structural Church. The world was also blessed in its physical, moral, and social life. Slavery, gladiator fights, and the killing of unwelcome children (abortion) were abolished. Crucifixion as a form of execution was abolished with the Christianization of the Roman Empire. Many humanitarian societies were established by the state through the influence of the Church. However, when the spiritual Church was in control in apostolic days, these humanitarian needs were met by the Church without state support or control.

The Church now entered its deterioration and great falling away. The First Reformation ended and the deformation of the Church began. Thus, the Church passed from its period of preservation and expansion during the time of persecution to its political prosperity and popularity, which brought about its decline and deterioration. The spiritual Church fades into obscurity and the structural Church begins to dominate until the beginning of the Second Reformation of the Church some 1,200 years later.

NOTES

1. Hamon, *The Eternal Church*, 61.
2. Bill Hamon, *Apostles, Prophets, and the Coming Moves of God* (Santa Rosa Beach, FL: Christian International, 1997), 61.

3. "Great Awakenings," http://www.theopedia.com/Great
     _awakenings.

4. Bill Hamon, *Prophets and Personal Prophecy* (Shippensburg, PA:
     Destiny Image, 1987); Bill Hamon, *Prophets and the Prophetic
     Movement* (Shippensburg, PA: Destiny Image, 1990); Bill Hamon,
     Prophets, Pitfalls and Principles (Shippensburg, PA: Destiny Image,
     1991); Bill Hamon, *The Manual for Ministering Spiritual Gifts*
     is taught several times each year at Christian International and
     various local churches. For more information, contact Christian
     International at 1-800-388-5308.

5. Hamon, *The Day of the Saints*, 81.

6. Adam Clarke, *Clarke's Commentary* (Nashville, TN: Abingdon
     Press, 1977), 230-231.

7. Ibid.

8. Bill Hamon, *The Eternal Church*, 68.

9. Ibid., 88.

10. Henry Halley, *Halley's Bible Handbook* (Grand Rapid, MI:
     Zondervan Publishing, 1965).

Chapter 4

THE DARK AGE OF THE CHURCH

Apostles Paul, Peter, and Jude wrote letters using different terminology that there would come a great falling away of the Church into a time of apostasy. (Greek *apostasia*, a forsaking or departure from former established truth, principles, and practices, a falling away from one's original religious faith.[1]) No time period was given except that it would begin some time after the first-century apostolic age and before the coming of the Lord. Paul wrote in his first letter to the Thessalonians about the resurrection/translation (R/T) of the saints at the second coming of Christ. They were going through great trials, persecution, and hard economic times. Paul told them to encourage each other with the truth that Jesus was coming soon to translate them to Heaven in a twinkling of an eye. Some who heard this twisted Paul's words to say the R/T had already taken place. Others quit their jobs and started just waiting in prayer for Christ's coming at any moment. Paul had to write his second letter to bring wisdom and balance to their understanding concerning Christ's second coming.

CHURCH RESTORATION BEFORE CHRIST'S RETURNING

To the Ephesians Paul wrote that the fivefold ministers had to keep ministering until the Church was functioning in all truth and had come to the maturity of Christ before the second coming could take place. Peter declared in Acts 3:21 that Jesus must be kept in Heaven until the restoration of all things prophesied by the prophets. Jesus declared that the Gospel of the Kingdom of God had to be preached in all the world for a witness to all nations before the end could come. And Paul told the Thessalonians that the Church would go through a great falling away before the R/T took place. The age of the great apostasy of the Church is the period of time we want to reveal now.

Thousand-Year Dark Age

The thousand-year Dark Age of the spiritual Church is the same time period historically and culturally.

Spiritual Church Dark Age

The Dark Age begins in the fifth century with the decline of the spiritual Church into its "Great Falling Away" to the beginning of the period of the restoration of the Church in the fifteenth century.

Natural History Dark Age

Historically, it was from the fall of Rome, A.D. 476, to the fall of Constantinople, A.D. 1453.

Dark Age Culturally

It was from the time when the civilized world was overrun by uneducated "barbarians" in the fifth century until the beginning of the Renaissance in the fifteenth century.

The Darkest Hour for Christ's Church

The Church that was established and demonstrated in the first century was no longer a Church of the supernatural. They no longer preached a supernatural born-again experience, the gift of the Holy Spirit with a spirit language, the casting out of devils, or miraculous healings. Most of the experiential doctrines of the early Church were no longer active. The morality and life of most of the Church leaders was as corrupt as the world. The 200-year period just prior to, and a little after, the year 1000 is called the "Midnight of the Dark Age."[2] Bribery, corruption, simony, immorality, and bloodshed among the clergy and throughout Christendom make it just about the blackest chapter in the whole history of the Church.

It looked like all the prophecies Jesus gave about the end times were happening. There were wars and rumors of wars. Entire nations were rising and falling to new conquerors. There seemed to be no mercy or justice in the world. The Christian Church was reduced to an empty form of godliness without any life or power to help suffering humanity. Mohammed had started the Islamic religion in A.D. 600 and had conquered Arabian and Asian nations. He established the Muslim religion in all those nations and even conquered Jerusalem. For a couple of centuries during the middle of the Dark Age, the European Crusaders and the Muslims won and lost the battle for Jerusalem several times. The majority of the world was enslaved to other religions and heathen practices: Hinduism, Buddhism, Shintoism, ancestor worship, and animist religions. The structural/political Church among the "Christian" nations had reached a place of political power and influence equal to the king. But as for the spiritual Church that Jesus birthed and established, it had now deteriorated from a brilliant thousand-watt searchlight to a flickering one-watt candle.

WHY DID GOD ALLOW HIS BELOVED CHURCH TO GO INTO THE DARK AGE?

Where was God, and what was He doing during this time? There are some things that are very mysterious and difficult for the natural mind to understand. The Dark Age of the Church is one of these mysteries.

Scripture shows that Jesus eternally ordained the Church (Rev. 13:8; Eph. 1:4). Then He died to redeem the Church. He sent the Holy Spirit to birth, empower, protect, and perfect the Church until it could be presented unto Himself, a glorious Church perfectly pure and mature.

Man's comprehension of love, concern, and wisdom is quite different from God's. God's ways are different from man's ways. His thoughts and methods of accomplishing His will are as far beyond man's as the heavens are far above the earth (Isa. 55:8-9).

GOD'S VIEW OF TIME

God's concept and attitude toward time is also completely different. Time is so relevant, pressing, and trying to mortal man. Our beginning was at a certain time. Every day our lives are controlled by a 24-hour cycle of time. As a young person looks forward to each year of new recognition and opportunity, the years seem to take forever. After reaching his twenties, entering marriage, and beginning his ministry, the time begins to "normalize." Then the years speed up from the thirties to sixties until it seems as though they are passing by faster than the speeding box cars on a railroad track. But *Jesus Christ is the same yesterday, today, and forever"* (Heb. 13:8). Peter said that time to the Lord is different from man's concept of it, for *"with the Lord one day is as a thousand years, and a thousand years as one day"* (2 Pet. 3:8). According to God's timetable, Jesus has been gone from the earth less than two days. Nonetheless, Hosea 6:2 says, *"After two days He will revive us* [full restoration]; *on the third day He will raise us up, that we may live in His sight* [resurrection and translation in the third day]."

ETERNAL PLAN TAKES PRIORITY OVER PROCESS

Considering the many millions of saints who were martyred in every diabolical, degrading, and humiliating method conceivable by men of demonized minds during the first 300 years of the Church, we must conclude that God considers suffering and death from a completely different perspective from mortal man. *God's eternal plan to bring forth His perfect man (Church) takes priority over the process and time period required to produce His Church/Bride.*[3]

The psalmist declares that God who knows everything, even the beginning from the end, foreknows every member in His Corporate Body and that He has numbered all the days of the Church (Ps. 139:15-16). The Church is being "curiously wrought," formed, and put together, not in the higher realms of Heaven but in the lower parts of earth. The Lord Jesus purchased the Church through suffering and death. His whole life and purpose is wrapped up in the Church. What purpose could He have then for allowing His precious Church to deteriorate into a thousand-year apostate Dark Age? His divine love for the Church did not diminish with its decline. However, His fellowship and functioning with the Church was greatly hindered.

GOD'S SOVEREIGNTY—MAN'S WILL

Did Jesus leave the Church to its own ways for a thousand years? As God is sovereign, why didn't He keep the Church doctrinally right, morally pure, and victorious over all her enemies? We know that God made man and that He can do anything He will with man. Or can He? Could it be that God has decreed that He will never overrule mortal man's will in relation to service to Himself?

God did not stop Adam and Eve from sinning when they willed to eat of the forbidden fruit (Gen. 3:1-8). He did not override the Children of Israel when they set their will against God's will for them to enter into and conquer Canaan. He left them to wander in the wilderness for 40 years (Num. 14:30-38). He started preparing a new generation and eventually had a people desirous and willing to fulfill His will.

Has God limited Himself in blessing mankind based on their willingness, faith, and receptivity to His grace and goodness? Why doesn't God make people do what is right? He convicts and constrains with His goodness and judgment, but if people will not yield, He will not force them to be properly related to Himself against their will.

GOD WANTS MATURE SONS

God does not want a kingdom of subjects or slaves under forced servitude. He did not want robots or humanoids preprogrammed to act without any choice and without any initiative of their own. He created a being in His own image and likeness as a compatible creature capable of creative thoughts, a free spirit with a separate will of his own, and the privilege of refusing or choosing to do God's will (Gen. 1:26-28). He created a son, not a slave. Therefore, He desires *sons,* not *subjects.* He desires intelligent, willful service from man. His joy is not to be an employer with employees, but a Father with a family of children. He does not even want laborers as children working for Him, but grown-up sons and daughters as co-laborers with Him. Jesus does not desire to rule and reign over His Church, but *with* His Church. He wants the Church to grow up to *"the measure of the stature of the fullness of Christ"* (Eph. 4:11-15) so that it can function on His level. An adult can come down to the level of a child and be in fellowship with him, but a child cannot elevate himself to fellowship as an adult. He must grow to that level. God came down to man's level in the person of Jesus to translate the Church into His Kingdom in the heavenly places in Christ Jesus (Gal. 4:4-5; Eph. 1:20). However, the Church cannot be *elevated* to maturity. It must *grow* to maturity. Growth requires submission and a willing participation in all that Christ is. God will settle for nothing less than a free, moral fellow being who chooses Him above all others and cooperates as a willing, loving companion: "Sons love because they choose to. Delight of heart to heart and mind to mind can occur only where one *freely chooses to cherish another.*"[4]

Therefore, if man is determined to go his own way, then God does not sovereignly force him to walk by His side. Jesus fully revealed and demonstrated the character of God in His dealings with mankind here on earth. Just as Jesus was God's perfect man, so the Church is to become Christ's perfected human race. The perfected Church-race of humanity will fully satisfy the original desire and plan that God had in His heart when He created the human race. God's original commission was for mankind to reproduce and fill the earth with a mankind creation in God's image and likeness. Adam was created in God's image and likeness, and he and his wife were to produce children in their physical image and likeness (Gen. 5:3). But those born of the Adam race would have to grow and mature into God's likeness in nature and character. Those born of the Second Adam, Jesus Christ, receive His DNA nature, but they must grow and mature into Christ's likeness and image of character and maturity.

Jesus Limits Himself to Church

Jesus, by His foreknowledge, and the New Testament writers, by divine inspiration, declared that there would be a great falling away of the Church. The Church willfully went its own way and fell away from God's original pattern. Jesus did not bind or restrict satan from leading the Church into deception and spiritual deterioration, nor did He sovereignly stop the Church from walking in her own willful way. Jesus has limited Himself to the Church. He will enlighten and perform according to the hunger, receptivity, and response of His people to the moving of His Spirit and to the cry of His ordained voices of reform.

Yet it is a mistake to conclude that God has left Himself to the whim and fancy of man. God is still sovereign. Though I do not presently fully understand the "why," I believe the Dark Age played a part in God's overall plan in purifying and perfecting His Eternal Church. God still rules in the affairs of man.

Egypt and God's People

God promised Abraham that his descendants would multiply until they became like stars of the sky and sand of the sea and that they would inhabit the land of Canaan (Gen. 12:1-3). He said they would first move to Egypt and be there for 400 years. For most of that time they would be slaves working for Egypt, but He promised there would come a time of deliverance, and they would return and possess Canaan as their own nation (Gen. 15:13-14). God chose Egypt as the place for Jacob's family of seventy to grow into a race of millions. They could not conquer and fully inhabit the Promised Land until they greatly multiplied. The Israelites were delayed in dispossessing all the inhabitants of the land until the cup of iniquity of the Amorites was full (Gen. 15:16). God could then pronounce His eternal judgments on them and send the Israelites in to execute the judgments written (Ps. 149:6-9).

God told Joseph to take Jesus into Egypt for a period of time to protect Him from Herod. Christ's Church went into the Egypt of dead religion for the thousand-year Dark Age. But just as God planned to deliver Israel out of Egypt and restore them to their Abrahamic inheritance, God planned to bring His Church out of religious Egypt and restore them to their original inheritance in Christ. Moses and miracles brought God's people out of Egypt and to the Promised Land (Exod. 12–15). But Joshua and the new generation conquered it and made it the inheritance and dwelling place of God's people (Josh. 10:40-43; 12:7-24). The Second Reformation and the restoration ministers are destined to bring God's Church out of religious Egypt and restore all that was lost during the Dark Age. The Third Reformation will take the Church into their inheritance and dispossess all who are in their inheritance, which is new earth.

CHURCH WHEN JESUS COMES

There are many unanswered questions about the Dark Age of the Church. Nonetheless, there is one thing that it definitely revealed and made perfectly clear—the Church that Jesus is coming back to receive unto Himself will not be like the Church of the Dark Age. He is not coming for an apostate Church. It will not even be a malnourished, worn-out, wrinkled, formal, lifeless, immature, retarded, lukewarm, falling away, or holding-on-until-Jesus-comes Church. If He had to prophetically wait until the "Great Falling Away" took place before He could return for it, then He had no need to wait any longer, for the Church of the Dark Age was in that condition. Thank God! He didn't even make a move toward coming for that Church. Jesus didn't come and rapture the Church off the earth when the first-century Christians were going through the tribulation of martyrdom, nor did He come for the Church that had fallen away from the faith. He had a thousand years in which He could have translated the remnant of the faithful few who were walking in truth. But He did not.

Rapture, Not Backdoor Escapism

When Jesus comes to translate His Church, it will not be God's heavenly helicopter coming to air-lift the saints out before they all backslide or before the devil has overrun their camp. When Jesus comes, it will not be because the battle is too great for the army of the Lord. Neither will it be to jerk the Church out before the antichrist system devours it or to provide a retreat or an emergency rapture to preserve the Church from extinction. It is not "backdoor" escapism before the devil kicks down the front door.

Jesus Cannot Be Intimidated

God is not motivated by fear, nor is He forced into action because of things happening on earth. Jesus has predestined His Church to be perfect in purity and maturity, conformed to His image and likeness by the time He returns. All the devils in hell or human rebels on earth cannot stop Him from working on His building. He will not be threatened or intimidated by the *"accuser of our brethren"* (Rev. 12:10) into catching away His Church before He has put every living stone in place and has completed the building to His satisfaction. He will not literally come for the Church until she has gone through the *"times of restoration"* (Acts 3:21). The Church-Bride has been retarded and restricted in her growth for more than a thousand years. Jesus will now begin the process of bringing full restoration to His Church by launching the Second Church Reformation.

Let us now follow the Holy Spirit as He launches the Second Reformation of the Church, which will cover approximately 500 years. There will be many revivals and times of refreshing making preparation for the numerous restoration movements needed to bring full restoration to the Body of Christ. When sufficient restoration has taken place, then the Third and Final Church Reformation can be launched. It will reveal and fulfill God's ultimate purpose for mankind, the Church and planet Earth. All things in Heaven and on earth will be consummated in Christ Jesus and His corporate body, the Church. Nothing is more important than understanding and preparing to participate in the final reformation of the Church. But first we must understand and incorporate into our lives all the truths that will be restored during the Second Reformation of the Church.

NOTES

1. See "apostasia," http://www.studylight.org/lex/grk/view.cgi ?number=646.
2. Hamon, *The Eternal Church*, 107.
3. Ibid., 112.
4. John L. Sandford, *The Elijah Task* (Plainfield, New Jersey: Logos International, 1977), 108.

Chapter 5

PREPARATION FOR THE SECOND CHURCH REFORMATION

GOD'S PURPOSE FOR THE SECOND REFORMATION

God's purpose for the Second Reformation was to bring the Church out of its dark age of religious Egyptian bondage and to set it on its journey to full restoration until everything is in divine order to begin the Third and Final Church Reformation.

PRODUCTS, PEOPLE, AND THE PROCESS FOR PREPARATION

When it's time for God's next major purpose to be fulfilled on the earth, He commissions the Holy Spirit to set certain things in motion. He begins to make preparation in certain areas. The Holy

Spirit knows the process required. He prepares a people, a product, and a place to perpetuate His plan. The Lord then raises up a man with a message and a ministry that produces a movement that further fulfills His purpose by various methods and means.[1]

ISRAEL OUT OF EGYPT— CHURCH OUT OF DARK AGE

When God's time and purpose was activated for His chosen people of Israel to be delivered from the bondage of Egypt, He used all the processes listed in the previous paragraph. The man He chose was Moses. His product used to bring about the desired result was His miraculous judgment on Egypt. God's purpose was not just to bring them out but to take them to a certain place—Canaan Land (Deut. 6:23). (Only God knew the time period for the journey and when they would possess their promised place.) When Moses made his public announcement that God Almighty was activating His removal of Israel, the same thing happened to the Children of Israel as did to Jesus when He was baptized in water—a time of testing and things getting worse took place before the movement produced the desired result.

THE GREAT NEED FOR DELIVERANCE

For more than a thousand years during the Dark Age, God's Church had been in bondage to a totalitarian religious system. Church members were slaves to religious ritual and to dead doctrines such as buying relics and doing penance. There were no Bibles available for the people, so they had no way of knowing if what the Church hierarchy was dictating to them was according to the truth of God's Word. They were at the mercy of the clergy just as Israel was at the mercy of the slave masters. The Church members were whipped by the lashes of asceticism, thrown into solitary confinement by monasticism, and terrorized by the fires of purgatory, living in constant fear of eternal judgment by a wrathful God. The Church system that arose in the Dark Age claimed to have power to open and shut the doors of Heaven to any human being. There was more condemnation, paganism, and superstition than there was grace, pardon, and peace.

The Church was in as much bondage spiritually as the Children of Israel were physically. The Holy Spirit began to raise up a modern-day Moses. Fifteen hundred years before Christ and the First Reformation, God raised up Moses to be the man with the message that would launch the Israelites into their "Out of Egypt, Journeying to Canaan Movement." Fifteen hundred years after Christ and the First Reformation, a man by the name of Martin Luther would receive and deliver the message that would bring the Church out of its Dark Age and launch the Second Reformation of the Church.

RENAISSANCE FOR THE WORLD— REFORMATION FOR THE CHURCH

The Renaissance prepared the world for the major change that would be brought about by the Second Church Reformation. It awakened Europeans to a new interest in literature, art, and science. This new knowledge stirred within them a desire to depart from ignorance, superstition, and religious domination of the mind and conscience. The revival of enlightenment and learning helped launch the reformers in the Church and the explorers of new worlds. Columbus discovered America in 1492, just 25 years before the launching of the Second Reformation in 1517. America was prepared to be the birthing place of most of the restoration movements that would take place during the Second Reformation. New places and products were being prepared to accomplish God's purpose for a major revolutionary reformation.

HISTORY RESULTS FROM GOD'S PURPOSE FOR HIS CHURCH

From God's perspective and purpose, world history—the Renaissance, the discovery of new nations, new inventions, the rise and fall of nations—revolves around His Church; in fact, the Church is the center of all of God's interest and activities on earth.

Thus, the Church, and only the Church, is the key to and explanation of history. Therefore, history is only the handmaiden of the Church, and the nations of the world are but puppets manipulated by God for the purposes of His Church (Acts 17:36). Creation has no other aim; history has no other goal.[2]

THE PRINTING PRESS

In 1456, Johannes Gutenberg invented the printing press—just 61 years before the launching of the Second Reformation. It would be the product that would help in the preparation and propagation of the world renaissance and the Church Reformation. Prior to this invention, books had been circulated only as rapidly as they could be hand copied. Before the printing press, it cost a working man his yearly wage to purchase a Bible. It is significant in showing the desire of that time that the first book printed by Gutenberg was the Bible. The press brought the Scriptures into common use and led to their translation and circulation in all the languages of Europe. It prepared the way for the Reformation. For the people who read the New Testament in their own language began to realize that the papal church was far from the New Testament ideal. This revolutionary invention enabled the Reformers to quickly produce multiple pamphlets and books, which greatly helped to propagate the truths of the Second Reformation.

PREPARING FOR HARVEST

The divine principle for Reformation works similar to the way God established the natural principle of seed time and harvest. I was raised on a 300-acre farm in Oklahoma (1934–1951). Our main crops were corn, cotton, and peanuts. Before we could plant the seeds, the soil had to be prepared to properly receive the seeds. We first plowed the ground about a foot deep, turning the soil over to make it more fertile. We then ran a disc-rake over it to break up the clods and level out the ground. Then we plowed it into straight rows with a furrow about eight inches deep, and within this row we drove a mule pulling a single planter that planted the seeds. After the corn seed sprouted and grew about a foot high, we cultivated, putting about three inches of soil around the corn stalks. This was done for two purposes—to stabilize the corn stalk so it would hold the ears of corn without falling over and to cover the weeds that had sprouted that would choke out the corn or reduce its production. This was repeated two or three times until the corn grew too tall to cultivate. After that, all we could do was wait until the corn matured to harvest time. Harvesting at the right time produced the greatest harvest. The corn was then sold for cash, and some was put in the barn to feed the animals during the winter. The same type of preparation is made in the field of humanity for harvesting a major reformation movement.

THE FORERUNNERS

There were several *men* and *movements,* forerunners of the Second Reformation of the Church. Several men sought to reform the Church from the twelfth century until the time of the Reformation. Many attempts were made to deliver the people from the bondage that the church system had heaped on them. The voices from within the Church were suppressed and were placed in obscure places. Those who moved outside the state church were repressed, and some were annihilated by bloody persecutions. These *men* and *movements* were seeds planted in the field of preparation for harvesting the Second Reformation. Others watered the plant as it grew, and the men of the Restoration period were reapers of the harvest: *"I planted, Apollos watered, but God gave the increase"* (1 Cor. 3:6).

Many *men* never see the fulfillment of their revelation and preaching, especially if they are ahead of their time. The apostle Paul was such a man. His vision of the Church overcoming the sting of death and mortality was beyond his day. He gave us that promise from the Lord (1 Cor. 15:51-57; 1 Thess. 4:14-17). The patriarchs of old *"died in faith, not having received the promises"* of the prophetically promised Messiah (Heb. 11:13-16). Likewise, Paul died in faith believing for physical immortality but, instead, was a seed planter and a forerunner to that day of deliverance for the Church. Paul spoke of himself as *"one born out of due time"* (1 Cor. 15:8). He was not born of God until after Christ's resurrection and departure from earth, and he was not privileged to live to see His second coming, though he had divine insight concerning both. God is the one who determines what divine plan will be activated in our day and what part we will play in its fulfillment. Our responsibility is to walk in the revelation He has given, be established in the present truth, and fulfill the will of God for our generation (Acts 13:36).

The forerunners of the great Reformation did the best they could with the revelation, ability, and authority they had from the Lord. There were many preparation movements, but we will mention only a few of the major ones.

300 Years of Preparation Movements

The Albigenses Movement—Twelfth Century

During the twelfth century, the Albigenses Movement grew to prominence in southern France. Members repudiated the authority of tradition, circulated the New Testament, and opposed the Church doctrines of purgatory, image worship, and priestly claims. They held some peculiar doctrines and rejected the Old Testament. To wipe out this nest of rebellion, Pope Innocent III declared them "heretic" and called for a crusade against them. The reformers were destroyed by the slaughter of almost the entire population of the region, Catholic as well as Albigenses.[3]

The Waldensians Movement—Later Twelfth Century

Peter Waldo, a rich merchant of Lyons, was concerned with the brevity of life and sought counsel from a priest. Because the priest suggested that Waldo should sell his goods and give them to the poor, he did so in 1177. He turned his attention to the Scriptures and decided to follow the example of Christ. His followers called themselves the "Poor Men of Lyons." They went around preaching in simple garb, circulating the Scriptures, seeking to conform others to the first-century apostolic Church. They denied the efficacy of the Mass and the existence of purgatory. They revived the Donatist attitude (similar to the Baptist beliefs regarding separation of church and state and the Churches of Christ belief in baptismal regeneration) and adopted a pious view of life. In 1184 they were declared heretics by the Pope. They left France and spread into the Netherlands, Germany, and Bohemia, as well as Spain and Italy.[4]

The John Wycliffe Movement—c. 1329–1384

John Wycliffe was born and educated in England. He earned his doctorate in theology and was greatly influenced by the writings of Augustine. He was the morning star that shone the brightest before the dawn of the Reformation. A high official in the affairs of England, Wycliffe provided England with a new proclamation of the pure Gospel, acknowledging the Bible as the only source of truth. Declaring that Christ, not the Pope, was the head of the Church, he rejected the Doctrine of Infallibility of either pope or council, and held that papal decrees or pronouncements had authority only insofar as they were in harmony with Scripture. The clergy was not to be lords over the flock but were to serve and help the people. He attacked the mendicant friars and the system of monasticism; wrote against the doctrine of "trans-substantiation" (i.e., that in the mass the bread and wine are transformed into the actual body and blood of Christ), regarding the elements as symbols; and urged that the church service be made more simple, according to the New Testament pattern.

His greatest work was his translation of the Bible from the Vulgate, the Latin version, into English. It appeared in the year of his death, 1382. His followers were called Lollards, who at one time were numerous. After Wycliffe was declared to be a heretic by the ecclesiastical system, his followers were severely persecuted and were virtually extinguished. John Wycliffe's strong influential preaching and his translation brought the plant of Restoration closer to harvest time. He added new life to the "babe in the womb" of the structural Church that was soon to be birthed in Restoration, soon to breathe and live on its own without the Church body of the Dark Ages.[5]

The John Huss Movement—c. 1372–1415

John Huss became the voice of reform in Bohemia as Wycliffe had been in England. He likewise was an educated man, having earned his bachelor's and master's degrees at the University of Prague. By 1398 he was lecturing on theology at the university. He was ordained to the priesthood in 1401, and the next year became Rector of the

University of Prague. Huss believed and preached all the teachings of Wycliffe. In his chief work, *On the Church,* Huss defined the Church as the *Body of Christ,* with Christ its only head. Although he defended the traditional authority of the clergy, he taught that only God can forgive sin. The clerical hierarchy of the world-dominating Roman Catholic Church branded him a heretic and his teachings as heresies. He was summoned to appear before the Council at Constance.

He agreed to go after safe conduct was guaranteed by King Wenceslaus, Emperor Sigismund, and by the Pope himself. But the pledge was violated upon the principle that "faith was not to be kept with heretics." He was condemned and burned at the stake, without a real opportunity to explain his views. However, his heroic death aroused the national feelings of the Czech people, who established the Hussite church in Bohemia until the Hapsburgs conquered Bohemia in 1620 and reestablished the Roman Catholic Church as the state religion.

According to tradition, one of the most profound prophecies concerning the coming reformation was made by John Huss just before he was burned to death. "You are now roasting the goose [*Huss* means goose in Bohemian], but in a hundred years there will rise up a swan whom you shall not roast nor scorch. His men will hear songs and God will allow him to live."[6]

Girolamo Savonarola—1452–1498

Savonarola (1452–1498) rose up as a voice of reform in Italy. He had no new revelation of Scripture to offer, but he preached against sin and corruption in commoners, government, clergy, and in the papal office. He gave some prophecies concerning the future development of Italy. There is one particularly interesting record of the results of his preaching. At the carnival in Florence in 1496, Savonarola inspired the burning of the vanities when the people made a great

THE FINAL REFORMATION & GREAT AWAKENING

bonfire of cosmetics, false hair, pornographic books, and gambling equipment. Savonarola suffered the same fate as the other reformers who dared question the authority of the pope, or the unscriptural doctrines and practices of the Dark Age Church.

A Changing World

There were many other contributions to the preparation necessary for the birth of the Second Reformation, such as the fall of Constantinople to Mohammed in 1453. Most historians place that incident as the dividing point between medieval and modern times. It is hard to grasp what it would have been like to live in those days. The whole world was going through a revolutionary change and evolving into a new era. Printing marked the end of mass ignorance. Gunpowder ended the usefulness of knights and changed the whole strategy of warfare. The compass put an end to man's limited knowledge about unknown lands and seas. Man rediscovered that the world was not flat, but round. Without the fear of falling off the end of the world, men began to explore the earth. They began to advance learning and gain new understanding of the earth, science, religion, and governments. Man slowly but steadily walked out of the shadow of the medieval Dark Ages and into the light of a new and modern world.

Eschatological Confusion

Theologians were at a loss concerning their eschatology (doctrine of end-time events). They did not know how to interpret what was happening in the light of biblical teaching concerning the end time. They did not want to make the same mistake as the theologians and people of the tenth century. Many were convinced that the world would come to an end in the year 1000. From their understanding of Scripture, most end-time prophecies had come to pass or were coming to pass. There had been a great falling away from the faith. It looked as though Islam was taking over the world, and it would be the antichrist system that would rule. There were wars and rumors of wars.

> The people who lived in the tenth century thought the Bible said something that meant the world was coming to an end in the year 1000, which was called the "millennium" from the Latin word meaning 1,000 years. Some people were glad the world was coming to an end. They were so poor and miserable and unhappy that they were anxious to go to heaven, where everything would be fine and lovely—if they had been good. So they were particularly good and did everything they could to earn a place for themselves in heaven.
>
> Others were not so anxious to have the world come to an end. But, they thought, if it were coming to an end so soon, they might as well get all the worldly pleasure they could while they still had a chance.
>
> The year 1000 came, and nothing happened. As time went on, without any change, people began to think the end was delayed for some reason they could not explain.[7]

Coming in Restoration First

The first-millennium Christians were just as convinced that the coming of the Lord would take place by the year 1000 as many present-day Christians are convinced it will take place before the end of the second millennium of the Church. (Church was birthed in A.D. 30; second millennium of the Church ends A.D. 2030.) Those living in the fifteenth century had no way of knowing what was about to break forth on the world.

The revolutionary Second Reformation of the Church was about to be launched into the world. God's initial purpose for the Second Reformation was to activate the fulfillment of Acts 3:21. Apostle Peter declared that Jesus' second coming could not take place until the Church went through its "times of restoration." Apostle Paul later declared that this restoration of truth and the ministry of the fivefold ministers must function until the Church reaches the maturity and ministry of Christ (Eph. 4:11-16). The Church becoming all God wants it to be means more to Jesus than the time it takes, even if it ends up taking another 500 years.

Let us now progress to the Restoration of the Church to determine the men, movements, methods, ministries, and restorational truths God uses to bring His many-membered corporate Body of Christ to the place where it is ready for the Third and Final Reformation of the Church.

NOTES

1. Hamon, *The Eternal Church*, 119.
2. Paul Billheimer, *Destined for the Throne* (Minneapolis, MN: Bethany House, 1996).
3. Hamon, *The Eternal Church*, 124.
4. Ibid.
5. Ibid.
6. Dr. David Huebert, "Outlined Study on Church Restoration," Chilliwack, B.C., Canada.
7. V.M. Hillyer and E.G. Huey, *The Medieval World* (New York, NY: Meredith Press, 1966), 54.

Chapter 6

REVELATION AND RESTORATION

Divine Purpose

God's main reason for the Second Reformation was to activate the Church into its prophesied "times of restoration." It was prophesied by the prophets in the Old Testament and apostolically decreed by Peter in the New Testament (Acts 3:21).

Jesus Kept in Heaven Until Full Restoration: Acts 3:19-25

This Scripture is at the core of this discourse and a key text on restoration, as John 3:16 is a key text that Christians use for salvation. It is expedient that this Scripture be given greater in-depth study than the other numerous Scriptures mentioned. The writer has used Acts 3:19-21 in teaching the restoration of the Church for 50 years. Nevertheless, before these things were put in writing, a thorough reexamination of this particular Scripture was made in the following areas: etymologically—to determine proper word usage; theologically—to evaluate the thinking of other theologians; exegetically—to derive the original Greek meaning; and topically throughout Scripture—to be sure the interpretation given is in agreement with the teaching of the whole Word of God. After applying all the principles of biblical hermeneutics to this passage, I am convinced its application to the restoration of the Church is in divine order.

NEW WAY AND A NEW DAY

In verse 19 Peter spoke to the Jews to repent and be converted, that their sins might be blotted out, for they had just crucified the *"Prince of life"* (Acts 3:15), God's promised Messiah. Jesus had recently fulfilled all the Scriptures concerning the suffering Savior. The majority of God's chosen people missed the "day of their visitation" by not recognizing that the coming of the Messiah had taken place (Luke 19:44; Acts 3:18). The First Church Reformation had established a new day and a new way.[1] Becoming a child of God would no longer be by ancestral descent as a Jew, but whosoever believed in Jesus would become a child of God. Now "both Jew and Gentile" are sinners in need of a Savior (Gal. 3:22; Rom. 3:9; 10:4). All must now repent and be converted. Peter declared that if they would repent and be converted, they would again become children of God by accepting Messiah Jesus whom God had sent for their redemption. The Jews who heeded his message of repentance were converted and became members of Christ's corporate Body, the Church.

PROPHETIC APPLICATIONS

Most prophetic Scriptures have two applications—natural and spiritual, individual and corporate. A prophetic Scripture can apply to natural Israel, the Messiah, and the Church, and not do injustice to the principle of biblical hermeneutics. It can have a natural fulfillment with Israel, personal fulfillment in Jesus, and then a spiritual corporate fulfillment in the Church. For instance, examine the Scripture in Hosea 11:1: *"When Israel was a child, I loved him, and out of Egypt I called My son."* The context of the Scripture definitely shows that the prophet is speaking of the time when God led the nation of Israel out of Egypt. He showed His love by delivering them from their Egyptian bondage and slavery. However, Matthew, in his book (Matt. 2:15), pulls one phrase from this Scripture to prove that it has a personal application to Jesus the Messiah. The Pharisee and Sadducee theologians could have argued with Matthew that he was taking the Scripture out of context. How could he use it to prove that this Jesus was the Messiah when it was clear that it was speaking of the nation of Israel? Regardless of the seeming contradiction, the Holy Spirit did inspire Hosea to prophesy this concerning Israel and also inspired Matthew to apply it to Jesus.

In the same manner, Hosea 11:1 can be applied personally to a sinner whom Jesus loved and called out of his Egyptian land of satanic bondage. It can also apply corporately to the Church, which consists of many of God's sons. At the beginning of the Second Reformation, God called the Church out of its Egyptian land of religious slavery and dead works that existed during the Dark Ages. His call brought the Church out of religious Egypt as well as started it on its goal to ultimate restoration.

GOD'S NEW RACE, NEW NATION: THE CHURCH

Christians today should get more excited about the Church and prophecies being fulfilled in it than about any other prophetic fulfillment. The Church is the highest realm, the most privileged people, and the greatest race of beings in God's eternal universe. Even Jews who become Christians are no longer Israelites in God's sight, but sons of God and members of the Body of Christ: *"There is neither Jew nor Gentile...for you are all one in Christ Jesus"* (Gal. 3:28 NIV).

SCRIPTURAL CRITERIA FOR SECOND COMING OF CHRIST

Dispensationalists see no prophecies to be fulfilled in the Church between Jesus' first coming and second coming. They believe in the imminent return of Christ regardless of the condition of the Church. Their criteria for the coming of the Lord are world events and the state of Israel. However, the foremost and greatest criterion for the second coming of Jesus is that which is taking place in the Church. He is coming back for the Church, but our text states that Heaven cannot release Christ to return *until* the "period of the great Restoration" has been accomplished in the Church. Notice, Peter declares in Acts 3:19 "times" of restitution or restoration indicating that there would come several restorational truth visitations to the Church. Jesus cannot be released from Heaven to return to earth to set up His literal Kingdom until His Church (His spiritual Kingdom) has been fully established and perfected.

Note how Acts 3:21 is rendered in different translations:

> King James: *"Whom the heaven must receive until the times of restitution of all things, which God hath spoken by the mouth of all his holy prophets since the world began."*
>
> The Living Bible: *"For he must remain in heaven until the final recovery of all things from sin, as prophesied from ancient times."*

Moffatt: *"[Christ] must be kept in heaven till the period of the great Restoration. Ages ago God spoke of this by the lips of his holy prophets."*

Amplified Bible, Classic Edition: *"Whom heaven must receive [and retain] until the time for the complete restoration of all that God spoke by the mouth of all His holy prophets for ages past [from the most ancient time in the memory of man]."*

CHURCH RESTORATION *UNTIL...*

Take note of the key word *until* or *till*: "Heaven must receive, keep, retain Jesus until..."; the Holy Spirit of promise *"is the earnest of our inheritance until..."* (Eph. 1:14 KJV); "Jesus must remain seated at the right hand of the Father until...." These and many other Scriptures reveal that certain things cannot happen until certain other things are revealed and fulfilled. The key emphasis here is that Jesus cannot return from Heaven to receive His Church unto Himself until it reaches its scripturally predicted state of purity and maturity and fulfills its predestined purpose. The Holy Spirit has been restoring truth after truth to the Church over the last 500 years. The Church has now obtained enough truth and maturity to begin fulfilling God's third purpose for the Church, which will be accomplished during the Third and Final Church Reformation.

WHAT ARE THE "ALL THINGS" TO BE RESTORED?

It is important that the words *all things* be restricted to *"that which God hath spoken through the mouth of His prophets."* There is no mention or prediction in the whole of God's book concerning the conversion and restoration of the wicked dead, fallen angels, or satan himself. The Bible talks about the Church being restored, Israel being restored, and the earth being restored. But no mention is made of satan, fallen angels, demons, or any wicked dead human soul being restored back to God (Heb. 1:13).

Of all the major commentaries I have read, I feel the following comments give the best exposition of Acts 3:21:

> *"Whom the heaven must receive."* The words have a pregnant force *"must receive and keep." "Until the times of restitution of all things."* The "times" seem distinct from the "seasons" as more permanent. This is the only passage in which the word translated "restitution" is found in the New Testament. Etymologically, it conveys the thought of *restoration to an earlier and better state,* rather than that of simple consummation or completion, which the immediate context seems, in some measure, to suggest. It finds an interesting parallel in the *"new heavens and new earth"*—involving, as they do, a restoration of all things to their true order—of Second Peter 3:13. It does not necessarily involve, as some have thought, the final salvation of all men, but it does suggest a state in which "righteousness," and not "sin" shall have dominion over a redeemed and new-created world; and that idea suggests a wider scope as to the possibilities of growth in wisdom and holiness, or even of repentance and conversion, in the unseen world than that which Christendom has too often been content. The corresponding verb is found in the words, *"Elijah truly shall come first, and restore all things."*[2]

Jesus declared that John the Baptist was the person who came in the spirit of Elijah (Matt. 11:10-11). He was the instrument used to restore and prepare the way for the coming of Jesus and the First

Church Reformation. The Church will be the instrument that will move in the power and spirit of Elijah, restoring all things that have been spoken by the mouth of all the holy prophets since the world began, releasing Jesus from the heavens and bringing about the *Third Reformation climaxing with the second coming of Christ.*

PROPHETS TO THE CHURCH, NATIONS, AND ISRAEL

The author of this book was not called and anointed to be a prophet concerning Israel or world conditions but a voice concerning the Church. He has no special revelation on God's eternal plan concerning the Jews, Israel, or the Jewish temple. He is not anti-Israel. He taught the Book of Romans for four years in Bible college and emphasized that chapters 9, 10, and 11 show the election, rejection, and restoration of Israel. Acts 3:19-21 evidently will have a natural fulfillment concerning God's chosen nation of Israel. For instance— God promised Israel that after He had dissolved their nation and scattered them, He would regather them to their land and give them their own national identity. This became a natural fulfillment in 1948 when the land was assigned to Israel as their own nation. "Natural" Israel and the Jews are having "times" of restoration that are gradually restoring them to all that the prophets predicted they would be and would have.

THREE MAJOR THINGS MUST REACH THE PEAK OF FULFILLMENT

There are three things that must dovetail together in order for the coming of the Lord to take place: Old Testament prophecies and New Testament teachings concerning the Church, prophecies concerning the state of Israel and the Jews, prophecies concerning world conditions. *All three areas are reaching the peak of fulfillment, but the*

Church is the key to the fulfillment of prophecy for Israel and for the world. Even the Christian prophets to Israel and extreme dispensationalists state that Jesus must finish His ministry to the Gentile Church and rapture it out of the world before He can turn to the Jews as their Messiah King. This still puts the Church on God's priority list as the determining factor in the second coming of Christ Jesus.

CHURCH IS DETERMINING FACTOR

This fact puts Jesus and His Church in the driver's seat. Christians are to "redeem the time" (Eph. 5:15-17) and "occupy until He comes" (Luke 19:13). This is not accomplished by getting excited about Israel or becoming discouraged over world conditions. The Church is *not* to sit around whining and pining for the coming of the Lord. If we are really serious about His coming, we should act on the apostle Peter's words, *"hastening the coming of the day of God"* (2 Pet. 3:12 LEB) or as the Living Bible says, to *"hurry it along."* This can be accomplished by us, the Church, going on to perfection in purity and maturity and becoming the last generation that overcomes all things, bringing about *"the final recovery of all things from sin, as prophesied from ancient times."*

WHY AREN'T MORE MINISTERS SAYING, "RESTORE"?

Throughout Christendom, just a remnant of ministers teach on the restoration of the Church. During the Dark Age of the Church, there came a desperate need for reformers to cry out for restoration. There is still a need today for reformers to cry out for restoration and transformation.

Through our study on the Dark Age of the Church we saw that the Church was left spiritually deaf and blind. Most of the spiritual leaders of the Dark Ages had lost touch with the *"Spirit of truth"* and the Spirit of revelation in the knowledge of the Son of God (John 16:13; Eph. 1:18). The Church had not only lost original reality in the doctrines of Christ and the experiential truths of the early Church, but they had also added man-made traditions, doctrines of devils, paganistic-type church practices, and ritualistic ways of worship. The Church was in the same condition before the days of the Second Reformation as Judaism was just prior to the coming of Christ Jesus. The pope and priests were "minoring in majors" and "majoring in minors" just as the Pharisees and Sadducees were in Jesus' day. The Scripture that most graphically describes the leaders of the medieval church is Isaiah 42:18-22. Of the leadership Isaiah says, *"Who is blind but My servant, Or deaf...as the Lord's servant?"* (Isa. 42:19). The people are described as *"a people robbed and plundered; all of them are snared in holes, and they are hidden in prison houses; they are for prey, and no one delivers; for plunder, and no one says, 'Restore!'"* (Isa. 42:22).

THOUGH NONE WERE SAYING RESTORE, GOD DECLARES, "I WILL RESTORE!"

The Book of Joel contains one of the most encouraging Scriptures of Israel's natural hope and the Church's spiritual hope for restoration.

> *Be glad then, you children of Zion, and rejoice in the Lord your God: for He has given you the former rain faithfully, and He will cause the rain to come down for you—the former rain, and the latter rain in the first month. The threshing floors shall be full of wheat* [Word of God], *and the vats shall overflow with new wine* [New Truth] *and oil* [anointing]. *So I **will restore** to you the years that the swarming locust has eaten, the crawling locust, the consuming locust, and the chewing locust.... You shall eat in*

*plenty and be satisfied, and praise the name of the Lord
your God, who has dealt wondrously with you; and My
people shall never be put to shame* (Joel 2:23-26).

THE THIRD REFORMATION
WILL BE GREATER

The end of the Church will be even greater than its beginning (Eccles. 2:9). God promised that the glory of the latter house (latter Church) will be greater than that of the former house (early Church) (Hag. 2:9). The Church flirted with the world and paganism as Samson did with Delilah. Samson's secret strength was discovered and taken away. His eyes were put out, and he was put into prison. Blinded and chained to the grinding mill, he went in circles until his seven locks of hair began to grow. When Samson's hair was fully restored, God gave him back his ministry of destroying the enemy and delivering God's people. More was accomplished after his restoration than had been accomplished in all his former years (Judg. 16:28-30). In like manner, the eyes of the Church were put out during the Dark Age. The Body of Christ was bound at the grinding mill of doing penance and trying to earn peace with God by religious dead works. It went in circles for a thousand years, but its locks of hair began to grow and will continue to grow until…. The last-century Church will accomplish more in its Third Reformation and will finalize God's purposes that He preordained the mortal Church to accomplish.

SPIRITUAL GROWTH: A
BIBLICAL COMMAND

The following Scriptures on progressive growth are included to clarify and amplify the fact that God desires and demands a going on and a growing up: Job 17:9; Psalms 84:7; 92:12; Proverbs 4:18; Isaiah 28:10; Hosea 6:3; 14:5-7; Malachi 4:2; Mark 4:32; John 16:13; Acts 3:19-21;

Romans 1:17; 8:29; Second Corinthians 3:18; Ephesians 2:21; 4:12,15; 5:27; Philippians 3:14; Second Thessalonians 1:3; Hebrews 2:10; 5:14; 6:1-2; First Peter 2:2; Second Peter 1:5-12; and First John 3:1-3.

SCRIPTURES ARE EMPHATIC

From these numerous Scriptures, it is evident that Christians who make up the Body of Christ, the Church, should be growing, increasing, and abounding continually. Three Scriptures speak of "going up," but 30 Scriptures speak of "growing up." At a 10 to 1 ratio, these Scriptures reveal that Christians should spend 10 times as much time on growing up as thinking about going up. Christians are to go from *"strength to strength," "faith to faith," "glory to glory"* to *"follow on to know the Lord."* Further, they must continue adding and growing in His grace and knowledge until they are *"changed into His same image,"* and have *"grown up into Christ in all things," "unto the measure of the stature of the fullness of Christ,"* becoming perfect in purity and maturity that Christ may present them unto Himself *"a glorious church, not having spot or wrinkle or any such thing, but that she should be holy and without blemish"* (Eph. 5:27).

"Beloved, now we are children of God; and it has not yet been revealed what we shall be, but we know that when He is revealed, we shall be like Him, for we shall see Him as He is. And everyone who has this hope in Him purifies himself, just as He is pure" (1 John 3:2-3). *"For whom He foreknew, He also predestined to be conformed to the image of His Son, that He might be the firstborn among many brethren"* (Rom. 8:29). Christ Jesus suffered and died that He might bring *"many sons to glory"* (that glory is Christ's image, likeness, and manifested presence and power; Heb. 2:10). The Holy Spirit is commissioned to take Christians from *"glory to glory"* until they reach Christ's perfect image, fullness, and maturity (2 Cor. 3:18). The corporate Church will have many progressive restoration movements

during the Second Church Reformation. Let us now cover the major restoration movements that were destined to take place during the Second Reformation. For no one will be qualified to participate in the Third and Final Reformation unless all the truths and ministries that have been restored to the Church are living realities within their lives. So it is essential that all Christians who are destined to participate know every truth and ministry that has been restored and then experience and practice them until they are their life and ministry.

God has predestined that His Third Reformation saints will mature to the place where they will be thinking Christ's thoughts, manifesting His majesty, demonstrating His Kingdom, portraying His power, and glorifying His grace. The Church will become a personification of the life and ministry of Jesus Christ. The end-time Church will be fully prepared to be joint heirs ruling and reigning as co-laborers with Jesus Christ in fulfilling all the purposes of God and executing all the written judgments.[3]

NOTES

1. John 14:6; 2 Cor. 5:17; Heb. 8:8,13; 9:15; 10:20

2. Charles John Ellicot, ed., *Ellicot's Commentary on the Whole Bible* (Grand Rapids, Michigan: Zondervan Publishing House, 1954), Vol. VII; *The Acts of the Apostles*, E.H. Plumptre, 19.

3. Rom. 8:17; Ps. 149:6-9; Rev. 19:1-10

Chapter 7

BIRTH OF THE SECOND REFORMATION

DIVINE PRINCIPLES FOR BIRTHING A REFORMATION

From the recorded history of the first and second reformations, we are able to derive the principles that God uses to birth a new restoration movement. There is usually a restoration movement that starts the labor pains for birthing a Reformation. The Protestant Movement was the movement that began the prophesied period of Church restoration and birthed the Second Church Reformation.

The main principle is—God chooses a man and then gives him a revelation of the message that will birth the new move of God. Then the Holy Spirit sends a sovereign move of God's presence that anoints and empowers His chosen vessels to demonstrate and propagate the truth. In the early years of the 1500s, the first requirement was for Heaven to find the man on earth that God wanted to be His voice of reform.

The Heavenly Host Looking for a Man

To make a restoration a reality, the business at hand was to find the right man. All Heaven knows that when God gets ready to do something on earth, He needs a human to be His instrument for its fulfillment. Therefore, the angels began to scatter around the earth in search of a man (Heb. 1:14). The *"eyes of the Lord run to and fro throughout the whole earth"* seeking for a man (2 Chron. 16:9). God sought for a man to stand in the gap and make up the hedge to begin the restoration to the Church (Ezek. 22:30).

The eyes of the Lord swept around the world. They came to Germany and zeroed in on a young man by the name of Martin Luther. The year was 1505. Jesus gave the command, "Start this man's preparation for his day of presentation for the liberation of My Church into its period of the great Restoration." Immediately, all of Heaven began to concentrate on fulfilling God's will.

God's Process for Choosing and Making His Man

God has several methods He uses in the calling and making of a person for divine ministry. A few of these methods are dissatisfaction, frustration, conviction, and consternation, which lead a person to the place of desperation. At this point, God brings a revelation that gives the person a deep appreciation of God's will for his or her life. This process makes that person willing to make God's truth known to the world regardless of the price.

The Man Chosen, Martin Luther

God put Martin Luther through this process until his day of presentation for the declaration of God's revelation of justification by faith. This truth established the doctrine of repentance from dead works, which is the initial truth to be restored during the restoration of the Church (Heb. 6:1-2).

At the young age of 22, Martin Luther had no idea what God had planned for him, nor the process that was being implemented to bring that plan into fulfillment. He was only time and earth-conscious. He only knew that at that moment he and a friend were caught in an electrical storm. It looked as though his life could be ended momentarily. He thought over his last 22 years of life. He remembered his peasant parents sacrificing and persisting until he had received a good education. He remembered attending the schools at Magdeburg and Eisenach and *singing* to support himself. (Remember the prophecy that John Huss gave that God would raise up a singing prophet who would bring restoration.) Now he was enrolled as a law student at the University of Leipzig and would soon graduate to enter a law career.

HEAVEN USES EARTH'S HAPPENINGS TO GET GOD'S CHOSEN MAN'S ATTENTION

As Martin Luther was horseback riding in the rain with his friend, his thoughts were interrupted by the sudden clap of thunder and flash of lightening. The next moment his close friend was dead, and he narrowly escaped death himself. Heaven had caught his attention! A consciousness of his sinful condition came upon him. He began to be motivated by a deep desire to find God. He started on his quest to find peace with God. He forsook his law career, and in 1505 entered the Erfurt monastery of the Augustinian order.

Luther became dissatisfied with the condition of his soul through the fear of death and the convicting power of the Holy Spirit. However, in his day, the surest road to earning one's salvation was the monastic life. He did everything his church order taught to make himself holy and at peace with God. He diligently practiced extreme asceticism, even to the extent of self-flagellation, endless fasting, and almost anything he could think of to inflict self-punishment upon his body. This type of self-denial and doing penance was guaranteed by the church to bring peace with God. But it only brought more sin consciousness and failure to find the peace he so desperately desired.

Luther became "frustrated" with his concept of God as a hard-hearted and tyrannical God, demanding so much and giving so little in return. The superior in his order suggested Luther give himself to the study of Scriptures and perhaps he could find his peace with God. It was the best advice he ever received from the church.

THE SPIRIT OF REVELATION

After two years in the monastery, he was ordained in 1507 at the age of 24. Four years later, at the age of 28, Luther became a professor at the University of Wittenburg. It was during his years as a researcher and professor of biblical studies that the spirit of revelation came. Romans 1:17 became a living reality to him: *"The just shall live by faith."* He realized it was *"not by works of righteousness which we have done, but according to His mercy"* (Tit. 3:5) and *"by grace you have been saved through faith, and that not of yourselves: it is the gift of God, not of works, lest anyone should boast"* (Eph. 2:8-9). The Scripture that finally brought his assurance and peace was Romans 5:1: *"Therefore, having been justified by faith, we have peace with God through our Lord Jesus Christ."* It is important to note that a restoration revelation gives the true interpretation and application of a Scripture. Luther's revelation resulted in a transforming experience. He recorded his experience, which is later described as being born again.

His personal testimony reveals how he was thinking and interpreting certain Scriptures until he received his born-again experience.

> I greatly longed to understand Paul's Epistle to the Romans, and nothing stood in the way but that one

expression, "the righteousness of God," because I took it to mean that righteousness whereby God is righteous and deals righteously in punishing the unrighteous. Night and day I pondered until...I grasped the truth that the righteousness of God is that righteousness whereby, through grace and sheer mercy, he justifies us by faith. Thereupon I *felt myself to be reborn* and to have gone through open doors into paradise. The whole Scripture took on a new meaning, and whereas before "the righteousness of God" had filled me with hate, now it became to me inexpressibly sweet in greater love. This passage of Paul became to me a gateway to heaven.[1]

RESTORATION REVELATION BRINGS DISSATISFACTION AND DISASSOCIATION WITH THE OLD

Luther received his born-again experience through faith in the accomplished work of Christ on Calvary and received the imputed righteousness of God according to His mercy. It transformed his understanding of the nature and character of God and his own teaching of the Gospels. He began to compare his Roman Catholic Church with the New Testament Church as revealed in the Book of Acts. He saw that many things were not biblical. Being a professor at Wittenberg University, he preached and lectured for more than four years after his revelation on justification. His convictions became stronger as he preached on this biblical truth and the errors of the structured Church system.

RELIGIOUS PRACTICES THAT PROVOKED

The degradation of the structural Church agitated Luther into making a declaration of 95 theological arguments against its unscriptural practices. Luther rebelled in his born-again spirit against the sale and worship of supposedly holy relics. He renounced these assumptions and the religious, superstitious adoration and awe of these objects. The last straw was the issuance of a special indulgence by Rome. The reigning pope, Leo X, needing large sums of money for the completion of St. Peter's church at Rome, permitted an agent named John Tetzel to go throughout Germany selling certificates signed by the pope himself. These certificates purported to bestow the pardon of all sins, not only on the holders of the certificates, but on friends living or dead on whose behalf they were purchased, without confession, repentance, penance, or absolution by a priest. Tetzel told the people, "As soon as your coin clinks in the chest, the souls of your friends will rise out of Purgatory to Heaven."[2] Luther vehemently preached against Tetzel and his selling of pardons, denouncing the pope's authority to issue such indulgences. He also decided to take some definite action to rectify the situation.

God started the process of preparation when His chosen vessel was age 22, but it was eight years later at age 30 that Martin Luther received his revelation of justification by faith that produced his born-again experience. It was another four years of teaching his revelation before, at the age of 34, Martin Luther took the action that resulted in the birthing of the Second Reformation.

THE SECOND REFORMATION'S OFFICIAL BIRTH DATE—OCTOBER 31, 1517

All Protestant historians mark this memorable time as the official day when the Reformation began. The hammer that caused an echo to be heard to the ends of the earth was the one Luther used to nail his *95 Theses* (declarations) to the Castle Church in Wittenberg, Germany. On the eve of All Souls' Day, October 31, 1517, Martin Luther's hammer sparked into flame "The Great Period of Church Restoration" and brought about what became known as the "Protestant Movement." News of his *theses* spread like wildfire throughout Europe. Within two weeks, every university and religious center was agog with excitement. All marveled that one obscure monk from an unknown university had stirred the whole of Europe.

They did not know that the God of Heaven had decreed that this man was the chosen instrument of the Lord to loose that rock (Church) that was hewn out of the mountain (Christ) and start it rolling. It would gain speed and size as it progressed like a snowball rolling down a snow-covered mountain. When it reached its objective, it would become judgment to the nations and bring the great giant image crumbling to the ground, putting all things fully under the feet of Jesus and His Church (Dan. 2:44-45).

OLD ORDER RELIGION: GREATEST ENEMY OF A CHURCH REFORMATION

The devil and the religious system tried to stop this voice of reformation as they tried to stop the reformers of the past. But this man was the swan that Huss had predicted would arise 100 years later and who God would not allow to be martyred but would cause to live. He would be the singing prophet who would open the door for the spiritual Church to emerge from the structural Church as a butterfly emerges from its cocoon and starts on its flight to full restoration. Luther was the man God used to lead the Church out of its religious Egyptian bondage 1,500 years *after* the coming of Christ, as Moses was the man who led the Children of Israel out of their literal Egyptian bondage 1,500 years *before* the coming of the Messiah.

You will notice from the beginning of the record of man that great changes take place in cycles and in multiples of 500 years. Even the Church has had similar experiences. It was birthed in A.D. 30 and around 500 years later had gone into apostasy. By the year 1,000

105

it had degraded to its depths, and 500 years later the period of the Great Restoration started. Hopefully, within another 500 years the *restoration of all things* will be finalized during the Third Church Reformation, thereby releasing Jesus from Heaven to return, bind the devil in the bottomless pit, and set up the Kingdom of God on earth.

THE REFORMER'S INITIAL OBJECTIVE

Martin Luther's only objective in making a public notice of 95 arguments against the church's abuse and use of indulgences, relics, etc. was simply to help delete some of these unscriptural practices from the Church. The 95 *Theses* were not intended as a call to reformation. Luther had no idea of breaking away from his beloved Catholic Church and starting another movement that would emerge into a whole new Christian era. Luther did not have this in mind, but it was in the mind of Jesus. Luther stood for reform within the Roman Catholic Church; nevertheless, he was excommunicated three years later, in 1520. He was commanded to recant, as were all his followers. They were given 60 days, and if they didn't recant from their so-called heresies, the penalty would be death.

LUTHER THE REFORMER EXCOMMUNICATED

Luther dared to defy the pope and his councils who claimed "authority to shut the gates of Hell and open the door to Paradise." The Roman Catholic Church made a decree that all of the faithful to the church were to burn all of Luther's writings. Luther met the excommunication with defiance and called it "the execrable bull of Antichrist." He publicly burned it December 10, 1520, at the gates of Wittenberg, before an assembly of university professors, students, and common people. This constituted Martin Luther's final separation and denunciation of the Roman Catholic Church. Luther's dramatic stand against both pope and emperor fired the imagination of Europe. He started a chain reaction that swept around the world. Other men in other countries arose to propagate the same truth: Ulrich Zwingli, John Calvin, John Tyndale, John Knox, Philip Melanchthon, and Martin Bucer. These are the men best known for their contributions to the great Protestant Movement.

STRUCTURED CHURCH SHAKEN

The Roman Catholic and Eastern Orthodox churches were the only representatives of Christendom until the reformation churches began to be established. This shook up the old order, causing them to begin persecuting the new as the old order Judaism persecuted the new order of Christians during the First Church Reformation. The Protestant Movement sparked wars between nations in the separation and ensuing battle between Catholicism and Protestantism. Halley states that "the number of martyrs under papal persecutions far out-numbered the early Christian martyrs under pagan Rome."[3] Confusion and chaos temporarily reigned in different countries until the lines were drawn between Catholic countries and Protestant countries: "The Reformation was followed by one hundred years of religious wars."[4]

RESTORATION TRUTH CAUSES PROBLEMS?

Could all this confusion, war, persecution, hatred, and division be the result of a restoration of truth? Yes! Consider what happened to God's chosen people Israel and to the religion of Judaism when Jesus came bringing the revelation of grace and truth! The revelation of Jesus Christ made provision for the restoration of man back to God, but it also brought riots, revolution, and a revolt of His followers against the established religious system. The Protestant Movement likewise created a worldwide revolution. One will notice in studying the restoration of the Church that each of the doctrines of Christ when restored bring about the same responses. Every restoration revelation brings a revolution. New wine cannot be contained in old, dried-and-set-in-their-ways wineskins; it will burst forth every time (Matt. 9:17). New wineskins must be prepared to hold the new wine (truth). "In every nation where Protestantism triumphed a National Church arose: Lutheran in Germany; Episcopal in England; Presbyterian in Scotland; etc."[5]

Regardless of the upset of religion, men, and nations, Heaven was thrilled, for the spiritual Church, the Body of Christ, had taken the first step in its journey to full restoration. The period of the great restoration of the Church was activated. Now the Second Reformation would continue bringing restoration to the Church until it was equipped enough to activate the Third Reformation.

ENDNOTES

1. Dr. Tim Dowley, *Eerdman's Handbook to the History of Christianity* (Grand Rapids, MI: Wm. B. Eerdman's Publishing Co., 1977); "Reform," by James Atkinson, 366.
2. Hamon, *The Eternal Church*, 122.
3. Halley, *Halley's Bible Handbook,* 793.
4. Ibid., 792.
5. Ibid., 794.

THE SECOND
REFORMATION:
1517 TO 2007

RESTORATION MOVEMENTS DURING
THE SECOND REFORMATION

Restoration Essential for God's Purpose

The plan and purpose of Jesus Christ from the beginning was to *build* His Church. During His ministry on earth, He made the unchangeable prophetic decree, *"I will build My church"* (Matt. 16:18). He emphatically declared that nothing would stop that decree from being fulfilled, even if all the gates of hell were opened against it. Jesus revealed to His disciples that He was in their midst as one greater than Solomon and the great temple he built (Luke 11:29-32). Jesus was saying that He was greater than Solomon and that the Church that He was building would be more glorious than Solomon's temple. Jesus loved the Church and provided everything needed to keep building the Church until He could present to Himself a glorious Church (Eph. 5:27). The Dark Age Church was far from being a glorious Church. It had none of the glory of the first-century Church. But the divine intention of Jesus was not to just restore back to a former glory but to an end-time majestic glory that was beyond anything the Church has ever been or done before. God spoke through the prophets that the glory of the latter Church would be greater than the former. Therefore, the restoration movements destined to take place during the Second Reformation were necessary before Christ could take the Church to its predestined glory that would be manifest during the Third and Final Reformation.

REBUILDING NATURAL JERUSALEM TYPIFIES RESTORING THE CHURCH

In the Book of Nehemiah, we have the story of Nehemiah being commissioned to rebuild the walls around Jerusalem and restore the temple. The Scriptures say that before they could begin building, they had to uncover the foundation, for it was covered with much rubbish (Neh. 4:2,10). This was also true concerning restoring the Church. Before the reformers could begin building the Church, much rubbish of dead religious works had to be removed. That is what Martin Luther was seeking to do when he wrote his *95 Theses* asking his Catholic denomination to remove all the religious rubbish that had accumulated during the Dark Age of the Church. The rubbish had covered the foundational doctrine of repentance from dead works (Heb. 6:1-2). All of Luther's restoration preaching was digging down to the true foundation of the Church. When revelation cleared the rubbish from his old religious thinking, he discovered that the true foundation for salvation was being justified by faith through divine grace with the blood of Jesus being the only way mankind could be forgiven and cleansed from sin. Martin Luther was fulfilling the ministry that Christ gave the apostle and prophet, which is to lay the proper foundation for the Church.

The unbelieving, wicked people around Jerusalem in Nehemiah's day did not want to see Jerusalem restored. They did everything they could to stop it. They did succeed in getting the building process stopped for a period of time, just as the devil succeeded in getting the building of Christ's Church stopped for a 1,000-year period. Nehemiah and Ezra were able to get the restoration process started again, and they continued on, accompanied by much harassment, until it was finished. Jesus and His reformers reactivated the building of Christ's Church and began the "Great Period of Church Restoration."

Church historians have established October 31, 1517 as the official time when the period of Church Restoration and the Second Reformation began. It started reforming the Church back to its original life and ministry as demonstrated by Jesus in the Gospels, established and demonstrated by the apostles in the Book of Acts, and taught in the epistles of the New Testament.

500 YEARS OF CHURCH RESTORATION MOVEMENTS

- 1500—The Protestant Movement
- 1600—The Evangelical Movement
- 1700—The Holiness Movement
- 1800—Faith Healing Movement
- 1900—The Pentecostal Movement
- 1950—The Charismatic Movement

- 1980—The Prophetic-Apostolic Movement
- 2007—The Saints Movement

The restoration movements happened about once every hundred years until the twentieth century; then three major restoration movements took place within the twentieth century. The last restoration movement was birthed in the twenty-first century in the year 2007. The Saints Movement became the restoration movement that launched the Third Reformation, just as the Protestant Movement launched the Second Reformation.

ABBREVIATED PRESENTATION OF EACH RESTORATION MOVEMENT

Literally thousands of books have been written covering the truths, people, times, and places of these restoration movements. It is reported that more books have been written relating to Martin Luther than any other person except Jesus Christ. I spent 20 years researching hundreds of books to gather the information I used to write my book on the history, restoration, and destiny of the Church. It then took three years of writing to publish. So much interesting and vital information was available that it became very challenging to choose the right material. The thousands of pages that could have been used were reduced to a 400-page book titled *The Eternal Church*.[1] Now the challenge is to take the 170 pages dealing with the actual restoration movements and condense them to 20 to 30 pages, yet present enough information to give sufficient understanding for those who are not familiar with Church restoration. Our purpose is to show the progressive restorational work of the Holy Spirit in bringing the Church to full restoration. Our purpose is to reveal what the Holy Spirit restored during each restoration movement. A minimal amount of the historical facts will be given concerning the voices of restoration God used and the times and places.

FROM RELIGIOUS FORM TO PERSONAL EXPERIENCE

Every restorational movement takes biblical truths and practices and brings new light on them revealing greater ways to experience and practice—the gifts of God, the fruit and gifts of the Holy Spirit, and the attributes of Christ. Also, each movement brings greater understanding and emphasis to one of the names of God such as Savior, Baptizer, Healer, Holy One, Everlasting Father, and Mighty Warrior.

Every restorational truth movement brings the scriptural meaning and experiential reality back to one of the fundamental doctrines of Christ. Each restorational movement takes certain Scriptures that religious men have placed in the mythical, allegorical, spiritual, and futuristic realm and makes them a living experience in the life of the believer. Most of the spiritual blessings and experiences we enjoy today were kept from Christians by religious leaders who spiritualized them into some ethereal realm or applied them to some future age.

For instance, the Dark Age Church explained being born again as being born into the church by confessing the Apostles' Creed or some religious dogmas of the church. Prior to the Divine Healing Movement, evangelicals explained "by His stripes we are healed" as the blood and grace of God healing our sin-sick soul (1 Pet. 2:24). They did not apply it to physical healing for our mortal bodies. The same type of interpretation was made concerning the gift of the Holy Spirit with speaking in unknown tongues, until divine revelation and application came with the Pentecostal Movement. The fundamentalists interpreted it as speaking in your natural language with a newly sanctified tongue instead of actually speaking in unknown tongues with a verbal language of the spirit. In each of these examples a truth that was meant to be literally experienced was spiritualized and made mythical during the Dark Age. Now with each restoration movement, Holy Spirit revelation and application will restore truth after truth until the Church is experiencing and demonstrating all biblical truth and ministries.

Jesus inspired the writing of the Scriptures, not to give man a set of idealistic philosophies and platitudes to be eulogized by great religious leaders, but to give mankind biblical truth—living principles and promises that will work in meeting every need of humanity. Every Scripture that has been spiritualized in the ethereal will be fulfilled in the literal.

THE PROTESTANT MOVEMENT—1600S

The Name "Protestant"

In A.D. 1529, just 12 years after the Reformation began, there was a legislative meeting of state and church hierarchy from several European states. The purpose was to settle the conflict between the Catholic church and the followers of the reformers. The Catholic rulers were in the majority, and they passed a bill condemning the teachings of the reformers, declaring that the Catholics could teach in the reformers' states but that the reformers, who were called Lutherans in Germany, were not allowed to teach in the Catholic states. To this unequal ruling, the Lutheran princes made a formal "protest." From that time on, they were known as "Protestants" and their teachings and practices as the "Protestant religion." That is why restoration historians call it the "Protestant Movement." From that time to the present, all churches that developed from a restoration movement are classified as *Protestant*. All Christendom is divided into two major groups. The two main denominations that represented Christendom during the

Dark Age were the eastern Greek Orthodox and the western Roman Catholic. Therefore, Christendom is divided and classified as either Catholic/Orthodox churches or Protestant churches. In America, if an application asks you for your religion as a Christian, you are only given two choices—Catholic or Protestant.

After 500 years of Church restoration, the Protestant churches are classified according to the restoration movement from which they originated. Ministers who are walking in currently restored truth identify and refer to Protestant Christians and church groups as Historic Protestant, Evangelical, Holiness, Pentecostal, Charismatic, and Prophetic-Apostolic.

Second Reformation—Restoration Movement

YEAR	MOVEMENTS	MAJOR TRUTH RESTORED
1500	Protestant Movement	Salvation by grace through faith (Eph. 2:8-9).
		(Lutheran, Episcopalian, Presbyterian, Congregational)
1600	Evangelical Movement	Water baptism, separation of Church and state.
		(Mennonite, Baptist, all Fundamental-Evangelical churches)
1700	Holiness Movement	Sanctification, the Church set apart from the world.
		(Methodist, Nazarene, Church of God, all Holiness churches)

YEAR	MOVEMENTS	MAJOR TRUTH RESTORED
1800	Faith Healing Movement	Divine physical healing in the atonement.
		(Christian Missionary Alliance, Church of God)
1900	Pentecostal Movement	Holy Spirit baptism with unknown tongues.
		(Assembly of God, Foursquare, United Pentecostal, Church of God in Christ)
1950	Latter Rain Movement	Prophetic presbytery, singing praises, and Body of Christ membership ministries.
		(Non-denominational churches)
1950	Deliverance Evangelism Movement	Evangelist ministry and mass evangelism reactivated with miraculous healings.
		(Independent churches and ministerial fellowships)
1960	Charismatic Movement	Renewal of all restored truth to all past movement churches. Pastors were restored to being sovereign head of their local churches.
		(Charismatic churches and denominational Charismatic)
1970	Faith Movement	Faith confessions, prosperity, and victorious attitude and life. Teacher ministry reestablished as a major fivefold ministry.
		(Faith and Word churches)

YEAR	MOVEMENTS	MAJOR TRUTH RESTORED
1980	Prophetic Movement	Prophetic, activating gifts, warfare praise, prophets to nations. Prophet ministry was restored, and a company of prophets brought forth.
		(Prophetic churches and networks)
1990	Apostolic Movement	Apostolic, miraculous, networking, great harvest. Apostle ministry restored to bring divine order, finalize restoration of fivefold ministers for full equipping of the saints.
		(Apostolic Churches and Network of Networks)
2007	Saints Movement	Saints manifesting mightily, and harvest reaped!

THE PURPOSE AND ACCOMPLISHMENTS OF THE PROTESTANT MOVEMENT

Protestantism came into existence because the Holy Spirit initiated the period of the restoration of the Church. The Protestant churches brought back into the Church the revelation, proper application, and reestablishment of the first foundational doctrine of Christ—repentance from dead works (Heb. 6:1-2).

The Holy Spirit's purpose for the movement was to bring reformation and restoration to the Church. Europe was the place of its birth and growth. The priests and people who came out of the Catholic Church were the ones who propagated the movement. Martin Luther was the first to receive and preach the revelation that launched the Second Reformation. Those who followed his teachings became known as Lutherans, which evolved into the Lutheran Church. The Lutheran Church is typical of all churches that would be established from the revelation of a restoration reformer. What is said here about the Lutheran Church could be said of all churches that originated from a reformer who pioneered a restoration truth.

Historically

The Lutheran Church came into existence because Martin Luther broke away from the Catholic Church and his followers fought for the right to be a church separate from Catholicism.

Spiritually

It came into existence because a man of God received a revelation of truth that made it impossible for him to continue in the same religious system he felt was contrary to the Word of God. He would have had to deny his knowledge of the Word of God, his conscience, and his newly received spiritual born-again experience in order to remain a priest who promoted the doctrines and practices of the Roman Catholic Church.

Restorationally

It came into existence because the man God chose to launch and establish Church restoration was named Luther, and those who followed his teachings were called Lutherans. The Lutheran Church became one of the Protestant Christian denominational churches that helped establish and maintain the truths and ministries that were restored during the first restoration movement of the Second Reformation. One of Luther's most revolutionary teachings was the "priesthood of the believer." He dared to teach that every born-again believer had as much access to the throne of God as any Catholic priest or the Pope himself. The Catholic hierarchy knew that

Luther's teaching was a threat to their whole church system. One can see why the old-order church had to condemn Luther as a heretic and his teachings as heresy. These same things happen with every restoration of a new truth. The same could be said for the reformers who pioneered the Protestant Movement in their nations—John Knox in Scotland, the Presbyterian Church; Thomas Cranmer in England, Church of England/Anglican/Episcopal.

KEY WORDS THAT REVEAL AND HELP SUMMARIZE

The history of restoration reveals that when God gets ready to do something new, He makes preparation in certain areas. He prepares a *people,* a *product,* and a *place* to perpetuate His *plan.* The Lord then raises up a *man* with a *message* and a *ministry,* which produces a *movement* that further fulfills His will by various *methods* and *means.* Let's look at a few examples of what key words can reveal.

People—Places—Products. In ages past when God was ready to activate His *"eternal purpose which He accomplished in Christ Jesus"* (Eph. 3:11), He made ready a *place,* planet Earth. God then brought forth His new creation, *man.* His mankind movement was named *Adam* and *Eve.* The *product* for man's use was all of earth's creatures, elements, and atmosphere.

Man—Message—Method. In the destruction of the world by a flood, Noah was the *man.* The ark was the *means* of preserving the righteous. Repentance was the *message.* Water was the *method* by which the wicked were removed. The *place* was in the ark on top of the water until planet Earth was ready for the migration of man again.

Using these key words, we can give abbreviated statements that reveal what was accomplished by the Protestant Movement.

God's *purpose* for the Protestant Movement was to activate the period of the Great Restoration of the Church and begin the Second Church Reformation. Europe was the *place* of its birth and growth. The priests and *people* who came out of the Catholic Church were the ones who propagated it. The *product* that publicized the restorational truth of the Protestant Movement was the printing press. The key *man* God used was Martin Luther. The main *message* was justification by faith and the priesthood of the believer. The *ministry* was the preaching of the Word. The *method* was by faith in God and by the use of every *means* available. The *result* was the corporate Body of Christ, His Church, awakened from her lethargy and apostasy. The Church came out of her religious Egypt by the blood of the Lamb and launched on her journey to possess her promised Canaan land. The kingdoms of Canaan were predestined to become the kingdoms of Joshua and God's chosen people. The kingdoms of this world are destined to become the kingdoms of Jesus Christ and His chosen people, the Church (Rev. 11:15). This will be the end result of the Third Church Reformation. Everything is progressively moving toward fulfilling God's purpose of restoring His Church so it can co-labor with Christ in restoring all things that were deteriorated by the rebellion of lucifer, the Fall of man, and the Dark Age of the Church.

The Evangelical Movement—1600s

The Holy Spirit's commission was to restore the second foundation stone in true Christian salvation: *"He who believes and is baptized will be saved"* (Mark 16:16). Water baptism by immersion was the major truth preached that created the greatest controversy and persecution of the Evangelical Movement. The movement was conceived in Europe, but America became the place of its birth and growth to maturity. The main word used to describe this movement was *Anabaptist* (meaning "re-baptizer"). All Catholic and historic

Protestant Churches practiced infant baptism and sprinkling water on adults for water baptism. The Anabaptists emphatically taught that infant baptism has no more saving grace than adult baptism does without a prior confession of faith. They would rebaptize any Lutheran, Anglican, Presbyterian, or Catholic who had only received baptism as an infant or was baptized by sprinkling as an adult.

Three other teachings were not acceptable to the national Protestant churches or the Catholics. The Lutherans had fought so hard against religious works of Catholicism to maintain that salvation was by faith only that the need for the works of righteous living were neglected. The first additional controversial teaching of the Evangelical Movement was on discipleship—that Christianity was more than mental faith and verbal confession; it must produce a transformed life and daily walk with God. The second was on the restoration of the Church. They were not interested in simply reforming the Catholic church or being a new Protestant church; they were committed to restoring it to the teachings and ministry of the first-century Church.

The third teaching was separation of church and state; that is, that there should not be only one church denomination recognized as the religion or church of the state or nation. They did not teach that Christianity should be separated from government as is now being propagated by some in America. The pilgrims came to America to have freedom from the dominance and persecution of the state churches. That is the reason the founders of the Constitution put in the separation of church and state. They did not want one church denomination ruling in the nation but freedom for independent churches and individual Christians to serve God according to their own Christian faith. In addition, the Evangelical Movement reformers taught that their followers should aggressively witness and seek to make converts. The Presbyterians who were established in the former Protestant Movement taught predestination; only the Holy Spirit was to draw people to Christ, and Christianity is a private matter not to be imposed on others.

NEW RESTORATION BRINGS PERSECUTION FROM ESTABLISHED RELIGION

The Protestant and Catholic churches joined forces to rid themselves of the evangelicals. To them, the Anabaptists were not only religious heretics but a threat to the social and religious stability of Christian Europe. Thousands of Anabaptist Christians were put to death by fire in the Catholic areas and by drowning in the Protestant areas. Only three groups were able to survive in Europe beyond the sixteenth century, the Brethren Churches in Switzerland and south Germany, the Mennonites in the Netherlands and north Germany, and the Hutterites in Moravia.

This will be the last persecution with a wholesale killing of the participants of a new restoration movement. The next restoration movements have their preparation in Europe but are birthed in the new religious freedom land of America. The laws of America prohibit the killing of people for religious reasons. During the following 300 years of restoration movements, persecution of the new by the old will follow the same pattern without the physical killings. Every major reformation and the restoration movements within it produce five groups of people.

FIVE GROUPS FORMED FROM A RESTORATION MOVEMENT

1. Persecutors

These are the ones from the old movement who restored a biblical truth back into the Church during their restoration movement.

They establish their doctrinal beliefs, which are then cemented into their denomination creeds. What was once a revelation now becomes a limitation. The newly restored truth was not a part of their revelation, doctrinal creed, or personal experience; therefore, the majority of the old reject the new as unacceptable teaching and as an experience a Christian should not seek to receive. The leaders feel the teachings are a threat to their denomination and way of life. Therefore, they call it heresy and not worthy of being a part of their Christianity, which gives them justification for rejecting and persecuting participants of the new restoration movement.

2. Passive

These are the religious leaders who are not for or against the new. They are either too far removed from the new restoration movement to be affected by it, or they are knowledgeable of it but choose not to persecute or to participate.

3. Participants

They may partially or fully participate in the movement. The partial participants are those who visit the revival, receive the blessings of the teaching and ministry, but stay in the security of their old denomination. Those who fully participate leave the old and join the new to be fully established in the newly restored truth, ministries, and refreshing presence of the Lord.

4. Proclaimers

These are the men and women who become ministers of the movement. They usually start a new local church so that they have the freedom to preach the new truth and establish a people in the restored truth and ministries. Up until 1948, these local churches always formed into a fellowship of churches with like faith and vision, which then evolves into a denomination. This happened in the Protestant Movement with the forming of the Lutheran and Presbyterian denominations.

5. Pioneers

These are the reformers, the ones who originally received the revelation of the new truth that the Holy Spirit wanted restored at that time. They are the men and women with the message that produces the movement. The pioneers preach, teach, and write books revealing the scriptural reality of the truths and ministries being restored. They pioneer the truth while most Christians are not aware that there is more truth than what their denomination is preaching. It takes several years and sometimes decades before the new restoration movement is accepted as worthy of being recognized as a legitimate Christian group.

EVERY RESTORATION MOVEMENT GOES THROUGH THE SAME CYCLE

When the movement is birthed, it creates great controversy within Christianity, especially in the denominations formed from the last restoration movement. The pioneers of the new restoration movement first receive much persecution and rejection from the old. It starts off as a hot war of rejection and persecution. Then after a few years, it turns into a cold war of toleration. The old allows the new to exist but does not believe them to be worthy of their fellowship. After several years, the new is finally accepted as a legitimate Christian group. The new can fellowship with the old without intimidation because they believe and practice all restored truth. But the old has problems fellowshipping with the new restoration movement churches because the truths they teach, their ministry, and ways of worship are beyond what their group believes and practices.

CHURCH DESTINED FOR UNITY FOR KINGDOM PURPOSES

Regardless of all the differences between restoration churches, unity will now be a priority. A new day has dawned with the beginning of the Third Church Reformation in 2008. God has now commissioned the Holy Spirit to fulfill the prayer of Jesus, "Father, make them one as We are one that the world may believe" (John 17:21). Jesus is very serious about His Church being fully restored and unified to demonstrate the Kingdom of God in all the world. Jesus wants to end the rule of wickedness in His earth and return for His Church to establish His rule of righteousness over all the earth (2 Pet. 3:13). But Jesus said the "end" could not come until this Gospel of the Kingdom is preached in all the world for a witness to all nations (Matt. 24:14). Apostle Peter declared that Jesus cannot return from Heaven until Christ's Church is fully restored (Acts 3:21). Jesus revealed that the world would not believe until His Church is unified; therefore, the Holy Spirit is intensifying the pressure on ministers of the Church to unify for God's greater Kingdom purposes or suffer the consequences. Jesus was crucified for the birthing of His Church, and He will crucify any of His ministers who hinder the restoration and unification of His Church. The Third Reformation brings advanced purposes, new responsibilities, and obedience for those who will participate and demonstrate God's Kingdom until God's purpose for His mortal Church is fulfilled.

But the need at hand in this book is to get on through the Second Reformation. The Protestant and Evangelical restoration movements established the foundation of Church restoration and revealed the guidelines, principles, and process of the restoration of truth and ministries back into Christ's Church. The remaining movements will

May 24, 1738

be given with a minimum of information and then a summarization of what the Holy Spirit accomplished in that restoration movement.

THE HOLINESS MOVEMENT AND THE FIRST GREAT AWAKENING—1700S

Over time, the passion for the Christian faith began to wane and churches became more institutionalized and less about one's personal faith. As spiritual life died out in churches, it resulted in moral and spiritual decline in both the church and society. A new philosophy called *The Enlightenment* emphasized man's ability, reason, and intellect and discounted the spiritual and supernatural. The Church had lost its fire and its relevance in culture.

It was into this setting God began to stir the flames of the First Great Awakening. Its purpose was to awaken a passion for the faith and to restore spiritual relationship with God in such a way that made Christianity relevant to the people of the day. This awakening served as the spark for the next restoration move of God known as the Holiness Movement.

John Wesley was ordained as an Anglican minister in 1728; however, he and his brother Charles did not personally encounter Christ and receive salvation until May 24, 1738 at a Moravian society meeting on Aldersgate Street in London. (It was not uncommon for clergy members of that time to not have a personal relationship with Christ.) In 1739 in Oxford, England, John and Charles Wesley, along with their friend George Whitfield, were seeking God with fasting and prayer on New Year's Day. They had an encounter with the Spirit of God that later became known as the Methodist Pentecost, for though they did not speak in other tongues they had a life-changing encounter with the Spirit of God that launched them into preaching the Gospel with great passion and dramatization.

The churches of the day did not know what to do with these fiery preachers, so the men were known to preach outdoors, often drawing crowds of twenty thousand or more. John Wesley became the father of the Methodist movement, preaching a message of holiness, sanctification, and personal transformation through prayer and study of the Word.

George Whitfield traveled to America and spread the message of this awakening, preaching over 18,000 sermons to over ten million people in his lifetime. The Great Awakening in America involved other men such as Jonathan Edwards (author of "Sinners in the Hands of an Angry God"), David Brainard, Samuel Davies, and Gilbert Tennett who were instrumental in stoking the flames of revival but also in shaping the future foundation of America as many of the founding fathers were impacted by the messages of this movement.

The people who participated and the ministers who propagated the truth came primarily from Protestant and Evangelical movement churches. But the power of the Holy Spirit and the restoration message of holiness and sanctification would awaken millions to personal faith over the course of several decades.

Restoration Message of Sanctification

Sanctification comes from a Greek root word that means holy, set apart, purified, and sanctified. In 1740, John Wesley started teaching that there were two separate works of grace. The first work of grace was justification by faith as the Protestant Movement taught; the second work of grace enabled a Christian to live a holy life. The second experience of sanctification purified the motives and desires and gave a pure love toward God that resulted in holy living. This experience also brought a release of great joy. There was a birth of new songs that portrayed the truth being restored. Charles Wesley published over 4,000 songs with words that expressed the messages that his brother John was preaching. John Wesley wrote over 400 publications in his lifetime emphasizing this new restoration truth.

The Methodist Church Symbolic of the Holiness Movement

John Wesley and George Whitefield were called *Methodist* because of their methodical method of Bible study, prayer, and anti-worldly Christian practices. The followers of Wesley became known as Wesleyan Methodists. Another great addition to the Church was the use of lay preachers who did not have a seminary degree. It was mainly the lay preachers who took the Protestant-Holiness gospel into the wild frontiers of America. There was also an emphasis on missions. God's purpose for the Holiness Movement was to bring the Church to victorious Christian living (sanctification) and to restore the fruit of the Spirit of joy expressed in shouting and singing joyfully. The Protestant Movement took God's people out of the Dark Age as the Passover took Israel out of Egypt. The Evangelical Movement took the Church through its Red Sea by water baptism, and the Holiness Movement established the Church on the other side separated from Egypt to be a set apart, holy people unto God.

THE SECOND GREAT AWAKENING—1800S

In August of 1801, in rural Cane Ridge, Kentucky, a Presbyterian minister named Barton Stone held a camp meeting revival that drew twenty to thirty thousand people. They were joined by the Baptists and the Methodists as the Spirit of God fell upon the people day and night causing them to fall to the ground weeping and crying out in prayer and worship. This began a period of time known in history as the Second Great Awakening, which over the course of the next century would see millions come to Christ.

The best-known leader of Second Awakening revivals was Charles Finney, an ordained Presbyterian minister who became known as "the Father of Modern Revivalism." Most of his revivals took place in New York, beginning in the Rochester area in 1830, where he saw over 100,000 saved in less than a year. He later preached continuous meetings in New York City. His preaching challenged the Calvinist theology of only the elect being saved, and declared that anyone could become a believer if he chose. Finney saw congregations respond to his preaching with people falling down under God's power and crying out in repentance. Entire cities were converted throughout upstate New York.

One young man who was saved in Finney's meetings went on to fan the flames of this awakening. In 1857 the nation was going through a period of deep political unrest prior to the Civil War. In 1857, the stock market crashed. Suddenly there was great spiritual disillusionment in the churches, and poverty and crime were on the rise in the cities. It was in this time of trouble a businessman named Jeremiah Lamphier began a noontime prayer meeting on Fulton Street in New York. The Fulton Street Prayer Revival swept the nation, as noontime prayer meetings sprang up all over the land with an estimated two million converts coming to Christ in less than two years. These prayer meetings went on worldwide for over seventeen years, with untold numbers coming to Christ. These meetings continued through the Civil War with an estimated one-third of the troops receiving salvation.

The Second Great Awakening fanned the flame of tremendous spiritual hunger and passion for God and His purposes. It resulted in millions of salvations, prayer meetings on every continent, the rise of charitable organizations and philanthropic endeavors, missionaries sent all over the world, and social reforms such as the end of slavery, temperance, and an impact on public education.

THE DIVINE HEALING MOVEMENT—LATE 1800S

This movement was for the purpose of restoring the truth that Jesus received the 39 stripes for the physical healing of the mortal body of mankind. The Dark Age church leaders had changed its truths from literal to spiritual, from real to ethereal, from a present manifestation to a memorial. The first-century Church believed and practiced biblical divine healing and deliverance from demonic activity.

Revelation That Brought Restoration

A.B. Simpson was a Presbyterian pastor who in 1880 received information from his doctor that he only had a few months to live. He decided that if he was going to die soon, he would die full of the Word of God. As he was studying the Word, the Holy Spirit revealed to him that divine healing was in Christ's atonement just the same as forgiveness of sins. He preached and wrote many books on divine healing. God confirmed His revelation to A.B. Simpson by healing his body and extending his life for 35 more years. His restoration message produced a worldwide movement that established the truth of divine healing back into Christ's Church. He had to leave his Presbyterian church to pioneer and practice this restoration truth. This resulted in the establishment of the Christian and Missionary Alliance church.

SUMMARY OF THE EVANGELICAL, HOLINESS, AND DIVINE HEALING MOVEMENTS

The message of these movements was threefold—believer's baptism by immersion, sanctification, and divine healing. The ministry was the preaching of the Word accompanied by special singers, great conviction, blessing, emotional manifestations, and physical healings. The new modes of transportation that carried the messengers with the message to the ends of the earth were the steamship and trains.

The result was that the eternal Church crossed its Red Sea of water baptism, became sanctified and separated from the world, and then journeyed on to receive Christ's redemptive work of divine healing at the waters of Marah (Exod. 15:22-25). Thus, three more major steps were taken in the walk of the Church to full restoration. It will now enter the twentieth century, which will produce several restorational movements to complete God's purpose of the Second Church Reformation. There will then come a restoration movement in the first decade of the twenty-first century that will launch the Third and Final Church Reformation. Let us continue on in restoration until we can enter the blessings and power of the Third Reformation.

THE CLASSICAL PENTECOSTAL MOVEMENT—1900

The movement's purpose was to restore the Holy Spirit to His powerful performance in the Church. By gifting the individual believer with "other tongues" in the baptism of the Holy Spirit and by releasing the gifts of the Spirit to the Church, Jesus restored the third doctrine of Christ to the Church—the doctrine of baptisms. There are three basic baptisms and three witnesses on earth—the baptism of repentance, witness of the blood; the baptism in water, witness of the water; the baptism of the Holy Spirit, witness of the Spirit (1 John 5:8). The Pentecostal Movement brought the fullness of the three-fold baptisms and witnesses. The place of its birth was the United States, after which it spread to the world with its greatest percentage of growth among Christians in Latin America.

The Pentecostal Movement claims no single person as its founder. However, Charles F. Parham and W.H. Seymour come as close as any of the men involved to qualifying for the role as the pioneers of the movement. The people who participated and the ministers who propagated the Pentecostal truth came mainly from the Holiness Movement churches.

The message was the baptism of the Holy Spirit evidenced by speaking in "other tongues." The ministry was the preaching of the Word accompanied by healings, miracles, speaking in other tongues, and gifts of the Holy Spirit. All types of musical instruments and singing were used to promote the Gospel and to worship God. "Dancing in the spirit" became an accepted form of Spirit-directed, uncontrollable expression of praise. The new methods of commuting and communicating this restorational truth to the ends of the earth were the automobile and the radio. Thus, the Church advanced in its restorational journey through the wilderness to its "water from the Rock" experience (Exod. 17:6-7). The result was more powerful performance in ministry, greater evangelism, and the "rivers of living water" flowing out of the saints' innermost being in other tongues (John 7:37-38).

The Pentecostal Movement was another progressive step in the walk of the saints of the Church progressing on to their prophesied destiny.

THE CHARISMATIC MOVEMENT—1948 TO 1988

I have made several references to the doctrines of Christ listed in Hebrews 6:1-2, and how different doctrines were restored during different restoration movements. In my book *The Eternal Church*,[2] the six doctrines are correlated with different restoration movements.

Because several movements were used to express different aspects of the doctrine, they were put under one restoration name. The Holiness Movement includes three restorations of truth—water baptism, sanctification, and divine healing. The same is true concerning the Charismatic Movement, the Latter Rain Movement of 1948, along with Deliverance Evangelism, the Charismatic Renewal of the 1960s, and the Faith Movement of the 1970s. Each of these demonstrated different ministries of the doctrine of laying on of hands.

The First Reformation established in the Church the six doctrines of Christ and implied a seventh, which is "going on unto perfection" for the ultimate fulfillment of all things.

The Second Reformation restored to the Church all the doctrines and ministries of Christ that were lost during the Dark Age of the Church.

The Third and Final Reformation activates the Church to begin establishing the Kingdom of God in all the earth and finalize the restoration and fulfillment of all things.

SIX DOCTRINES OF CHRIST (HEB. 6:1-2)	RESTORATION MOVEMENTS
Repentance from Dead Works	Protestant
Faith Toward God	Holiness
Doctrine of Baptisms	Pentecostal
Laying on of Hands	Charismatic
Resurrection Life	Prophetic-Apostolic
Eternal Judgment	Saints/Army of Lord
Ultimate Fulfillment ("go on to Perfection")	Kingdom of God

THE LATTER RAIN MOVEMENT—1948

God's purpose for the Latter Rain Movement was to restore the experiential reality of the biblical practice of laying on of hands, thereby restoring to the Church the fourth doctrine of Christ—the laying on of hands. The place of its birth was Canada.[3] It then spread throughout the United States and around the world.

Latter Rain Leaders

The Latter Rain Movement has never recognized any man or group as head of the movement, but certain men were notable in making known and maintaining the doctrine of laying on of hands. Numerous men and churches practiced the laying on of hands with personal prophecy by the presbytery (called a "prophetic presbytery"). Reginald Layzell was the one who pioneered the truth with wisdom and balance. The Latter Rain Movement developed certain protocols for where, when, how, and who could receive prophetic presbytery. In *The Eternal Church,* a thorough coverage is given concerning all that was restored in the Latter Rain Movement. As many new truths and ministries were restored during this movement as there were in any of the previous movements.

Deliverance Evangelism—1948

These were the men of God who demonstrated the laying on of hands for healings and miracles. Hundreds of ministers arose as healing evangelists in the 1950s. Oral Roberts was the best known for demonstrating laying on of hands for healing. He laid hands on more than a million people during his years of ministry. William Branham demonstrated calling out the disease with a word of knowledge and discerning of spirits. T.L. Osborn demonstrated miracles for the masses. In a gathering of hundreds of thousands, he would pray a prayer for certain diseases, lameness, or hearing, etc. Hundreds would come forward to testify and demonstrate their miraculous healing. Benny Hinn has been one who has continued this type of ministry to the present time. I have been in stadiums filled with thousands of Latin American people and watched one of my spiritual sons, Guillermo Maldonado, pray an anointed prayer of faith, and hundreds would come forward to testify of their healing. Most charismatic pastors and evangelists minister to the saints with the laying on of hands.

THE CHARISMATIC RENEWAL

This was a sovereign move of the Holy Spirit around the world to give everyone a chance to be established in all restored truth. God was pouring out His Spirit on all flesh, including Catholics. In one day a Catholic could be justified by faith, baptized in water, sanctified, receive the gift of the Holy Spirit with praying in his spirit language, and receive personal prophecy; in other words, he could experience all the truths and ministries that had been restored to the Church. During the Charismatic Movement, most denominations from Catholic to the Holiness Movement churches developed a Charismatic group within their denomination.

The Faith Movement

God's purpose in this movement was to deliver the Church from false teaching that developed during the Dark Age of the Church. They taught that being poor and miserable were synonymous with spirituality. The monastic orders exemplified self-denial of worldly goods and riches, seeking to become more spiritual. The Faith Movement teachers taught strongly from 3 John 2 that it was God's will that Christians "be in health and prosper even as their soul prospered." Examples from the Old Testament were used to show how

God prospered His people. Money is needed to take the Gospel to the ends of the earth. Kenneth Hagin and Oral Roberts were two of the pioneers of this truth.

The Charismatic Movement Leaders

Key men who were originally instrumental in activating and spreading the Charismatic Renewal were Dennis Bennett, David du Plessis, and Demos Shakarian. Derek Prince helped make the historic Charismatic conscious of the reality of the spirit world of demon activity. Kenneth Hagin became known as the father of the faith message for prosperity and health.

The majority of the people who participated and the ministers who propagated deliverance evangelism and Latter Rain truths came mostly from the Pentecostal Movement churches.

Those who originally were called Charismatic were ministers and members of historic Protestant denominations, but then came those from the Catholic and Orthodox, Holiness, Evangelical, and Fundamentalist churches. Finally, many Pentecostal and Latter Rain leaders reluctantly accepted the word *Charismatic* to identify those who were Holy Spirit-filled, tongues-talking, God-praising, present-truth Christians for that day and hour.

The Message of the Charismatic Movement

The message of the Latter Rain-Charismatic Movement was threefold:

1. The laying on of hands for healing, Holy Spirit baptism, deliverance, Body of Christ membership ministry, and activation of three more gifts of the Holy Spirit—gifts of healings, prophecy, and word of knowledge.

2. The proclamation of all the Pentecostal and Latter Rain Movement truths to denominational Christians. This was mainly done by denominational ministers who were newly baptized in the Holy Spirit.

3. The proclamation by present-truth and faith ministers concerning the maturing of the Body of Christ and of Christians living victoriously—spiritually, physically, and financially.

The ministry was the preaching of the Word accompanied by healings, prophecy, and revelation gifts. This caused many salvations, extensive spiritual growth in individual Christians, the numerical growth of churches, and the prosperity of the saints.

Time to Move On

The result was that the Church-Saints reached their Mount Sinai experience and remained there until divine order was established so that all Christendom had an opportunity to move to the front line of present truth. The Church was encamped at that mountain of truth (Charismatic Movement) for 40 years (1948 to 1988). I believe that in 1988 the angel of the Church in Heaven started trumpeting a message in Heaven that began to be echoed on earth by the emerging company of apostles and prophets, declaring, "Church, we have been here long enough; it is time for another restoration movement!" (Deut. 2:3).

THE PROPHETIC-APOSTOLIC MOVEMENT

God's purpose in this movement was to bring full restoration and activation of the fivefold ministry of prophets and apostles. Several other truths and ministries were restored during this time. Not only was the fivefold office of prophet restored, but a whole company of prophets were brought forth to corporately fulfill the prophecies concerning the Elijah to come, which was to "prepare the way and make ready a people" for the coming of the Lord. This company of prophets and apostles with that "Elijah" anointing would fulfill those Scriptures for Christ's second coming as John the Baptist fulfilled them for Christ's first coming.[4]

The Prophetic Movement brought the revelation of how to activate saints into their spiritual gifts of prophecy, word of knowledge, and wisdom. The Apostolic Movement did the same for the saints in the power gifts of healings, faith, and working of miracles. In correlating the progressive journey of Israel from Egypt and into Canaan, the Prophetic-Apostolic Movement crossed the Church over Jordan to be prepared and in position for the warfare of possessing their promised Canaan Land. They taught that the Canaan Land of the Church-Saints individually is driving out of oneself all the "-ites" of everything contrary to the character of Jesus until they are conformed to Christ's image with no "-ites" of selfishness and sin left. The corporate purpose and Canaan Land of the saints is for them to keep fighting and subduing the enemy until the kingdoms of this world become the kingdoms of our Lord Jesus and His Church (Rom. 8:29; Rev. 11:15). That is the reason they taught and demonstrated warfare praise and prophetic/apostolic intercessory prayer. Another key message and ministry that was not restored in the Charismatic Movement but was restored in the Prophetic Movement is revealed by the word the prophetic ministers chose to describe it—*activation.*

The core teaching on activation was that all saints can be prophetic in that they can hear the voice of God and minister the mind of Christ to others. Saints can be activated into the gifts of the Spirit just as a sinner can be activated into the gift of eternal life or a born-again Christian can be activated into the gift of the Holy Spirit.

They taught that the gifts of the Spirit are received and manifest the same as the gift of eternal life and the Holy Spirit. All three are sovereignly given, received by grace, and manifested by faith (Eph. 2:8-9; 1 Cor. 12:7). Their passion was to teach, train, activate, mentor, and mature the saints into their membership ministry in the Body of Christ. Emphasis was given to the Scriptures that state, *"You can all prophesy one by one," "desire spiritual gifts,"* but *"desire earnestly to prophesy,"* and *"let us prophesy in proportion to our faith,"* not by physical sensations or emotions of the soul (1 Cor. 14:1,31,39; Rom. 12:6).

Other major teachings included the appointment of apostles and prophets to the nations, usually ministering to the heads of those nations. They believed that the Prophetic Movement brought with it the baptism of fire for intensified purifying of the saints (Mal. 3:1-5; 1 Cor. 3:13). The apostolic portion gave more emphasis to God's divine order for building the Church, unity of the Body of Christ, world harvest, miracles, and deliverance. However, the major purpose of God for restoring the prophets and apostles was to complete His fivefold ministers from just three being recognized and activated to all five so that they could fulfill their commission of equipping the saints for their membership ministries (Eph. 4:12). This is necessary for there to be qualified saints ready to participate in the coming Saints Movement.

The movement was birthed in the United States of America and then spread around the world. The two leaders recognized by *Charisma* magazine as the original pioneers and leaders of the Prophetic Movement were Paul Cain and Bill Hamon. The Apostolic in the late 1990s was championed and propagated by Bill Hamon, Peter Wagner, and hundreds of others around the world. No one person was given great recognition because they taught "team ministry" and networking all together for the corporate good of God's purpose. There was much teaching on the "Joshua Generation." One book listed 10 major things that the Prophetic Movement restored that were not active in the Charismatic Movement and 15 transitions that took place when the Church crossed over its Jordan prepared and equipped to begin possessing its promised Canaan Land.[5]

The new products of commuting and communication that helped spread the message of the movement were jet planes, computers, books, the internet, and all the new and advanced technology. The sons of Issachar apostles and prophets who know the times, seasons, Holy Spirit refreshings, and restoration moves of God are making declarations like the following:

The apostolic-prophetic "Joshua Generation" is leading forth, and the priestly pastors have carried the ark of God's restorational presence across Jordan. The journey of the Charismatic Movement has fulfilled its purpose of bringing the Church to its Jordan River. Now the cloud by day and the fire by night that covered and led God's people have been replaced by the fiery prophets and covering apostles (Exod. 13:21-22). The apostles and prophets have arisen to provide protection, direction, and timing for the forward move of the Church. The manna has ceased, and now it is time to eat the corn of Canaan, drink the milk, and be energized by the honey to destroy the wicked enemies out of the Promised Land and inheritance of the Church (Josh. 5:11-12).

The prophetic voice is sounding forth the trumpet call: *"Prepare for war! ...Beat your plowshares into swords and your pruning hooks into spears"* (Joel 3:9-10). We have now entered into a warfare that cannot be ended until the Church of Jesus Christ has possessed the promised possessions that God has preordained for the perfected saints.

A Gigantic Final Tidal Wave of Awakening, Restoration, and Reformation Is Coming

Many major waves of restoration have taken place during the last five hundred years, with smaller waves of restoration and renewal between each of those. Several of these smaller waves of restoration and spiritual renewal of various truths and ministries have taken place from 1948 to 2008, and now in this twenty-first century of the Church, the Third and Final Church Reformation has been launched.

A Time Unlike Any Before

The prophets and apostles, however, are seeing on the horizon of God's purpose for His Church a Reformation wave of such incomprehensibly gigantic proportions—like a thousand-foot tidal wave—that it staggers the imagination and faith of both those who have prophetically seen it and those who have heard of it. The Saints Movement has activated the great swelling of the wave and launched the Church into the Third and Final Church Reformation.[6]

Just as previous Great Awakenings have occurred during times of division in the land, economic shaking, and moral decline, so the stage is being set for the Greatest Awakening the earth has ever seen in which billions, not just millions, come to Christ, signs, wonders and miracles are poured out, and nations are changed. As the Third and Final Church Reformation converges with this next Great Awakening, it will be the time we see the fulfillment of God's prophetically declared purposes. It will be the most exciting time the earth has ever seen.

As the prophet Joel declared, there has never been a time like it before, and there never will be again (Joel 2:2). As the prophets and apostles continue to reveal the mysteries of God and echo on earth what the angels are sounding in Heaven, it will be the time of Revelation 10:7: *"But in the days of the sounding of the seventh angel, when he is about to sound, the mystery of God would be finished, as He declared to His servants the prophets."* The Third Reformation will activate within the Church the revelation, wisdom, power, and grace to co-labor with Christ in fulfilling the prophetic decree in Revelation 11:15: *"Then the seventh angel sounded: And there were loud voices in heaven, saying, 'The kingdoms of this world have become the kingdoms of our Lord and of His Christ, and He shall reign forever and ever!'"*

The Saints Movement that was activated in 2007 will complete the Church restoration portion of Acts 3:19-25. Now the Third Reformation will bring fulfillment concerning the *restoration of all things* that God has spoken by the mouth of all His holy prophets since the world began.

This Time Will Fulfill All Things Necessary for the Release of Jesus from Heaven

The tidal wave of the Third Church Reformation will have such a force and height that it will sweep all evil principalities from earth and out of the heavenlies, subduing all the kingdoms of this world under the Lordship of Jesus Christ. It will cause the Kingdom of our Lord Jesus and His Christ-anointed Church to be established in the heavenlies and over all the earth.

The "Snowball" Principle of Restoration

There was a thousand-year Dark Age of the Church, and then restoration movements took place every hundred years until 1900.

Another major movement took place within 50 years; then in the last 50 years there has been a restoration move every 10 years—the Latter Rain Movement (1950s), the Charismatic Renewal (1960s), the Faith Movement (1970s), the Prophetic Movement (1980s), and the Apostolic Movement (1990s).

Most Church theologians agree that the "stone" that the prophet Daniel saw hewn out of the mountain is the Church (Dan. 2:3-35). The Church in its restoration has progressed like a rolling snowball gaining momentum and size as it progresses to the bottom of the mountain. If you make a hard snowball and roll it down the steep, smooth slope of a snow-covered mountainside, it begins to get bigger and go faster. That is the same way Church restoration has progressed. The Protestant Movement was the making of the snowball at the top of the mountain. Then, with each restoration movement, the snowballing Church became greater and the movements began happening faster (1,000-100-50-10).

God said He would do a quick work, and Peter declared we need to hasten the coming of the Lord (2 Pet. 3:11-13). We can do that by preparing the way, making ready a people, reaping the great end-time harvest, and restoring all things that the prophets have spoken for the launching of the Third and Final Reformation to accomplish its purpose of fulfilling all things. Thereby, we are enabling Christ to be released from Heaven and return as the conquering King of kings and Lord of lords to rule and reign with His Church over all the earth.[7]

WHY HOLY SPIRIT?

Why has the Holy Spirit been so relentlessly restoring more and more truth back into the Church? If all that was needed was to restore the saints back to the Church of the first century, then the second coming of the Lord Jesus should have already happened. He wants to return and shall return, but why hasn't He returned? With the new revelation that God has brought, we now realize that the restoration of the Church is not an end in itself but a means to an end. God has purposed for the Church to come to full restoration and maturity to be God's instrument to subdue all things under Christ and restore *all things* that the prophets have spoken concerning the Church, mankind, the heavenlies, and earth. This is all divinely destined to take place during the Third and Final Church Reformation. The Church has been reformed to bring full reformation to all creation.

NOTES

1. Hamon, *The Eternal Church*, 117-287.
2. Ibid., 151-288.
3. Ibid., 225.
4. Mal. 4:5; Matt. 11:9-14; Isa. 40:3-5; Luke 1:16-17; Matt. 17:11; Acts 3:21
5. Hamon, Apostles, *Prophets, and the Coming Moves of God,* Chapter 6.
6. Hamon, *The Day of the Saints.*
7. Matt. 24:22; 2 Pet. 3:12; Rev. 11:15; 19:11-16

Chapter 9

REVELATION AND PREPARATION OF THE THIRD REFORMATION

PREPARATION FOR THIRD REFORMATION

Technically, ever since Adam and Eve sinned and were cast out of the Garden of Eden, all things have been progressing toward fulfilling God's original purpose for creating mankind (Gen. 3:1-8). God's original purpose was for mankind, who was made in God's own image and likeness, to reproduce and multiply themselves until they filled the earth with a mankind race in God's own image and likeness. The end purpose of the Third and Final Church Reformation is to establish God's original and eternal purpose for mankind and planet Earth.

GOD STARTS FROM HIS VISION OF THE END BEFORE HE BEGINS

Before God created the universal heavens and earth, He had man in mind. Everything is designed according to its place to function and purpose for being. The Milky Way Galaxy with its millions of stars and solar systems was made with man in mind. Earth was one special planet among eight rotating around a particular star called the sun. In God's eternal mind, it was planned for man's habitation.

In the beginning, planet Earth was headquarters for one of God's great created beings. He was like the archangels, a covering cherub who was the worship leader of God's universal choir of angels. They filled the throne of God and the eternal realms of God with heavenly music. The name of this bright musical being was *lucifer*. He had approximately one-third of the angels under his charge. The earth had rivers and oceans with great forests and fruit trees of every kind. Gigantic creatures like dinosaurs roamed the earth. However, lucifer developed the thought in his heart that he should be governing the universe and not just planet Earth. He led a rebellion to overthrow God and take His place as supreme ruler.

God sent Michael and the war angels out to fight with lucifer and his angels (Rev. 12:7-9). The war ended by lucifer and his angels being defeated. They were thrown back down to earth, which caused a cataclysmic destruction of the earth and everything on it (Gen. 1:2). Lucifer and his angels had all light removed from them. The earth was immediately frozen in utter darkness and became one big ball of ice for millions and millions of years. It remained in that timeless, eternal state until God's original purpose in the beginning for creating the heavens and the earth was ready to be activated. God allowed all of His heavenly creatures to join Him and watch and behold as God prepared to manifest His master plan.

God extended His Spirit of light and warmth to brood over the ice ball of earth (Gen. 1:1-2). This was the first preparation movement to ready earth to be a habitable place for God to birth His master plan on earth. His master plan was to create His masterpiece in His own image and likeness and make mankind master of all that God created on earth. There were six successive preparation movements required for everything to be ready for God's major purpose to be brought forth on the earth. Earth was made for man, and man was made from the earth (Gen. 2:7). Man and earth were made for each other and have an eternal destiny together in God's eternal purpose. It is essential to understand this in order to grasp God's full purpose for the Third and Final Church Reformation.

EVERYTHING DESIGNED ACCORDING TO ITS PURPOSE

We take note that everything God created was designed to function in its place and to fulfill its purpose. Birds were designed with a body with feathers and wings so that they could function in their appointed area of the air. Fish were made with bodies that could swim and breathe in their designated habitat of water. Animals were made to function on land. Mankind was made with a body created from earth and an eternal spirit from the breath of God, thereby enabling him to communicate and function in both the natural and spirit realm. Man was made with ability that no other earth creature had—the ability to talk, with a creative mind like God's, which could create and speak many languages.

MAN'S PHYSICAL BODY WAS DESIGNED TO FULFILL MANY PURPOSES

The human bodies of Adam and Eve were designed to reproduce like kind by the power of procreation. The human body expresses what

God would look like in physical form. God made man in His own image and likeness. One of God's major purposes was to make the human body be the exact type of body that God wanted His only begotten Son to have as His own. In fact, the human body of Jesus would become the dwelling place of the Godhead. Colossians 2:9 declares that the fullness of the Godhead dwells in the body of Jesus. The body of Jesus was the full expression of Eternal God. The human body was made flesh, bone, and blood in order to suffer, bleed, and die for the redemption of mankind.

Every design of the body of man was to fulfill a particular purpose of God. The body was not designed as a throw-away body after a short period of use. Total man is a trichotomy of body, soul, and spirit (1 Thess. 5:23; Heb. 2:5-10). Man is a spirit being as well as a physical. The body of man was made with the capability of being subject to death. If the physical body dies, the spirit being of man continues to live on in the spirit realm. The spirit being of man can continue to live without the body, but the physical body of man cannot live without the spirit man. If God had not designed man this way, he would not be redeemable. God designed man to be redeemed. Spirit beings like the angels who fell with lucifer are not redeemable. Since our forefather Adam did sin and separate us from God and set death in motion, thank God, we were created redeemable. The spirit, soul, and body are important and relevant to God. Apostle Paul prayed that our spirit, soul, and body be preserved blameless unto the coming of the Lord. He also declared that not only our spirit man but our natural bodies are members of the Body of Christ (1 Cor. 6:19-20; 2 Cor. 4:10-11).

HUMAN BODY DESIGNED AND DESTINED FOR ETERNITY

The flesh and bone body of man is part of God's eternal purpose. The flesh and bone body of Jesus was resurrected for Jesus to live and reign in that body forevermore. Adam's body was made with the capability of living forever as long as he ate of the tree of life that God planted for him in the middle of the Garden of Eden. God warned man that if he ate of the tree of the knowledge of good and evil he would be denied access to the tree of life causing death to begin to work in his body (Gen. 3:11). Adam did eat and was cast out of the Garden, being denied access to the tree of life, which resulted in the death of his body 930 years later. Because of one man's sin of disobedience, the whole human race became subject to the mortality of death (Rom. 5:12). Now it is appointed unto all men once to die and then stand before the judgment seat of God (Heb. 9:27).

It is essential to understand that God's purpose for the body of man is for it to eternally be a part of man. The Christians who have lost their bodies through death will get them back at the first resurrection (1 Cor. 15:51-52). The Christians who are living at the time of the coming of Christ will have their bodies changed from mortal to immortal in a moment's time. The wicked will have their bodies resurrected to indestructible bodies that will burn in the fires of hell forever and ever. Every human body who has ever lived on planet Earth will be resurrected, the righteous to eternal life and joy with the Lord and the unrighteous to eternal damnation and torment with the devil (Dan. 12:2).

REDEEMED HUMAN BODIES BELONG TO GOD

We can see why the apostle Paul told us to present our bodies as a living sacrifice to God for we have been cleansed and purchased by His blood (Rom. 12:1; Acts 20:28; 1 John 1:9). The body of a Christian does not belong to himself but to God. Our body is God's temple and dwelling place on earth. We are therefore to glorify God in our spirit and body, which both belong to God. The life of Jesus is to be lived and manifested in our mortal flesh-and-bone bodies. That is the reason sins in the flesh and body are sins against God. One of the restoration movements in the Second Reformation was the Holiness Movement. The truth revealed was that there is grace sufficient to live a sanctified life—spirit, soul, and body. The body of man is to be sanctified, set apart wholly for the Master's use and glory (1 Cor. 6; 2 Cor. 4:10-11).

To be full participants of the Third Reformation, every restoration truth restored in the Second Reformation must be a living, practiced reality. We must progress from revelation head knowledge to heart belief so that it is at the core of our being, motivating every action from the heart and mind of God (Col. 3:1-3; Gal. 2:20; 1 Cor. 2:16). The last generation of the mortal Church must overcome the last enemy (1 Cor. 15:26). The last enemy to be destroyed is death to the physical body. Jesus will triumph over this enemy at His second coming; that is Christ's part to play. However, the corporate Body of Christ has their part to play also. The Church must be transformed continually until it reaches the fullness of resurrection life and faith (Rom. 4:11; Heb. 11:5). Every restored doctrine of Christ required the sovereign move of God from Heaven and the participation of mankind on earth to receive, believe, participate, and then, as joint heirs with Christ, bring God's purpose into experiential reality and prophetic fulfillment. Let us now venture on to discover what all the Church must come to know and do to fulfill God's purpose for the Third and Final Church Reformation.

TWO REFORMATIONS PREPARE THE WAY

First Reformation

The purpose of the First Reformation was to birth the Church into the world. The Church was built on the foundation of the apostles and prophets with Jesus Christ as the chief cornerstone (Eph. 2:19-22). It required several movements to establish the Church in all the world. The First Reformation Church fulfilled God's purpose for it.

The Second Reformation

The Church declined into a thousand-year Dark Age. It had a great falling away from the original pattern. The living truths of the first-century Church were deadened by religious tradition and doctrines of men (Matt. 15:3,6; Mark 7:13). The purpose of the Second Reformation was to restore these living truths back into the Church. This took place during 500 years of truth restoration movements, from 1517 through 2007. The last two restoration movements made the final preparation for Heaven's decree to be trumpeted in Heaven and echoed on earth by God's restoration apostles and prophets (Rev. 10:7).

The Third Reformation

The decree has been made that the time of the Third Reformation has begun. But like the beginning of the First Reformation (which started with the birth of Jesus), it was several years (30) before there were any public manifestations that a new day was dawning and a new covenant of God was about to be established. As we saw in the study of the First Reformation, it required several movements over many years before the world realized that God had done something major in the earth. I believe Revelation 10:7 is symbolic of the beginning of the Third Reformation, and Revelation 11:15 is symbolic of the finishing of the Third Reformation.

> *Then the [mighty] angel whom I had seen stationed on sea*
> *and land raised his right hand to heaven (the sky), and*
> *swore in the name of (by) Him Who lives forever and ever,*

Who created the heavens (sky) and all they contain, and the earth and all that it contains, and the sea and all that it contains. [He swore] that no more time should intervene and there should be no more waiting or delay, but that when the days come when the trumpet call of the seventh angel is about to be sounded, then God's mystery (His secret design, His hidden purpose), as He had announced the glad tidings to His servants the prophets, should be fulfilled (accomplished, completed) (Revelation 10:5-7 AMPC).

The mighty angel begins the first note of the sounding of the seventh trumpet, and that trumpet sound continues until the last note is finished in Revelation 11:15. All Heaven begins to shout with loud acclamations that *now* the kingdoms of this world have become the kingdoms of our Lord and His Christ.

The seventh angel then blew [his] trumpet, and there were mighty voices in heaven, shouting, The dominion (kingdom, sovereignty, rule) of the world has now come into the possession and become the kingdom of our Lord and of His Christ (the Messiah), and He shall reign forever and ever (for the eternities of the eternities)! (Revelation 11:15 AMPC)

APOSTLES AND PROPHETS REVEAL FINAL MYSTERIES

When the seventh angel lifts the trumpet to his mouth to begin the sounding of the seventh trumpet, it sets certain things in motion in Heaven and on earth: *"The mystery of God would be finished, as He declared to His servants the prophets"* (Rev. 10:7). This phrase has a twofold prophetic application. One, it declares all that the prophets have prophesied in the past that have been mysteries to man will now be revealed and fulfilled. Second, it reveals that present-day prophets and apostles will receive revelation, understanding, and application of those mysteries and make them known to the present generation.

This is why the Prophetic-Apostolic Movement was so timely and essential. This movement restored more truths and ministries back into the Church than any other restoration movement. The two major ministries restored back into the Church were that of the prophet and apostle. As revealed in my other books and in our short presentation of the Second Reformation movements in this book, we find that since the Evangelical Movement, their teachers have taught that apostles and prophets were no longer valid, active ministries within the Church. Although all of the restoration pioneers were prophets and apostles, yet the denominations that were established from their restoration revelation did not recognize them as such. The teaching, recognition, acceptance, and promotion of the ministries of prophets and apostles did not take place until the Prophetic Movement was birthed in 1988. In the 1980s the main emphasis was on the prophet and then in the 1990s that of the apostle was magnified within the Church. Those pioneers of the restoration of apostles and prophets during the first decade of the twenty-first century Church were giving equal recognition to the gift-of-Christ ministers of prophets and apostles.

WHY SO ESSENTIAL?

Ephesians 3:3-5 reveals that God makes known His mysteries to His holy apostles and prophets. Paul explains to them that a dispensation of the grace of God was given to him to be an apostle, and they had heard how he had received the message that he had preached to them. His restoration revelation was that the Gentiles have equal access with the Jews to the salvation made available in Jesus Christ. This was a revolutionary teaching of which not all first-century Church leaders had full revelation. Paul let them know that his teaching did not come just from study of the Scriptures or reading some book but by divine revelation.

> *How that by revelation He made known to me the mystery (as I have briefly written already, by which, when you read, you may understand my knowledge in the mystery of Christ), which in other ages was not made known to the sons of men, as it has now been revealed by the Spirit to His holy apostles and prophets* (Ephesians 3:3-5).

Paul lays the foundation stone in the Church that it is the anointing of the prophets and apostles to receive revelation of the mysteries. This is especially true concerning the pioneering prophets and apostles of restoration truth. They are like the sons of the tribe of Issachar who had special understanding concerning what Israel should do (1 Chron. 12:32). This was only one tribe out of the twelve, and out of this tribe only 200 had this special anointing. That equates to about one tenth of one percent of all the Israeli soldiers who came to make David king over all Israel. This would be about the percentage of Christian ministers who have this special "sons of Issachar" anointing to know the times and purposes of God for His Church and what the Church should do to fulfill that purpose in God's timing.

Amos the prophet declared that God does nothing secretly on earth without first revealing His secrets unto His servants the prophets (Amos 3:7). Most of the books in the Old Testament were written by prophets, and most of the books of the New Testament were written by apostles. One can see why it is essential for God to fully restore the ministry of prophets and apostles in order to bring forth the revelation of God's mysteries, which are God's secret purposes that have not been revealed up to this point, but are now being revealed unto His holy apostles and prophets. There are a few mysterious, secret purposes of God yet to be revealed, understood, appropriated, and established in the earth. It is destined in the purpose of God that as the seventh angel begins to sound the trumpet, the spirit of wisdom and revelation is released on the apostles and prophets, causing the final mysteries of God to be revealed and fulfilled. This is absolutely necessary for the fulfillment of everything that is destined to be accomplished during the Third and Final Church Reformation.

The trumpet sound of the seventh angel is not one short blast, but the Scripture says, *"in the days of the sounding of the seventh angel."* Revelation 10:7 reveals what happens when the first sound begins, and Revelation 11:15 reveals what happens when the final sound is made. There is an indefinite period of time that the trumpet is sounded. It probably continues for many decades. For many things must transpire—nations must be transformed into goat or sheep nations (Matt. 25:31-33); the Kingdom of God must manifest mightily in every nation for a witness to them that Jesus is the only true God and redeemer of mankind (Matt. 24:14). We will cover the many things that must take place during the Third Reformation. It will definitely include Church Reformation for Kingdom demonstration, producing world transformation until the kingdoms of this world become the kingdoms of our Lord Jesus and His anointed one, His Church. Jesus is the Head of His Church and His overcomer saints are the universal corporate Body of Christ who will co-labor with Christ in subduing all things under His feet.

THE PROPHETIC-APOSTOLIC MOVEMENT WAS ALSO CALLED THE SECOND APOSTOLIC AGE

Some referred to the time of the restoration of the apostles and prophets as "The Apostolic Reformation." It was the time when God was reforming the Church with the ministry of the apostles and prophets being fully active within the Body of Christ. Peter Wagner was brought forth as a pioneer apostle to help propagate the ministry of apostles and prophets. He wrote several books on the apostle and apostolic ministry. Apostle Peter also spearheaded an organization called the International Coalition of Apostles. I served with Peter as one of the Apostolic Council members from its founding to the present. It was an opportunity for hundreds of apostles from around the world to gather once a year to fellowship, share revelation, develop spiritual relationships, and validate one another concerning calling and commissioning. Many members were apostles of networks who oversaw hundreds and thousands of ministers and churches. I was the bishop/apostle over my Christian International Apostolic Network with hundreds of churches and thousands of ministers with international headquarters on every continent of the world. There was a spirit of humility and unity among the apostles that made them not feel they were an island unto themselves or the only anointed apostolic ministry within the Church.

Peter Wagner states that he believes that the year 2001 was the time that the Apostolic Movement reached a critical mass, for it was the time when thousands of ministers and churches around the world openly recognized present-day apostles and prophets. Thousands of ministers who had the calling and were doing the work of an apostle began to take the title of *apostle*. The titles *apostle* and *prophet* began to become acceptable as the title *pastor* had been since the

Protestant Movement. The Prophetic-Apostolic Movement fulfilled its major purpose of restoring the ministry of the prophet and apostle back into Christ's Church. Jesus knew that His gift-ministry of prophet and apostle had to be fully restored and active in order for the Church to advance to the Saints Movement and then launch into the Third and Final Church Reformation.

SAINTS MOVEMENT—LAUNCHING PAD FOR THIRD REFORMATION

Restoration Movement Launches Reformation

The Protestant Movement of 1517 launched the Second Church Reformation. The Saints Movement birthed in 2007 was the catalyst and launching pad for the Third Reformation to be launched in 2008.

Church history proves that there is usually a revival or time of refreshing just before a restoration movement takes place. For instance, there was the Welsh Revival just before the birthing of the great Pentecostal Movement in 1901. In 1947, there was the great healing revival that swept around the world. The next year in February of 1948, the restoration movement called Latter Rain was birthed. The main truth restored was the doctrine of laying on of hands, many other spiritual blessings in worship, and the gifts of the Holy Spirit. 1948 was a major restoration year; for instance, Israel was restored as a national state of its own in May of that year.

There was a sovereign move and intercession in October 1987 for the birthing of the great company of prophets that Malachi prophesied would come forth to prepare the way and make ready a people for the second coming of Christ as prophet John the Baptist prepared the way for Christ's first coming. It was one year later in October 1988 that the Prophetic Movement was birthed.[1]

In April of 2007 the Saints Movement was birthed and witnessed to by several major national and international prophets who were present at the meeting. The full explanation of the ministry and purpose of the Saints Movement is presented in *The Day of The Saints.*[2] The revelation and teaching of the Saints Movement was essential in preparation for the Third Reformation. Some of the key revelations included the following: every saint is a minister and Kingdom demonstrator in the marketplace as well as in the local church; the saints need to be activated in their divine gifts and ministries; saints possess and demonstrate the Kingdom of God; every saint has the power and privilege of demonstrating the supernatural works of God and taking that power outside the walls of the local church and meeting the practical needs of mankind, plus many more truths and ministries.

These were truths that would prepare the Church to manifest all restoration truths in full power and authority during the Third and Final Church Reformation.

NOTES

1. The full history of the Prophetic Movement is described in detail in my book, *Prophets and the Prophetic Movement* (Shippensburg, PA: Destiny Image, 1990), 88-100.
2. Hamon, *The Day of the Saints.*

Chapter 10

PROGRESSIVE REVELATION TO ULTIMATE DESTINATION

One translation of Proverbs 29:18 says, *"without a progressive revelation the people wander aimlessly"*; other translations say, *"when there is no prophecy, the people cast off restraint"* (LEB), and *"where there is no vision, the people perish"* (KJV), *"without prophecy the people become demoralized"* (NAB). Prophets have always been Heaven's choice for revealing God's will and purpose to mankind on earth. Prophetic revelation is absolutely essential for the Church to continue progressively fulfilling the will of God on earth. During the 400 years between the Old Testament and the New Testament, there were no prophets speaking prophetic revelation; therefore, the people wandered aimlessly for that period of time. During the thousand-year Dark Age of the Church, there was no progressive revelation; therefore, the Church was demoralized and wandered aimlessly for that period of time. But at the beginning of the Second Reformation, pioneering prophets and apostles began to receive revelation of truth that needed to be restored back into the Church. These prophetic revelations came about every 100 years starting with the 1500s into the 1900s; then in the last 50 years of the twentieth century, there was progressive revelation coming forth in the Church every decade. Now in the first decades of the twenty-first-century Church, God's progressive revelation has revealed the birthing of the Saints Movement in 2007 and the divine decree for the launching of the Third and Final Church Reformation in 2008.

PRESENT HISTORY OF PERSONAL PROGRESSIVE REVELATION

What makes us who we are today? Each one of us should ask ourselves, how did I develop my core values, beliefs, and convictions? How did I become the person I am today in my total being—body, soul, and spirit? We know how we came to be who we are physically. The color of eyes, hair, and skin is determined by that of the parents, grandparents, and genealogical history. Our soul—intellect, emotional makeup, and personality—is determined some at birth. However, the way we think and function is mainly determined by our environment, education, experience, and all things that have influenced us. The sum total of who we are at the present as a physical and soulish person is determined by all the things just mentioned.

Who we are in our spirit is determined by our relationship with God, who is a Spirit. Our experiences with Jesus Christ, our salvation, our revelation and experience with His truth and Spirit-life determine what type of Christian or minister we are in Christ's Church. In reality, a person cannot think or act any differently than what his total being has become over the years, just as a computer cannot perform and respond any differently than what has been programmed into it (Prov. 23:7). Our decisions in life are normally made based on our core values and what we believe to be the real purpose of life. Receiving God's grace over the years and developing an understanding of human motivation and action enables me to have patience with people who do not believe the way I do about God's purpose for His Church.

REVELATION MAKES AN EXCEPTION TO THE RULE

The only exception to seeing things according to the conditioning of past experiences and environment is to receive divine enlightenment. The Holy Spirit can suddenly illuminate our minds to see things never understood before, enabling us to respond differently. Apostle Paul is a living example of this truth. As a strict Pharisee, he was convinced that the followers of Jesus were heretics and needed to be destroyed (Acts 9:1-9). But when Jesus struck Paul blind, knocked him off his horse, and spoke revelation to him, it transformed Saul the persecutor into Apostle Paul, the promoter of Christianity (Acts 9:1-9). The same was true with Peter. Because of the past teaching he received from his Jewish rabbi, he did not believe that non-Jewish people could receive salvation from Jesus Christ without first becoming a proselyte Jew. While praying, he received a vision of a sheet full of unclean creatures being lowered toward him from Heaven. The voice of God told him to eat the creatures; he refused, declaring they were not clean according to the law of Moses. God told him not to call anything unclean that He had cleansed and declared clean.

Peter did not understand what this meant, but when he went with the men to a non-Jewish household, they asked him to share what God had given him for them (Acts 10:33-48). When Peter made the statement in his message that *"whoever believes in Him will receive the remission of sins,"* the people believed, and the Holy Spirit witnessed to it by gifting them with their own spirit language of unknown tongues. Apostle Peter based his conclusion that God had forgiven and Spirit-baptized them on the fact that the Italian household of Cornelius spoke in unknown tongues just as the 120 did on the day of Pentecost (Acts 10:44-48; 2:5-12; 11:15). This revelation and experience changed Apostle Peter's belief and helped him fulfill his calling as a New Testament apostle. Our degree of divine revelation determines what type of Christian minister we will be. Apart from revelation, the teaching and ministry we receive determines what type of Christian or minister of the Church we will be.

OUR MENTOR IS A PHOTOGRAPH OF OUR FUTURE

The teaching we receive and the anointing we respect are the beliefs we establish and the type of ministry we become. The fivefold minister who attracts and enthuses us the most becomes the model for our lives, and normally we will become a reproduction of them. We cannot choose our biological parents, nor can we decide what set of parents will raise us to adults. Sinners normally do not choose which minister will bring them to a saving knowledge of Jesus Christ. However, Christians can choose which church and minister they want to mentor them, especially if where they were birthed is not growing them beyond their babyhood Christianity.

ADVANCING BEYOND OUR PRESENT TRUTH

As a general rule, a minister will not advance beyond the restoration truth, doctrines, and bylaws of his or her denomination. And a congregation will not advance beyond their pastor's restoration truth and Christian maturity. The exception to the rule is when the minister or church member receives advanced teaching and spiritual experiences outside his local church or denomination.

An Example

Apostle Paul met several disciples who had been mentored by the teaching and ministry of John the Baptist. They had been Baptist Christians for quite some time before this incident took place, some twenty years after John the Baptist was beheaded and some twenty-two years after the Church was established. They had been faithfully living and practicing their faith as good Baptist believers. Apostle Paul asked them:

> *"Did you receive the Holy Spirit when you believed?" So they said to him, "We have not so much as heard whether there is a Holy Spirit." And he said to them, "Into what then were you baptized?" So they said, "Into John's baptism." Then Paul said, "John indeed baptized with a baptism of repentance, saying to the people that they should believe on Him who would come after him, that is, on Christ Jesus." When they heard this, they were baptized in the name of the Lord Jesus. And when Paul had laid hands on them, the Holy Spirit came upon them, and they spoke with tongues and prophesied* (Acts 19:2-6).

In present-day terms, we would say that Paul was a charismatic minister who met some evangelical Christians who had never heard about the baptism of the Holy Spirit with the evidence of speaking in other tongues. He enlightened them on truth more advanced than they had been taught. He then prayed for them to receive the gift of the Holy Spirit. They received and spoke in tongues that updated them in Christian truth and experience. If these Baptist Christians had never been exposed to the present truth from Apostle Paul, which was beyond what anyone was teaching and experiencing in their circle of Christian fellowship, then they would have stayed on that level of Christianity for the rest of their lives.

During the Charismatic Renewal, millions of Christians who were in denominations that were established in past restoration movements were exposed to the teaching on the gift of the Holy Spirit with speaking in other tongues. Hundreds of thousands received the experience and came out of their denominations in order to fully receive, practice, and propagate that truth. Many ministers and saints who received the experience stayed and formed a charismatic group within their denomination. Even now, some 30 to 40 years later, major denominations like Lutheran, Methodist, and Baptist have 20 to 30 percent of their ministers who are charismatic. However, most of those denominational Charismatics have not advanced beyond the initial experience they received during the Charismatic Renewal. And most of those who started independent charismatic churches have not advanced beyond their original charismatic experiences and teachings.

Many Never Make the Transition

There are people in Christendom who have never advanced beyond their first involvement with Christianity. We could say there are Christian groups who have their camps set up all the way from Egypt to within the promised Canaan Land. Some families have been camped in the Catholic Church for numerous generations and have never to this day advanced on to the first restoration truth that was established some 500 years ago. Likewise, some have been Historic Protestants for years and have never experienced Evangelical/ Holiness Movement truths. In like manner, Pentecostals have not advanced beyond what was restored in the Pentecostal Movement a hundred years ago. Even many Charismatics have not advanced on into the Prophetic-Apostolic Movement truths and spiritual experiences. No doubt many who are now involved in the prophetic and apostolic will not move on to be leaders and participants in the Saints Movement.

As for me and my house, I do not want to stop anywhere short of the fullness of restored truth. With the mentors I have had and the exposure to teachings on restoration and revelation concerning God's overall purpose for His Church, I should always be a follower and promoter of restoration truth. Thanks be to God for keeping me open to new restored truth. My long, in-depth study of Church history makes me knowledgeable concerning the failures of past movements. We must be open to new truth but not gullible to false revelations or the reviving of old, erroneous teachings and practices. Like all others, I am the total sum of all my past, but it might be helpful if the reader had a better knowledge of who the author is, how he arrived at his present understanding, and how he became a twenty-first-century prophet-apostle fivefold minister of Jesus Christ to His Church.

HOW THE AUTHOR CAME TO BE A RESTORATION MINISTER

Spiritual DNA of the Author

Let me share some personal background so that you can see how this author has developed in his concepts of Christ and His Church. I was born in southeastern Oklahoma, July 29, 1934. My dad and mom were farmers, and my two brothers, two sisters, and I were raised on the farm. We lived five miles from the small town of Boswell, Oklahoma. Electricity was not brought to our community until I was 15 years old in 1949. Telephone lines were brought in later. When my dad and mom were married, they never attended church. The main reason was that my dad's family background was Methodist, and my mom's was Baptist. Because one sprinkled and the other immersed people in water baptism, they could not agree on which church to attend, so they never attended any.

After I had become a minister, my mom revealed to me that she had received a born-again experience when she was nine years old and felt called to preach. My dad had never had an experience with God. I was never inside a church to be part of a church service before I became a Christian. That came about when some ministers came to our community and built a brush arbor about two miles from where we lived. About ten young men, including my brother, cousins, and friends, rode our horses to those meetings. We mainly went because many young girls were attending. That was my initial motivation also, for I was dating one of the young ladies whose mother was a strong Christian and had helped sponsor the brush-arbor meetings. Her daughter, whom I was dating, was not a Christian.

Because there was no electricity in that area, they hung kerosene lanterns on the poles that were holding up the brush covering. They played string instruments and sang beautifully and loud. They preached every night and then gave a long, persistent altar call for people to get saved.

BIBLE REVELATION AND CONFIRMATION

After attending a few nights, I noticed that they were preaching out of a book they called a Bible. I wanted to check out what they were telling me, so I asked my mom if we had one of those books. We had an old Gideon Bible with the back torn off and some of the pages missing, but I took that book and without letting anyone know, I began reading the Bible. I found that the Bible really did talk about life after death and that people would spend eternity in Heaven or hell. A deep desire was developed within me to escape that hot place called hell. I figured if it was much hotter and more miserable than where I lived was in July, it should be avoided by all means.

GOD CAN USE DREAMS TO MOTIVATE

During this time, a dream made me even more desperate. In the dream, a person was standing on a platform announcing that it was the platform for Heaven and everyone who wanted to go should get aboard. I jumped on, and it began to ascend to Heaven and pass through some clouds. A voice said, "Give your ticket for Heaven now." Suddenly everyone went into Heaven, and I was back on earth. What was this ticket needed to get in, and where did you get it? I had never been involved in anything that needed a ticket except when we rode our horses five miles to town and paid our dime to purchase a ticket to see the weekly movie. A few nights later, I had the same kind of dream. The same things happened in this dream, only this time I pulled out a gun and was going to force them to let me enter through the gate to Heaven. But again everyone else went in, and I was back on earth. Finally, during the brush-arbor meetings, the preacher said in one of his messages, "Jesus is the ticket to Heaven."

In the second week of the five-week revival, I began to seek God. Each night I walked my girlfriend home while leading my horse and then rode three miles back to my house. After unbridling and unsaddling my palomino horse "Smokey," I would shuck ten ears of corn for his feed. Then I would kneel and lift my hands as I had seen the saints doing at the brush-arbor meetings. This continued for two weeks, but nothing seemed to happen until the night of my sixteenth birthday. My girlfriend had allowed her mother to talk her into getting me a particular present. She gave it to me in a box, which I tied on the back of my saddle. When I arrived home and had gone through my regular routine, I opened the box, and there was a Bible with a beautiful cover and a zipper that closed the cover around it. As I held it in my hands, something started happening within me. I do not remember that what I prayed was any different from what I had for the last two weeks, but suddenly I felt clean and pure with a light and glow filling my inner being. I started laughing and crying at the same time. I was kneeling beside my bed and did not realize I was getting louder and louder. My dad awoke and threatened to come in and give me a whipping if I did not shut up and go to sleep. I slipped out to the smokehouse where we kept our smoked hams hanging and worshiped the Lord for two hours.

DOWN THE SAWDUST TRAIL

The next night, after working in the fields all day cultivating corn with a team of mules, we attended the meeting again. They gave the same persistent altar call, only this time my girlfriend wanted to go and said she would go forward to the altar if I would. As I stood up, she and three of her friends stood and we all walked down to the altar, which was a rough two-by-twelve bridge board laid across some blocks of wood with sawdust covering the ground. As we started walking forward, all the singers and the preacher started shouting, "Hallelujah!" I wondered why they were getting excited when we were the ones going for the goods.

RECEIVING THE GIFT WITH THE EVIDENCE

As we knelt and began praying, I saw a vision of Jesus hanging on the cross speaking to me that He died for me that I might live for Him. As I was viewing this scene, words were pouring out of my mouth. In my natural conscious mind, I was expressing thanks to God. A little ole brother started praying with me. I wasn't conscious of his presence for a while until I heard him praying loudly, asking God to send the fire and send the rain. He then said, "Let it go; that's it!" I did not know what I was to let go of, so I took my hands off of the altar. He then started saying, "That's it; just talk it out!"

When he said *talk,* I thought to myself, *What is he trying to say, for I am talking as fast and loud as I can.* However, I was surprised at what was coming out of my mouth. It was not the Okie English that I had been speaking when I came to the meeting. For the next 30 minutes, that other-tongues language flowed through me with great joy as I continued pounding that altar bench with my hands. They told me later that I was preaching in the Spirit. All four young people who went to the altar with me received their gift of the Holy Spirit and began to speak in tongues. As I was carrying on at the altar, I could hear my horse-riding buddies laughing and making fun of me, but I did not care, for I had something going on that was better than what they thought about me.

After the five-week revival was over, they had those who had accepted Christ meet once a week with a preacher in a little one-room country schoolhouse, which was about three miles from my home. This discontinued after three months, and then for the first time I rode my horse five miles to attend the church in town where many of the saints had come from to help in the meetings.

INITIAL CHURCH GROUP INVOLVEMENT

I did not know one church group or denomination from another. They said they were Pentecostal, and the name on the outside of the church building said Assembly of God. Those old saints shouted and "danced in the spirit" and sang with great enthusiasm. They sang some songs such as, "Power in the Blood," but most of the songs were about "the old account settled long ago," or the future glories of going to Heaven: "when I die, hallelujah, bye and bye, I'll fly away." The majority of the songs were about leaving this world and going to Heaven. They preached often on living separate from the world. Anything to do with sports or entertainment was sinful. A statement that I make sometimes is comical but has some reality: "Everything was a sin but breathing, and that had to be done in church to be sanctified." I was the only teenage young man in the church, but God's grace kept me faithful to the Lord though none of my family or former friends were Christians.

My family moved to Hollis, Oklahoma to work in the cotton fields because all of our hogs and some of our cattle developed a disease and died. The move was just six weeks before I was to graduate from high school. Somehow, I finished and graduated while I was still 16 years old. That fall, we moved across the state line to Wellington, Texas. I lived with my parents until we had finished picking cotton that fall. It was during this time that an experience established a truth within me that would end up determining the way I would train saints in prophetic ministry more than 30 years later.

GOD'S PROVIDENTIAL PREPARATION

A brother whom I had met at church told me that he could pull 1,200 pounds of cotton in one day. It didn't sound possible, for the most I had ever picked or had seen anyone do was less than 400 pounds. He challenged me to come and work in the same field with him the following week. He worked with a 14-foot cotton sack and I worked with a 12 foot. He took two rows at a time, and I took one and worked off of one of his rows so that I could stay right with him. We worked over 12 hours that day from dawn to dark. When he had his 14-foot sack full and went to the weighing wagon to weigh and empty the cotton, I went with him. I stuck with him like Elisha did Elijah. The first day I broke my record and pulled over 400 pounds of cotton, on Tuesday over 500, over 600 on Wednesday, 700 on Thursday. On Friday, our last day together, I pulled 818 pounds, and that same day he finally pulled his 1,200. Just by working alongside someone who was a professional in his field and doing everything he did, I more than doubled my greatest ability and production. This is the way I trained our core prophets who are now national and international prophets and apostles. My dad used to say, "The way to train a young, untrained mule is to harness him with an old mule who knows how to pull the plow properly." If you are a young, untrained Christian who wants to be much more fruitful and successful, then get harnessed with a mature man or woman of God who knows how to be a productive minister.

MAKING A TRANSITION TO NEW RESTORATION TRUTH

In October of 1951 at age 17, I moved away from home and got a job in Amarillo, Texas and lived in a boarding house. While I was attending the First Assembly of God church, some of my church friends started visiting a church that was having a great move of the Holy Spirit. They would sing their praises to God instead of shouting them. They would do this for an hour or so with several prophecies being spoken when the worship would become lower in volume. They would have waves of worship and prophecy. It seemed strange to me compared to what I was used to in the Pentecostal shout and frenzied dance unto the Lord. After a few weeks, I was birthed into that worship and started attending that church in October of 1952.

Their preachers proclaimed a victorious Church with a glorious future. They also emphasized that every Christian has a membership ministry in the Body of Christ. For the first time, I heard teaching on the Church not being a denomination or church building but the many-membered corporate Body of Christ. I had been given tongues and interpretation of tongues in my Pentecostal church, and now I was prophesying in the congregation during the church service.

BECOMING AN ORDAINED PREACHER

There was a great desire in my heart to be a preacher, but I did not know if God wanted that and, if He did, how to become one. In February of 1953, a prophet came to the church and spoke to me my first personal word of prophecy. It gave me hope and encouragement that God was going to call me into the ministry. In late August, I drove my 1948 Studebaker to Portland, Oregon to attend Bible college. In October of that school year, I was called forth to receive prophetic presbytery where four ministers prophesied much of my gifts, calling, and destiny. The following year, I was ordained on February 4 and launched into ministry at the age of 19. I evangelized for a month and then took a pastorate in Toppenish, Washington.

ESTABLISHED IN CHURCH HISTORY AND RESTORATION

After being a single pastor for almost two years, I married Evelyn Hixson on August 13, 1955. During our six years of pastoring, we traveled to an annual restoration conference in North Surrey, BC, Canada. There is where the seeds of Church restoration were planted into my spirit. The following 25 years my studies majored in Church history. I did research into everything I could find recorded concerning the revivals and movements that had transpired in the Church since its beginning. I started teaching on Church restoration in 1959.

PROGRESSIVE REVELATION OVER 67 YEARS: 1954 TO 2021

During the first 25 years of my ministry, I taught and preached on all restored truths that had been restored up to that time. My main ministry in the Spirit was prophesying and getting people filled with the Holy Spirit, and joyfully liberated in praise to the Lord. During my five years (1964 to 1969) of teaching in a Bible college, I taught all of the Old Testament books, which greatly broadened and deepened my biblical knowledge. I also taught Church history and the makeup of the Church mainly from the Book of Ephesians.

RESTORATION MOVEMENTS PARTICIPATION

I became a Christian while attending a Pentecostal meeting and then attended Pentecostal churches from 1950 to the fall of 1952. I then attended a church that was embracing the restoration truths and ministries that were being restored in what became tagged the Latter Rain Movement.[1] I attended a Bible college that was seeking to incorporate the new ways of worship, laying on of hands, and prophecy. I received personal prophecies from the prophetic presbytery formed from the faculty of the Bible college on Thursday night on October 1, 1953.[2] While pastoring in Washington State for six years, I attended the annual restoration movement camp meeting in North Surrey, BC, Canada. The apostle over the two-week conference was Reg Layzell, who was an apostolic teacher who had a balanced and biblically sound teaching on all the truths and ministries being restored at that time. The seed to the tree of restoration ministry that I have today was planted in my spirit during those days.

So my progressive revelation and experience began with a born-again, Spirit-baptized experience in a Pentecostal meeting and was established in Pentecostal truth and ministry. I began my ministry as a minister of the restoration movement and then participated in the Charismatic Renewal of the 1960s and the Faith Movement of the 1970s. Then in 1973 God gave me that sovereign experience of an endless prophetic flow. (The details of the prophetic presbytery received in 1953 and the sovereign anointing and release of personal prophecy in 1973 is described in detail on pages 306–317 in my book, *The Day of the Saints*.) This divine experience and the revelation that came with it launched me into the ministry of activating the saints in the prophetic ministry of the gifts of the Holy Spirit. In 1977, I started activating saints in the gifts as I traveled in ministry, and then in 1979 we started a Friday night School of the Holy Spirit. Hundreds of Christians were taught and activated into spiritual ministry, and many received personal prophecy every Friday night. This experience and revelation established the major ministry we would have for the Body of Christ for the next 40 years.

In 1977–1978, I received two major prophecies that I was to write a book. I really didn't pay that much attention to the word. I felt I was too busy traveling in ministry to stop and take time to write a book. Writing and producing a book back in the 1970s was not nearly as easy as it is today with computers. The Lord was more serious about the book writing than I was. In May of 1978, I had a kidney stone attack while ministering in Atlanta, Georgia. That night, instead of presenting degrees to our extension graduates, I was in the hospital having kidney stones removed from my body.

During the six weeks recovery time back at home in Phoenix, Arizona, God spoke to me to find all the prophecies I had on tapes or written out and to type them and put in chronological order, starting with the first prophecy received in 1952. I was surprised when I typed the two major prophecies received in 1977–1978, both of which stated, "Yea, the Lord says stop traveling and take time to write the book." One part of the prophecy repeated "the book, the book" nine times.

I started to write on my bachelor's thesis, which was dealing with Jesus and God's purposes for creating the human race. I couldn't get the writing to flow. I prayed to the Lord telling Him that I wanted to write about Jesus, who was the nearest and dearest thing to my heart.

Jesus finally spoke and said, "I do not want you to write about the nearest and dearest thing to your heart, but to write about the nearest and dearest thing to My heart, which is My Church."

Over the next three years, I handwrote the book on Christ's Church and titled it *The Eternal Church*. Much more revelation was received on the five divisions of the book covering the origination of the Church, its deterioration, times of restoration, and the ultimate destiny and purpose of the Church, including its last generation ministry. It came off the press in 1981, and I did continual preaching concerning the Church.

OBEDIENCE OPENS THE DOOR TO NEW REVELATION AND COMMISSIONING

A couple of years after the book was finished and distributed throughout the Church world, God brought revelation that would bring a new vision and commissioning. God brought revelation on Malachi 4:5-6. The core of the message was that the prophecy had a twofold application—personal and corporate. It first applied to one prophet preparing the way for the first coming of Christ and then a company of prophets preparing the way for Christ's second coming. The revelation was written in Chapter 2 of *Prophets and Personal Prophecy*.[3] In October of 1988, the Prophetic Movement was birthed at one of our conferences after I had preached a message on the great company of prophets God wanted raised up. The sovereign move of God that birthed it is described in my second book on the prophetic called *Prophets and the Prophetic Movement*.[4] We then started schools, seminars, and conferences on prophets and prophetic ministry. The third book on the prophetic was *Prophets, Pitfalls to Avoid and Principles to Practice*.[5] I then wrote a 300-page manual of teachings and activations to train prophets, prophetic ministers, and prophetic saints in prophetic ministry.[6] After 30 years of using the manual, more than

500,000 saints and ministers have been trained on every continent of the world.

Being an apostle of restoration, I knew that the apostle had to be fully restored, so I wrote the book *Apostles, Prophets, and the Coming Moves of God.*[7] The apostles were restored back into the Church in the 1990s. For me and Christian International, the apostolic was fully birthed at our October conference in 1998.

The Lord had revealed to me in the 1970s that He was going to take the last five decades of the twentieth century to clarify and reemphasize the ministries of the evangelist, pastor, and teacher that had been restored, and then restore the ministry of the prophet and apostle back into the Church.

DECADE	FIVEFOLD MINISTRY	MOVEMENT
1950s	Evangelist	Deliverance Evangelism
1960s	Pastor	Charismatic Renewal
1970s	Teacher	Faith Teaching Movement
1980s	Prophet	Prophetic Movement
1990s	Apostle	Apostolic Movement

ALL FIVE EQUIP THE SAINTS FOR THE SAINTS MOVEMENT

When fivefold ministers were active in the first-century Church, it produced a Saints Movement. By Church history and revelation knowledge, I knew that when all five ascension gift ministers were active and fulfilling their commission of equipping the saints it would produce a Saints Movement (Eph. 4:11-13). I preached the coming Saints Movement from 1997 until it was birthed within the Church in 2007. I wrote the book *The Day of the Saints* to reveal what would be accomplished in the Saints Movement and God's divine purpose for it.[8]

EXTENDED AND EXPANDED VISION AND GOAL

During all of my 67 years of ministry, I have preached that God's ultimate purpose is to have a perfected Church/Bride. The main purpose of Christ giving the fivefold ascension gift ministers to the Church was to bring the saints to Christ's maturity and ministry. My goal was to co-labor with Christ to fulfill Ephesians 4:11-16; 5:23-32; Hebrews 6:1-2; and Romans 8:17—that He might present the Church to Himself a glorious Church without spot or blemish, a mature Church ready to be joint heirs with Christ in all that God planned for Jesus to be and do throughout eternity. When the Church was fully restored and perfected, then Christ could come resurrect and translate His Church to Heaven to enjoy eternal life with Christ Jesus forevermore.   *stop*

A KAIROS TIME TO FULFILL PROPHET ISAIAH'S PROPHETIC COMMAND

Enlarge the place of your tent, and let them stretch out the curtains of your dwellings; do not spare; lengthen your cords, and strengthen your stakes. For you shall expand to the right and to the left, and your descendants will inherit the nations, and make the desolate cities inhabited (Isaiah 54:2-3).

Notice the key descriptive and directive words: *enlarge, stretch out, lengthen your cords, strengthen,* and *expand.* These are words to all who would enter the Third and Final Church Reformation. If we obey this command, then His promise is that we will inherit the nations and make the desolated cities inhabited, which speaks of transformation of nations and the restoration of all things.

EXPAND AND EXTEND THE ULTIMATE PURPOSE FOR THE CHURCH

This is what happened to me when the revelation came concerning the Third and Final Church Reformation. I had to extend my vision and understanding of God's purpose for the Church from Ephesians 4:11-16 to Revelation 11:15. My vision and revelation now was not just to have a perfected Church to be presented as the Bride of Christ, but to have a perfected Church that has been built into the Army of the Lord executing the judgments written concerning the world until the kingdoms of this world have become the kingdoms of our Lord Jesus and His anointed one, the Church. Previously, my thinking was that the perfecting of the Church in Christ's maturity and ministry was the end of God's purpose. Now the spirit of revelation has stretched out my understanding, expanded my vision, and extended God's purpose for the Church.

WHAT HAS THE CHURCH BEEN COMMISSIONED TO ACCOMPLISH?

The Third Reformation revelation reveals that God's purpose for perfecting and restoring the Church is to have a corporate Body of Christ on earth that can be instrumental in bringing about the restoration of all things. A new look at Acts 3:21 reveals that Jesus was not only held in the heavens until the restoration of the Church, but until the restoration of *all things.* The Living Bible says, *"For he must remain in heaven until the final recovery of all things from sin, as prophesied from ancient times."* The final recovery of *all things* from *sin* expands and extends the restoration to include everything that was lost by the sin of lucifer and Adam. This brings us to the reality that Jesus has been restoring the Church to His maturity and ministry to be His major instrument for restoring all things. What has not yet been revealed or made clear is how much restoration of all things the Church will bring while still mortal and how much will be left to be done after the Church is immortalized. It is not too relevant to those who are committed to co-laboring with Christ in all He shall ever be and do from now to throughout eternity. My personal preference would be to receive my immortal body as soon as possible; then my work would be with unlimited power without pain or confusion in my performance of God's will on earth as it is in Heaven. It is the same attitude I have about when the R/T (rapture-resurrection/translation) takes place. If I had a vote on the matter and it counted for anything, I would vote for a seven-year sabbatical before I had to start ruling and reigning. If seven years was not an option, then I would take three and a half years, and if that wasn't in the plans, then I would take five minutes, and if none of those were available, then I would gladly be changed in a moment, in the twinkling of an eye, receive my immortal body, and immediately continue co-laboring with Christ in executing dominion and rule over all the earth until all that dwells therein is God's holy people living on *"new earth in which righteousness dwells"* (2 Pet. 3:13).

END-TIME PREDICTIONS VERSUS PROPHETIC REVELATION

In the early years of teaching, my eschatological viewpoints were based on the writings of dispensational theologians. I was expecting the imminent return of Christ as I had been taught by my Pentecostal mentors. In fact, they implied that one was not a full believer if one did not expect Christ to return any moment.

Between 1954 and 1963, I taught in the local church, where I was pastoring, and in my travels that the second coming of Christ would have to take place by the end of 1963. Clarence Larkin's dispensational charts were spread across the front of my church to show how it was all going to happen. I don't think you need to be told that Christ's second coming did not take place at that date. Being a theologian, I figured all this in my head, but my prophet anointing made me sense in my spirit that something was going to happen in the early 1960s. Something did happen; the Charismatic Renewal began to sweep through the Church world in 1963. Some 25 years later, another dispensational minister predicted that Jesus was going to return in 1988 and even wrote a book giving 88 reasons why it would happen then. The second coming of Jesus did not take place; nevertheless, something spiritual and significant did happen in 1988—another restoration movement took place, which was called the Prophetic Movement. Ever since dispensationalism became popular among Evangelical and Pentecostal Christians, hundreds of dates have been set for the second coming of Christ during the last few centuries.

I am more of a restoration-reformation theologian now than a dispensational. Let us now look at the difference in the two beliefs and how they affect one's view of God's purpose for His Church.

DIFFERENT THEOLOGICAL CONCEPTS

God has a purpose for His Church. How a person views God's purpose is determined by his theological background. This, in turn, affects his expectations about the second coming of Christ and end-time eschatology. It affects his beliefs concerning what part the Church will play in the fulfillment of all things. There are basically two major concepts—one is the dispensation viewpoint, and the other is the reformed restoration viewpoint.

THE DISPENSATIONALIST VIEWPOINT: "GOING UP"

The dispensational viewpoint was established during the Evangelical Movement. It is the view that the ministry of apostles and prophets was brought forth to lay the foundation of the Church Age and write the books of the New Testament. When the foundation was finished and the Bible completed, the ministry of the apostle and prophet was no longer necessary and therefore dispensationally deleted from the Church. Dispensationalists also believe the same about the miraculous element of the Church. They do not believe that supernatural miracles, healings, demonic deliverance, or speaking in unknown tongues with the baptism of the Holy Spirit are still to be active in the Church today. The only supernatural experience they accept is that of a born-again experience by the work of the Holy Spirit. Most of them accept the gift of eternal life as being a sovereign, supernatural work of the Holy Spirit. The main reason they could accept that truth-experience was because it had already been restored in the Protestant Movement.

Dispensationalists' Concept of the Church

The only purpose dispensationalists see for the Church is for the saints to be witnesses of Jesus Christ for the salvation of others. Their view of the end-time Church is a lukewarm "Laodicean church" based on Christ's words to the church in Laodicea in Revelation 3. They believe there will be a remnant holding on in faith until Jesus comes and rescues the Church from total annihilation. They see the rapture—the translation of the saints—as God's heavenly helicopter coming to evacuate the saints off of the earth before the antichrist takes over the world and the great tribulation begins. The only purpose for Christ's second coming is to remove the saints from the earth so they will not be here when the woes and judgments of God's wrath are poured out on the wicked of the earth. With this concept, most of them are premillennial and preach a pretribulation rapture. This means that they believe the next item on God's agenda is the "going up" of the saints out of this world, which they believe will occur before the great tribulation. Dispensationalists see wickedness and world calamities in the world as evidence that Jesus is coming any moment, and they believe the only thing preventing Him from returning is His grace in giving the unsaved more time to be born again.

The dispensationalist viewpoint is currently held by many Christians who describe themselves as evangelical or fundamentalist. Even many Pentecostals, who believe the baptism of the Holy Spirit is a valid experience in the Church today, agree with the dispensationalist viewpoint of the end-time purpose of the Church. Some groups emphasize that there will be merely a "remnant" or "chosen few" left in the Church when Jesus returns, and therefore their primary goal is to keep themselves apart from the corrupt world system until they are rescued to Heaven. Many others emphasize the need to witness to as many people as possible in the short time left before Christ returns. Basically, they believe the purpose of the Church is to win more Christians so more people will be saved from hell. Then God will have a big family of redeemed people that He can take to Heaven to love on and enjoy throughout eternity. They look forward to going to Heaven to have an eternal vacation and get away from their problems on earth. This was some of my thinking when I was expecting the second coming of Christ to take place in 1963.

Evangelicals Are Missionary Minded

Because these groups have a greater vision for the "quantity" of the Church than for the full restoration or "quality" of the Church, they have been used of God to introduce many to a saving knowledge of Jesus Christ. Through their preaching of the Gospel of salvation, multi-millions have been led to the Lord. Some of the largest denominations in the world have grown because they have a vision for outreach and missions. Many of these believers read their Bibles regularly, pray, disciple others, and are committed to abstaining from sin. They are faithful to the amount of vision they have received.

Eternity with Christ—Eternal Vacation or Vocation?

God gave me some revelation and insight concerning what the saints will be doing in Heaven, on God's new earth, and in the ages to come. Now I seek to give saints a greater vision of their inheritance in Christ as joint heirs with Jesus in all that He is going to be and do both now and throughout eternity. Saints need to know that eternity with Christ is not eternal vacation but an eternal vocation (Eph. 3:1-7). We will not be hallelujah hobos, drifting clouds, or wandering stars, nor will the saints ever become angels, cherubim, or seraphim; we will forever be redeemed mankind saints.

Eternity with Christ is living in a real heavenly world where there is God's government, the work of carrying on God's business, and a social order of saints relating to one another and ministering to one another with God's love. Membership in the Body of Christ is an eternal calling (Eph. 1:18). The Body of Christ is as eternal as its head Christ Jesus.[9] Saints need to get delivered from the Dark Age concept of Heaven being a mythical, spooky place where people float around in long robes with a strange look on their face and a halo over their head doing nothing but praising the Lord continuously as they drift through eternity. God's new heaven and new earth will be a real place with real people living and working together doing realistic things. Read Isaiah 65:17-25 to discover some of the things that take place after God creates new heavens and a new earth.

THE RESTORATION VIEWPOINT: "GROWING UP"

Reformation/restoration theologians propagate that the whole New Testament is the blueprint for the building of the Church. Every truth, ministry, and supernatural manifestation found within the Bible is for the Church to receive, believe, and manifest today. They believe the first-century Church was the pattern for the whole age of the mortal Church. But there came a great falling away of the true Church that began around the third century and continued until nearly all the truths and supernatural ministries of the Church were lost. The Church went into a thousand-year period of time called by historians the "Dark Age of the Church" that lasted until the 1500s. At that time, the period of the Second Church Reformation began.

The restoration of the Church has progressed since that time by "restoration movements." Each restoration movement has restored back into the Church some of the truths and ministries that were lost during the great falling away. Restoration theologians believe that the greatest apostasy of Christ's Church has already taken place. Although the world's cup of iniquity will continue to increase and false voices will go out seeking to deceive even the elect, the progressive Church as a whole will overcome and grow more and more glorious. Restoration Christians believe that before Christ returns the Church will be fully complete in maturity as well as in the *number* of members needed: *"Then each of them was given a white robe, and they were told to be patient a little longer, until the number of their fellow-servants and of their brethren, who were to die as they had died, should be complete"* (Rev. 6:11 PNT).

THE CHURCH WILL NOT "GO UP" UNTIL IT HAS "GROWN UP"

Part of "growing up" for the Church includes the restoration of all things as well as conforming to the image of Christ. Not only will the Gospel of salvation be preached to the entire world, but also the Gospel of the Kingdom of God (Matt. 24:14; John 14:12), which includes speaking the words of Jesus and doing all the supernatural works that Jesus did. In this way, the Church will truly be the manifested Body of Christ on the earth. The Bible reveals that all of creation is anxiously waiting with earnest expectation for the Church to fulfill God's purpose during the Third and Final Reformation. It will release them into the glorious liberty of the children of God (Rom. 8:19-22).

When the saints receive their immortal bodies, it will cause a chain reaction throughout all of God's creation that was affected by the fall of lucifer and the sin of man. All the heroes of the faith and the saints who have lost their bodies through death are waiting for the Church to fulfill all things and thereby release Jesus from Heaven to return and restore their bodies by His resurrection power. Even the saints are groaning inwardly, earnestly looking forward to the redemption of our bodies from deterioration and death (Rom. 6:19-23; Heb. 11:39-40). Even Jesus is excitedly looking forward to the Third and Final Church Reformation bringing about the restoration of all things so that He can return and be joined to His Church/Bride to cleanse the heavens and earth of all wickedness and evil spirits and set up His rule and righteousness over His cleansed and restored new heavens and new earth.

God Uses His People to Fulfill His Purpose on Earth

Noah built the ark to preserve and transition the human race from the old world to the new (Gen. 6–8). *Abraham* was used to start a special chosen race of God's people, which became the nation of Israel. God promised Abraham He would bless him and the race that he fathered and all people on earth would be blessed through them (Gen. 12:1-5). *Moses* was used to bring God's people out of their bondage in Egypt and to give them God's law—their pattern for living according to God's ways and not those of the nations around them. He built God's tabernacle, the place designated for God's presence to dwell among them (Book of Exodus). *Joshua* was instrumental in taking the people of Israel across the Jordan River and by military force destroying the inhabitants and establishing Israel as a nation in their "promised land" of Canaan.[10]

Samuel started the school of prophets that launched hundreds of prophets who became God's main voice of communication to humankind. He also established the reign of kings over Israel.[11] *King David* was the man after God's own heart who defeated the enemies of Israel and established her as a godly nation chosen to fulfill God's purpose. David was the only one who conquered all the land to the borders that God promised Abraham, from the Mediterranean Sea to the Euphrates River (1 Sam. 19:20; 2 Sam. 8:15).

God could not find a man who could fulfill His next major purpose to bring redemption and reconciliation of man back to God (Isa. 59:16). Therefore, God sent His own Son to become a mortal man (John 3:16; Heb. 2:5; Gal. 4:4). *Jesus* became the only human to be fathered by God Himself. Adam was created by the hand of God, but Jesus is the only begotten Son of God (Gen. 2:7; John 1:14; Eph. 1:3). God's perfect man, the only sinless man to ever live, became the perfect and only acceptable sacrifice for the redemption of man (Heb. 5:5). Through the man Christ Jesus' death, burial, and resurrection, a new creation of humankind was brought into being (Eph. 1:3-6; 1 Cor. 15). A people who were not a people now became the people of God (1 Pet. 2:9-10). They became a new race upon the earth called the Church race.

The only way to become a part of this new race is to be born again—not by a natural birth, but by a spiritual birth (John 3:3-5). By believing in the heart and confessing with the mouth that Jesus Christ died for our sins and rose again, a person receives Christ into his or her life, becoming born again and a new creation in Christ (Rom. 10:9). Old things pass away, and all things become new (2 Cor. 5:17; Eph. 2:11-13). When a person becomes a new creation by being born of God, Almighty God becomes their Father, and Jesus Christ becomes their Lord and Savior (Rom. 8:14-17). They are baptized into a Body of anointed believers called the *Ekklesia* or the Church (1 Cor. 12:12). Other names for this new creation race of special called-out people are believers, members of the Body of Christ, Christians, and the saints.[12] New names will now be used during the Third Reformation, such as Kingdom demonstrators, seven-mountain ministers, Elijah revolutionaries, Davidic company, Joshua generation, transformers, and the Omega-transition generation.

Who Are Restoration Christians?

Basically, every Protestant is a restoration person. In other words, they are a member of a church denomination that came into existence because of a restoration movement. The restoration movement restored certain truths, ministries, and practices that were present in the early Church but were not active in the existing churches at that time. In order to propagate and practice these truths, they found it necessary to start a new church group or denomination.

Restoration Churches

Every mainline Protestant church denomination came into being and exists today because of a restoration movement that has taken place during the last 500 years. Every mainline Protestant Christian belongs to a denomination that became established because of a major restoration movement. All are restoration saints; the question is, how much truth do they want to see restored? Did the Holy Spirit's work of restoring all truth cease after their denomination was brought forth from a restoration movement?

How will we know when the period of the restoration of the Church is completed? Which restoration movement restored all the truths and spiritual experiences that Christ has predestined for the fully restored Church? None has thus far, but each has restored some of the total truth that God intends for His Church. There is a statement of truth that is a trustworthy criterion for determining if there are more restoration movements coming to the Church: *if the literal second coming of Christ has not taken place yet, then there is more spiritual restoration coming to the Church.*

Acts 3:21 emphatically states that the second coming of Christ cannot take place until all things are restored. This means that as soon as the last thing that the apostles and prophets have prophesied and written in Scriptures is restored, Jesus will immediately return to earth in a moment, in the twinkling of an eye (1 Cor. 15:52). Based on this scriptural truth, if we believe the second coming of Jesus Christ has not taken place yet, then we must believe for more restoration. For if all things were now restored, then Christ Jesus would have already returned as sovereign Lord and King over all the earth. If all things have been restored, then we should now be the saints resurrected and translated into the immortal Church (Rev. 20:4-6). Because we have not received that experience and are not functioning as an immortal Church, then Christ has not returned, and all things are not restored and fulfilled in and by the mortal Church.

WHAT IS NEXT ON GOD'S AGENDA?

The next major thing to take place on God's divine timetable is not the second coming of Christ but another major restoration movement. For if, within this last minute, all things had been restored, then the second coming of Christ would be taking place right now. Jesus is extremely desirous to return for His Church. The moment the last thing is restored, Christ will give a great shout, and Gabriel will blow his trumpet as Jesus returns accompanied with the spirits of the departed saints (1 Thess. 4:13-18). Jesus Christ will resurrect the bodies of the saints and reunite them as His redeemed spirit, soul, and body people. During the same moment, He will immortalize the bodies of the saints still living on earth, instantly lifting them up in the air to join with the other saints. By this miraculous act, Christ Jesus reunites His Church from Heaven and earth into one eternal Church to be His Bride and co-reign with Him over Heaven and earth. For this reason, present-day saints should be working toward and believing for more restoration, rather than just gazing into the heavens hoping for an imminent second coming.

There can be *no second coming until there is a full restoration of all things* spoken by the prophets. This is what the apostle Peter was making reference to when he told us to "hasten" the coming of the Lord (2 Pet. 3:12). We cannot hasten Christ's coming by just preaching that it is going to happen soon, but we can by "preparing the way and making ready a people" for His second coming.[13] We prepare the way by receiving prophetic revelation on what needs to be restored and then becoming instruments in the hand of the Holy Spirit to bring about the restoration of all things so that Christ can be released from Heaven to return. We make ready a people by transforming every saint into the image and likeness of Jesus so that they can manifest Christ's full manhood and ministry (Rom. 8:29).

The Omega Generation

Present-day fivefold ministers and saints must accept the reality that there are things that the last generation of the mortal Church must fulfill and accomplish before Christ can return. In order for the Omega-generation saints to fulfill God's purpose, they must come to the fullness of the way, truth, and life of Christ (John 14:6). The saints must come to the unity of the faith until they become one even as Jesus and His Father are one. Jesus declared that the world would not believe and be won to Christ until the saints are one with one another in Christ (John 17:20-23). The greatest harvest ever recorded in Church history will happen when this unity takes place. Apostle Paul declared by divine revelation that all fivefold ministers must continue ministering to the saints until every member of the Body of Christ is fully functioning in their membership ministry (Eph. 4:13).

Preach More on the Truths That Produce God's Purpose

These scriptural realities are just a few of the things that must be accomplished first before Christ Jesus can return. We should be preaching more about these things than the imminent return of Christ. Preach His second coming, but also prepare the way and make ready a people so that Christ can return. We are not waiting on Him; He is waiting on us! Evangelical ministers have been declaring the immediate return of Christ for hundreds of years. While they have been asking for His literal coming, Christ has been coming spiritually again and again to the Church as present truth in several major restoration movements.

Evangelicals and Pentecostals have been declaring for years that the next thing on God's agenda is the second coming of Christ. Like Noah proclaiming for a hundred years that there was a flood coming, one of these days they will be right. He will come! However, if Noah had preached about the flood but had not at the same time prepared the ark so he and his family could be the transition generation, they would not have been prepared to make the transition from the old world to the new. There is a transition generation today who are preparing their ark of conformity to the image of Christ so that they can make the transition from old earth to new earth. Christ's prophesied second coming will soon be history just as the prophesied flood is now history. His coming is real and will happen, but it cannot happen until all things are revealed and fulfilled. We cannot hasten His coming just by longing for it, but we can hurry it along by co-laboring with the Holy Spirit in restoring all things.

God's Provision and Preparation for Restoration

While Jesus was on earth, His natural body was the home and headquarters of God here on earth (Col. 2:9). Now the Church, as the corporate Body of Christ, is the home and headquarters for Jesus Christ here on earth (1 Cor. 12:27; Eph. 2:22). The personal body of Jesus was used of God to provide all things, overcome all things, and fulfill all things necessary for the redemption of mankind. The shedding of His life's blood paid the price for the purchase of His Church (Acts 20:28). He authorized it by His resurrection from the dead and birthed the Church by His Holy Spirit on the day of Pentecost (Rom. 1:4; Acts 2:4). The body of Jesus contained the fullness of God and was used to accomplish all of God's will and purpose for the human race (Acts 3:18).

Jesus and His Church Will Co-Labor Together Forever

God's purpose for the human race was to have a special group of redeemed people to be in relationship with Him and to show forth

His glory on the earth (Heb. 2:10; Eph. 1:6,11). These special people make up His Church. It was God's purpose for the Church to be the Bride of Christ, thus making the saints who are part of the Church/Bride heirs of God and joint heirs with Christ Jesus.[14] This means that the Church is one with Christ and participates with Him in all that He shall ever do or be both now and throughout eternity. Does God have a purpose for the Church? Yes, just as much as He had and has a purpose for Christ Jesus. God has purposed for the Church to be the full expression of Christ Jesus as Jesus was the full expression of His heavenly Father (Eph. 4:7-16; Col. 2:9; Luke 14:17).

JESUS PERSONALLY FULFILLED HIS PART

In His physical body on earth, Jesus fulfilled every prophecy concerning Himself personally until His second coming: *"Those things which God foretold by the mouth of all His prophets, that the Christ would suffer, He has thus fulfilled"* (Acts 3:18). When Jesus declared, *"It is finished,"* and *"I have finished the work which You have given Me to do,"* it revealed that Jesus had finished the work that had to be done by Himself personally, alone (John 19:30; 17:4). After Jesus had fulfilled all things, He ascended back to His Father who then said to Him, *"Sit at My right hand, till I make Your enemies Your footstool"* (Heb. 1:13).

JESUS' MAIN MINISTRY NOW

Jesus now sits at the right hand of God in that heavenly place, making intercession for the saints (Rom. 8:34). He is praying that they may finish all He began and accomplish all that He appropriated for His Church. That part of Jesus' ministry as a lone minister is over forever. Never again will He have to do anything alone. Whatever else is to be done will be done with, in, and through His saints (Eph. 3:20)! Jesus is interceding for His saints that they will work with His heavenly Father to make all His enemies His footstool, to restore and fulfill all things, and to prepare the way and make ready a people for His second coming.

JESUS HAS ETERNALLY JOINED HIMSELF TO HIS CHURCH

He united Himself with His Church in its origination and did not forsake His Bride during the period of deterioration. He has continued to give Himself to His Church time after time in restoration, and will continue until His Church/Bride reaches her ultimate destination. Jesus has delegated His power of attorney unto His Church for the performance of His eternal purposes (1 John 4:17; Eph. 3:10-11; Matt. 28:18-20). Just as Jesus declared that the Father had delegated all authority unto Him, so has He now delegated all of His authority unto His Church (John 17:18; Matt. 28:18). This does not take glory from Him any more than Jesus having all the power of the Father detracted from God's glory. The authority of Jesus was based on Him doing the will of His Father. In like manner, the authority of the Church saints is based on them ministering with the mind of Christ according to God's word, will, and way.

All things yet to be revealed, restored, or fulfilled will be accomplished in, by, and through Christ's Church. Jesus knows that His Father has decreed that He must be held in Heaven *"until the times of restoration of all things, which God has spoken by the mouth of all His holy prophets since the world began"* (Acts 3:21). Father God has declared to His Son, "You have paid the extreme price. You have provided all things and have accomplished all things necessary for every purpose of God to be fulfilled. You have done it all; now set here at My right hand and enjoy watching Your Church, which You purchased with Your own blood and empowered by Your Holy Spirit, subdue all Your enemies and put them under Your feet as Your footstool" (Acts 3:21; Heb. 1:13).

The Saints Are Christ's Instruments for Prophetic Fulfillment

The twenty-first-century Church has a destiny to fulfill prophetic Scriptures just as Jesus fulfilled prophecies. There are many Old and New Testament prophetic Scriptures yet to be fulfilled by the Church. The mortal Church must fulfill all Scriptures pertaining to God's purpose for the last-generation Church before Jesus can return. Therefore, it is *necessary for us to understand those prophetic Scriptures that must be restored and activated into reality before Jesus can be released from Heaven.* When we know the things that must yet be activated, restored, and fulfilled in order for Christ to return, then we can knowingly co-labor with God for their full restoration. We can be like Daniel, who received a revelation that Jeremiah's prophecy concerning Israel's 70-year captivity was reaching fulfillment and that it was time for full restoration (Dan. 9:2; Jer. 25:1-14). He began to intercede in prayer for the prophetic fulfillment of Israel's restoration to their homeland. Ever since God created mankind, He does nothing on earth without a person participating with Him in bringing it to pass.

We do not want to be guilty of the failure of the generation to which Isaiah gave the prophetic indictment, *"None saith, Restore"* (Isa. 42:22 KJV). None of the leaders of that time were believing for and working toward bringing restoration to God's people and the nation of Israel. No one had a vision for restoration. Though none were saying restore, yet God declared, *"I will restore"* (Joel 2:25). There are over 30 Scriptures speaking of restoration, growing from faith to faith, strength to strength, glory to glory, and growing in grace and knowledge until we *"grow up into Christ in all things,"* until we are *"conformed to His image,"* *"a glorious Church without spot or wrinkle,"* *"like Him,"* *"unto a perfect man even to the measure of the stature of the fullness of Christ Himself.*" The Scriptures definitely teach there will be *"line upon line, precept upon precept,"* restoration of truth upon restoration of truth, until the Church comes to its divinely predestined purpose. There are three Scriptures that talk about the saints "going up," while there are more than 30 that talk about the saints "growing up." That reveals that God puts ten times more importance on our maturing into Christ's image and ministry than He does on us being raptured to Heaven. Let us major on what God majors on.

NOTES

1. Hamon, *The Eternal Church*, 227.
2. Hamon, *Prophets and Personal Prophecy*, 5-7.
3. Ibid., Chapter 2.
4. Hamon, *Prophets and the Prophetic Movement*, 92-96.
5. Hamon, *Prophets, Pitfalls, and Principles.*
6. Bill Hamon's The Manual for Ministering Spiritual Gifts is taught several times each year at Christian International and various local churches. For more information, contact Christian International at 1-800-388-5308.
7. Hamon, *Apostles, Prophets, and the Coming Moves of God.*
8. Hamon, *The Day of the Saints.*
9. 1 Cor. 12:27; Eph. 3:21; Col. 1:18,24; Eph. 1:22-23
10. Book of Joshua; Josh. 1:1-18; Gen. 15:18
11. Hamon, *Prophets and the Prophetic Movement*, 17-28, 198.
12. Hamon, *The Day of the Saints*, 21-42.
13. Hamon, *Prophets and Personal Prophecy*, 21.
14. Rom. 8:17; Hamon, *The Eternal Church*, 345.

Chapter 11

THE THIRD AND FINAL REFORMATION: THY KINGDOM COME

TRANSITIONING TO KINGDOM MENTALITY

What do we mean by Kingdom attitude, mentality, and thinking? What is the difference between Kingdom thinking and the prevailing thinking of the Church world today? Most denominational seminaries and Bible colleges teach their students how to be a successful minister and how to build a growing local church. Pastors in training are taught to win people to Jesus Christ and then establish them in their local church. This was good teaching, but we who have pastored have often found that our motivation became more personal. We wanted to get people saved and make them and other Christians faithful members of our local church. But our measure of success was to build a larger and larger church congregation. Most pastoral thinking was along the lines of *what can the community and city do for my church*, rather than *what can my church do for the community*. We saw the city more as a resource of people to convert and fill our local churches.

Kingdom mentality is asking, *What can I and my local church do for my community and city? How can we be instrumental in bringing the Kingdom of God to our area?*

Romans 14:17 declares that the Kingdom of God is righteousness, peace, and joy in the Holy Spirit. There is imputed righteousness that puts us in right standing with God, and then there is the righteousness that means that everything is right according to biblical standards and Kingdom principles.[1] The Church can bring the Kingdom to government by praying and working to remove corruption and by providing the wisdom to do things right. We can bring peace to troubled families and marriages, and we can work with the police in reducing lawlessness. We can bring joy by bringing greater harmony and working relationships between different groups in the city.

The Church can do this when it is full of the Holy Spirit; we can hear the voice of God and receive divine strategies that will provide solutions for the needs of mankind. Kingdom thinking will make us ask this question: "If Jesus had just returned and commissioned us to do what was necessary for God's Kingdom to come and His will to be done on earth as it is in Heaven, what could we do to make our community and city operate according to Kingdom principles?" We talk about ruling and reigning with Christ, but how many church members have any idea of what to do or how to bring transformation to their city until it becomes a righteous Kingdom of God city? It is for sure that those who will rule and reign with

Christ over all the earth will have to know the constitutional government of the Church/Kingdom. The Bible, which is the thinking, convictions, and principles of God revealed in written form, is the Constitution. The life, nature, character, and Spirit of God are the motivating forces for living and enforcing the Constitution. Jesus was the Word of God made flesh and demonstrated in a human life and body (John 1:1,14). When the Scripture says that we must come to the fullness of Christ, it means we must come to the fullness of the Word of God. The Third Reformation saints must become saturated with the Word of God and life of Christ until they can say with all reality, "It is not I who live, but Christ living in me, for my life is hid with Christ in God" (Gal. 2:20; Col. 3:1-3). It would require a whole book to reveal this part of Third Reformation truth.

TRAINING FOR REIGNING— SCHOOLING FOR RULING

Fivefold ministers must begin now to give intensified training to their saints if we are to fulfill all the prophetic statements in the seventh chapter of Daniel, which declares that the saints shall possess the Kingdom and establish it on earth (Dan. 2:34-35).

> *Then to Him was given dominion and glory and a kingdom, that all peoples, nations, and languages should serve Him. His dominion is an everlasting dominion, which shall not pass away, and His kingdom the one which shall not be destroyed (Daniel 7:14).*

> *But the saints of the Most High shall receive the kingdom, and possess the kingdom forever, even forever and ever... until the Ancient of Days came, and a judgment was made in favor of the saints of the Most High, and the time came for the saints to possess the kingdom (Daniel 7:18,22).*

But the court shall be seated, and they shall take away his dominion, to consume and destroy it forever. Then the kingdom and dominion, and the greatness of the kingdoms under the whole heaven, shall be given to the people, the saints of the Most High. His kingdom is an everlasting kingdom, and all dominions shall serve and obey Him (Daniel 7:26-27).

The kingdoms of this world have become the kingdoms of our Lord Jesus, and His anointed one, the Church, and they shall reign forever and ever (Rev. 11:15). Most High, You are our Father God, and we pray for Your Kingdom to come and Your will to be done on earth as it is in Heaven, for Yours is the Kingdom and the power and the glory forever and ever. Amen (Matt. 6:10; Rev. 11:15).

DEVELOP KINGDOM MENTALITY

A prophetic statement that was made in the first prophetic presbytery I received in 1953 stated, "For thus saith the Lord, I have even kept thee unto My own purpose."[2]

It was 30 years later before prophetic revelation made me to understand what the Lord meant by that statement. The understanding came after God brought revelation and application of the Scripture in Malachi 4:5-6. Jesus declared that John the Baptist fulfilled the prophecy of the Elijah prophet who would come and prepare the way for the coming of the Messiah (Matt. 11:10-11). The new prophetic revelation that came to me was that now in the last days of the Church God would raise up a company of prophets in the spirit of Elijah to prepare the way for Christ's second coming as John the Baptist prepared the way for Christ's first coming.[3]

CALLED AND PREPARED FOR GOD'S SPECIAL PURPOSE

The Lord spoke to me, "I did not make you a pioneer and major minister in the past movements you have been involved in. I have kept you for My own timing and purpose. All your years of testing, training, and ministry have been preparing you for what I originally chose you to do for Me and My Church: raise up My great company of prophets to prepare the way and make ready a people for My second coming."

I began to preach the revelation everywhere I ministered around the world to bring the Church into the Prophetic Movement. I began to impart to those I taught a prophetic mentality, which is saints and ministers having the attitude and faith that they can hear the voice of God and minister God's prophetic word to others. Through our Christian International ministers, we have taught and activated more than 500,000 Christians in prophetic ministry who have in turn trained hundreds of thousands around the world. I have functioned in my calling as a prophet for most of my 67 years of ministry and have given personal prophecies to more than 50,000 individuals. These individuals have been in every walk of life and positions from presidents of nations to little babies. Yet with all these years of experience, it still requires an exercise of faith for me to prophesy the word of the Lord. That's the reason the apostle Paul wrote that if our divine gifting was prophecy, then *"let us prophesy in proportion to our faith"* (Rom. 12:6).

I do not automatically have a prophecy just because I am a spirit-filled believer or a prophet. In other words, if I do not activate my faith to receive a prophetic word, then I do not receive anything. I teach saints that if I don't look for it, I don't see it; if I don't actively listen, I don't hear; if I don't believe, I don't receive; and if I don't have confidence in the faithfulness of God to give me the accurate word, I will not have the faith to prophesy the word received.

KINGDOM MENTALITY, MINISTRY, AND MIRACLES

The same is true for training saints to have a Kingdom mentality. Kingdom thinking is understanding and believing that you can demonstrate the attributes and miracles of the Kingdom. It is believing that you are called to bring the Kingdom of God to your area of influence. To know that the Kingdom of God is within you just as the Holy Spirit is within you, and therefore you can minister the Kingdom just as you can minister the Spirit (Luke 17:21). Apostle Paul declares in Second Corinthians 3:6 that we are ministers of the Spirit. Pastors must bring this truth to their saints so that they can demonstrate the Kingdom in their lives, family, profession, and in all their areas of influence.

APOSTLE AND PROPHET PIONEERS MUST WRITE THE TRUTH

The pioneers of restoration truth movements, like Martin Luther and others, immediately wrote books giving the biblical reality of the truth being restored. Knowing this restoration principle was part of my motivation for writing the three books on prophets and prophetic ministry. The first of the trilogy of prophetic books, *Prophets and Personal Prophecy,* was published in 1987. It contains revelation and understanding concerning prophetic ministry and the office of the prophet.

A SOVEREIGN VISITATION FOR ACTIVATION

A sovereign visitation of God took place in October 1988 at our second conference of the International Gathering of Prophets. I was caught up in the Spirit and received a vision of the great company of prophets that God was going to bring forth.[4] Jesus stated that He wanted me to take a pioneering and fathering role in raising up this great company of prophets. I accepted His commission and have labored ever since in doing my part to pioneer and father the Prophetic Movement. At that time, I thought it was just for the purpose of restoring the prophets and apostles. All fivefold ministers would then be active and able to mature and equip the saints sufficiently to produce the Saints Movement.

PROGRESSIVE REVELATION

By biblical knowledge, I knew that the final fulfillment of all things was the second coming of Christ Jesus. So I knew that the company of prophets would prepare the way of the Lord for Christ's second coming just as Prophet John the Baptist prepared the way for Christ's first coming. By moving in progressive revelation, I have come to realize that God had not revealed all that was to take place before His literal coming. He has now revealed that there is a Third Reformation preordained to bring about the restoration of all things, just as the Second Reformation was ordained to bring about the restoration of the Church. The restoration of all things and the Final Reformation have to be fulfilled first before the literal second coming of Christ can take place. The company of prophets and apostles had to come forth first and make known the mysteries of God to the Church so that all things could be restored and fulfilled (Eph. 3:3-5; Rev. 10:7). This then prepares the way by making the final preparation and restoration necessary for Christ to be released from Heaven for His second coming (Acts 3:21-25; Isa. 40:3-5).

NEW EMPHASIS, NEW TRUTH, NEW TERMINOLOGY, AND EXTENDED VISION

This is why we use different terminology to express the truth and ministry that we are now propagating in the Body of Christ. Themes are given to different conferences, such as Kingdom Enforcers, Church Reformation for City Transformation, Kingdom Demonstration for World Transformation. If the Third and Final Reformation could be condensed to one sentence, it might look like this: The Final Church Reformation brings Kingdom demonstrations for the transformation of nations and the restoration of all things for Christ's glorious return to earth as sovereign owner and ruler of the earth.

KING JESUS: THE DOMAIN AND KINGDOM OF GOD ON EARTH

John the Baptist came preaching, *"Repent, for the kingdom of heaven is at hand!"* (Matt. 3:2). Then, in Mark 1:15, Jesus came to Galilee, preaching the Gospel of the Kingdom of God, saying, *"The time is fulfilled, and the kingdom of God is at hand. Repent, and believe in the gospel."* Jesus was the King and the domain of God. Jesus was the Kingdom of God who had come to be manifested. Time was fulfilled for Him to now demonstrate the Kingdom of God on earth. That is why it says the Kingdom of God is within us, for Christ is in us. Jesus taught and demonstrated what the Kingdom of God is. At the end of His earth life, He was crucified, buried, and resurrected to bring forth His Church. The Church would contain the Kingdom until the time was fulfilled for the Church to demonstrate the Kingdom in every nation. The Third Reformation is the time appointed by the Father for the full demonstration of the Kingdom of God.

THE NEW MAN CREATION—THE CHURCH-KINGDOM RACE

Within the four Gospels, Jesus spoke about the Kingdom of God more than 100 times, but then He made a revelation statement that would start a new creation of mankind—the Church race. They would be different from all other human beings on planet

Earth. They would have a natural birth like the rest of humanity, but then they would be born again by the Spirit of the living God. They would actually be born of God and become children of God. They would be spiritually translated out of the dark-world into the light-world of God's Kingdom (John 3:3-5; Col. 1:13). The place of provision and authority for God's newly created man was the Garden of Eden. The place of power and provision for the new man in Christ Jesus is being seated at the right hand of God in the heavenly places in Christ Jesus (Eph. 1:20; 2:6). The Church race would be the most revolutionary thing God had created since the original creation of mankind. However, the Third Reformation will produce a Kingdom race who will demonstrate the Kingdom of God for many years, and then the last act of redemption will transform them into the eternal Kingdom race. The Church race has eternal life in mortal bodies. The bodily redeemed Kingdom race will have eternal life in immortal bodies. God is progressively moving everything toward fulfilling His ultimate purpose for creating mankind on earth.

JESUS PREACHED TO BUILD THE CHURCH AND TO ESTABLISH THE KINGDOM OF GOD ON EARTH

Jesus declared to His apostles, *"I will build My church"* (Matt. 16:18). But during the more than three years that the apostles were with the Lord Jesus, they had no idea what He was talking about. The Jewish rabbis taught that when their Messiah came, He would restore Israel and make their nation the head of all nations. Proof that this was the thinking of the apostles is found in the question they asked Jesus after He was resurrected and ready to ascend back to Heaven: *"Lord, will You at this time restore the kingdom to Israel?"* (Acts 1:6). It was not until the Holy Spirit birthed the Church on the Jewish day of

Pentecost that the spirit of revelation gave them understanding and application of what Jesus had been teaching.

Jesus had promised them that when the Holy Spirit came He would bring all things that Jesus had taught them to their remembrance and give illumination for proper application that would lead them into all truth (John 14:6-17). As we discovered in the first reformation, it took several years before the apostles fully understood that a whole new covenant and church age had been ushered in. It was really a latecomer, the apostle Paul, who received the full revelation and wrote it in his letters to the churches, which became 14 books of the New Testament (Eph. 3:3-5).

THE LORD'S PRAYER TO BE ACTIVATED INTO LITERAL REALITY

Jesus told His followers to pray to Father God, *"Your kingdom come. Your will be done on earth as it is in heaven"* (Matt. 6:10). The Evangelical and Pentecostal preachers rightly preached the spiritual application of this prayer decree, but there seemed to be no revelation of a present-day literal application. They preached that after the rapture of the Church, there would be a thousand-year millennial Kingdom age. They could pray for God's Kingdom to come and His will to be done in bringing transformation to their personal lives, but they had no revelation for God's Kingdom to come and bring transformation to cities and nations now. Remember that one of the principles of restoration is that it takes a truth that preachers have placed in the past or future and makes that truth into an experiential reality for the present generation.[5]

Now, Third Reformation revelation is challenging the Church to become Kingdom demonstrators and enforcers. It is now time to pray, work, and believe that the Kingdom of God can come and His will be done, not only in our personal life and family but also in our community, state, and nation. The new revelation, application, faith, and challenge from the Lord is for Christians to believe that God has purposed for the overcomers in the Church to be the ones God uses to fulfill this prophetic prayer.[6]

> *Father God, we are believing that Your Kingdom can come now and Your will can be done now in all the earth as it is in Heaven. Start with me, and let it extend to my family, community, state, and nation until the kingdoms of this world come under the government and dominion of Jesus Christ and His Church.*

AS IT HAS BEEN DECREED, SO SHALL IT BE!

It has been prophetically decreed in Revelation 11:15 that *"the kingdoms of this world have become the kingdoms of our Lord and of His Christ."* Prophecies of future events speak of them as factual realities and call those things that are not as though they are (Rom. 4:17). A true prophecy comes from Eternal God who functions in the eternal dimension where there is no past, present, or future. He is the beginning and the end (Rev. 1:8). God speaks from what He sees us being and doing in our future. God speaks prophetically of those things that shall be as though they already exist. God's prophetic decrees are natural events that will happen and be recorded by mankind as history. Prophecy is history that has not happened, and history is prophecy that has been fulfilled.

For example, there were 4,000 years of prophecies about a coming Messiah who would provide redemption for mankind. Jesus came and fulfilled all those prophecies concerning the coming Messiah: *"But those things which God foretold by the mouth of all His prophets, that the Christ would suffer, He has thus fulfilled"*

(Acts 3:18). Now those prophecies have become history for the last 2,000 years. Likewise, ever since the Book of Revelation was written during the first century of the Church, the prophecy that the kingdoms of this world have become the kingdoms of our God has remained just a prophetic decree. Now the Church has entered into a new era of Christianity, a new purpose of God, and a commission to the Church—to co-labor with Christ for the fulfillment of this prophecy into literal reality.

IS THE CHALLENGE AND COMMISSION TOO MUCH FOR THE CHURCH?

This challenging commission to the Church is no greater than the one God gave to Joshua and the Children of Israel. They were commissioned to enter into Canaan Land and dispossess all the inhabitants. There were more than 30 kings with walled cities and military garrisons and an army of powerful fighting warriors. Plus, there were several million people living in the land. There were seven major nations God named that they would have to conquer and destroy in order to inhabit their promised inheritance.

> *When the Lord your God brings you into the land which you go to possess, and has cast out many nations before you, the Hittites and the Girgashites and the Amorites and the Canaanites and the Perizzites and the Hivites and the Jebusites,* **seven nations greater and mightier than you,** *and when the Lord your God delivers them over to you, you shall conquer them and utterly destroy them. You shall make no covenant with them nor show mercy to them* (Deuteronomy 7:1-2).

Notice that the Lord acknowledged that those nations were greater and mightier than Israel, but God would equal that out by joining them in all their battles. Before they entered the land, Moses charged them, saying, *"You must not fear them, for the Lord your God Himself fights for you"* (Deut. 3:22). Then, after many years of military campaigns, it is recorded in Joshua 10:42, *"All these kings and their land Joshua took at one time, because the Lord God of Israel fought for Israel."* The Church serves the same God whom Joshua served. God has not changed (Mal. 3:6; Heb. 13:8). Jesus is a mighty Man of War who fights for His people (Exod. 15:3). He is declaring for us to enter into our inheritance, which is the kingdoms of this world, and He will join us to win the battles (Eph. 1:17-19; John 17:20-26).

ARE ALL THINGS POSSIBLE WITH GOD?

The thought of the Church influencing the nations of the world, executing the judgments of God, and supernaturally demonstrating the Kingdom of God until they become Christian nations is beyond the comprehension of the natural mind. It is as inconceivable as the promise and challenge that Gabriel gave to Mary when he told her that she would have a baby boy without ever knowing a mortal man. But she believed without understanding how it could possibly be. The angel assured her that it would not be by natural ability but that the Holy Spirit would come on her and the procreative power of God would cause her to conceive and birth a son. He would be the Son of God, and He would build a Kingdom that would never end. Then Gabriel told her not to try to figure it out, but just to believe, for with God all things are possible (Luke 1:26-38). Later, Jesus told His followers, *"If you can believe, all things are possible to him who believes"* (Mark 9:23; Matt. 17:20; John 11:40), and "If you really believe in Me, the works that I do you can do also" (John 14:12).

Likewise, we must not base our faith on what we know and have experienced up to the present. God is going to do something new and special for His Third Reformation people. God is about to do for us what we cannot do for ourselves. God is making the same decree for this day of nation transformation that He did for Israel in Deuteronomy 2:25: *"This day I will begin to put the dread and fear of you upon the nations under the whole heaven, who shall hear the report of you, and shall tremble and be in anguish because of you."* God is going to begin putting within people a respect and honor of God's Kingdom people, plus a fear of not accepting and working with them. The *Lord* promises us that if we allow Him to establish us as a holy people to Himself, keep His commandments, and walk in His ways, *"Then all peoples of the earth shall see that you are called by the name of the Lord, and they shall be afraid of you"* (Deut. 28:9-10).

ISRAEL—SEVEN NATIONS; THE CHURCH—SEVEN KINGDOM CULTURES

In his book *The Seven Mountain Prophecy*,[7] Johnny Enlow correlates the seven nations Israel had to conquer with the seven cultures, societies, or activities of mankind. He refers to Isaiah 2:2 in calling these groups "mountains": *"Now it shall come to pass in the latter days that the mountain of the Lord's house shall be established on the top of the mountains."*

CANAANITE NATION	MOUNTAIN/ KINGDOM OF:
HITTITES	Media—all means of communication
GIRGASHITES	Government—military and cities, states, and nations
AMORITES	Education—all schools, universities, and medical kingdom

CANAANITE NATION	MOUNTAIN/ KINGDOM OF:
CANAANITES	Economy—business world, kingdom of finances
HIVITES	Celebration—entertainment, arts, and sports
PERIZZITES	Religion—all religious groups (except the true Church)
JEBUSITES	Family—father, mother, children, and relatives

Pastor Enlow describes in his book what each of these "-ite" tribes represent by their anti-Kingdom-of-God characteristics. For example, the Hittites (Media) represent bad news rather than the good news of the Kingdom; Amorites (Education) represent the mind of reason rather than Kingdom-mindedness and the mind of Christ. He also lists the evil principality assigned to each of the seven, what ministry can best overcome each kingdom, its basic mission, and what attribute of God can best counteract each one of the seven. Many apostles and prophets are writing books about this Third Reformation although they may describe it in different terminology.[8] But many ministers from many nations are preaching and writing about the new era of Christianity that the Church has entered into. They are emphasizing that Isaiah 43:19 is applicable now more than ever before: *"Behold, I will do a new thing, now it shall spring forth; shall you not know it?"* This verse applied to the First Reformation and the Second Reformation—and now applies especially to the Third and Final Church Reformation.

EIGHTH KINGDOM MOUNTAIN RULES OVER ALL OTHER KINGDOMS

The Eighth Kingdom Mountain is the Kingdom of God:

> *Now it shall come to pass in the latter days that the mountain of the Lord's house shall be established on the top of the mountains, and shall be exalted above the hills; and all nations shall flow to it* (Isaiah 2:2).

> *And in the days of these kings the God of heaven will set up a kingdom which shall never be destroyed; and the kingdom shall not be left to other people; it shall break in pieces and consume all these kingdoms, and it shall stand forever* (Daniel 2:44; see also Daniel 7:22,27).

Eight is the number of new beginnings. The Kingdom of God has been predestined to rule and reign over all the nations and kingdoms of this world. Eight is the number representing the transition to a new order. Eight was the number of people who made the transition on the ark from the old world to the new world. Eight represents the end of the old and beginning of the new. God created all things in six days and rested on the seventh; the eighth day was a new beginning. Under the law, the Jews met on the seventh day, but when the new age of the Church came, the Christians met on the eighth day, which is the first day of the new week. David was born the eighth son of Jesse, and he established the new order of the tabernacle of David (1 Sam. 16:10; Acts 15:16). There are seven colors in a rainbow spectrum; the eighth begins a new spectrum. The eighth note on a piano begins a new octave. There are numerous other eights in the Bible that represent the same. God required Jewish baby boys to be circumcised on the eighth day, according to the Abrahamic covenant, to demonstrate that they were beginning their new life on earth in covenant with God.

In our generation, years ending with eight have been significant in restoration movements—in 1948, the Latter Rain Restoration Movement began, and Israel became a nation again; in 1988, the Prophetic Movement started; 1998 and 2008 marked the beginnings of the Apostolic Movement and the Third and Final Church Reformation, respectively. During this Third Reformation, the Eighth Kingdom—the Kingdom of God—will possess and rule over all kingdoms of this world. On the wall of our Christian International Family Church, we have a four- by twelve-foot colorful banner portraying the seven kingdoms of this world with the Church-Kingdom over all of them. If every decade on the eighth year continued to be the pattern, then we might see the Army of the Lord Movement in 2018, the Kingdom Establishing Movement in 2028, and the second coming of Christ by 2038. These projected dates are only interesting speculation, not prophetic revelation. God acts according to the fulfillment of prophecies, not certain days, months, and years, although certain times, seasons, and numbers are significant to God. The Bible exhorts Christians to know the times and seasons of God. Know that it is the time and season for the Third Reformation (1 Thess. 5:1-5).

TRANSFORMATION—GOAT/SHEEP NATIONS AND WORLD KINGDOMS

Jesus declared in Matthew 25:31-34 that there would be righteous sheep nations and evil goat nations on earth when He returns at His second coming. He is speaking of nations, not just individuals. When we state that the kingdoms and nations of this world shall become the kingdoms of our God, we realize that not all nations will be transformed into sheep nations, but will become goat nations that will be removed from the earth. The sheep nations that remain will become

Kingdom of God nations. These are nations that have an eternal destiny in God. This is exemplified in the nation of Israel. However, they will not be the only sheep nation on earth when Jesus returns.

ALL THINGS MADE NEW FOR NEW JERUSALEM AND SHEEP NATIONS

In Revelation chapter 21, God cleanses the old heavens and earth and transforms them into a new heaven and a new earth. He then declares that the tabernacle of God is now with men on earth, for God has made all things new (Rev. 21:1-8). The New Jerusalem descends from Heaven to orbit around the earth, and it does not need sun or moon for light, for the Lamb of God illuminates it brighter than any sunlight. And verse 24 states that the *nations* of those who are saved shall walk in its light, and the kings of the *earth* shall bring their glory and honor into it. Revelation 22:2 says the leaves of the tree of life are for the healing of the *nations*. Jesus gives the promise in Revelation 2:26 that the person who overcomes and keeps His works until the end, Jesus will give him power over the *nations*. And the overcomers shall rule the *nations* with a rod of iron.

It was shocking to me to discover, according to Scripture, that there will always be nations, not only on the present earth but also on new earth. Evidently, the sheep nations that are set on God's right hand will be allowed to continue on into the millennial age and live and function on new earth.

*When the Son of Man comes in His glory, and all the holy angels with Him, then He will sit on the throne of His glory. All the **nations** will be gathered before Him, and He will separate them one from another, as a shepherd divides his sheep from the goats. And He will set the sheep [nations] on His right hand, but the goats [nations]*

*on the left. Then the King will say to those on His right
hand, "Come, you blessed of My Father, inherit the kingdom prepared for you from the foundation of the world."
...Then He will also say to those on the left hand, "Depart
from Me, you cursed, into the everlasting fire prepared for
the devil and his angels"* (Matthew 25:31-34,41).

The righteous sheep nations placed on God's right hand will
receive the Kingdom that has been prepared for them by Father God.
Those placed on the left hand of God will be cast into that place of
everlasting fire prepared for the devil and his angels. Every sincere
Christian who really believes in the reality of Heaven and hell should
work with all diligence to get individuals prepared to spend eternity
with Christ Jesus. If we really believe Jesus' presentation of sheep and
goat nations, then we need to work with all diligence to make our
nation a sheep nation. Can we make a difference? Yes, for God is
releasing new strategies, wisdom, grace, supernatural power, and pro-
visions to those who will volunteer to be Kingdom demonstrators in
their societal mountain sphere of influence.

Apostle Ed Silvoso of Argentina is a major pioneer in this Third
Reformation, especially in the field of the transformation of nations.
He wrote a book called *Transformation* that gives the best teaching and examples of how all this can become a reality. He also has
made 12 DVDs portraying people who have brought transformation
in the mountains of business, government, and in some of the other
mountains. I was a speaker at Ed's conference in Argentina in 2008.
Hundreds of businessmen, government officials, and many other
major Christian leaders attended. They were committed to the transformation message that is one of the major truths of the Third and
Final Church Reformation. Cindy Jacobs wrote a book on ways and
means of establishing God's Kingdom called *Reformation Manifesto*.

GREATEST SIGN AND DETERMINING FACTOR FOR THE *END* OF THIS AGE?

The greatest sign of the times in the first 50 years of the 20th century was in 1948 when Israel was restored as a nation of its own. The greatest sign of the times in the last 50 years of the 20th century was the great company of prophets that began to come forth at the birthing of the Prophetic Movement in 1988. The restoration of all fivefold ministers during that same time was also a great sign revealing the times and purposes of God. Now in the Third Reformation one of the greatest signs of the times will be the Gospel of the Kingdom being demonstrated in every nation (Matt. 24:14).

SIGN OF CHRIST'S COMING AND *END* OF THIS AGE

In Matthew 24, it is recorded that the apostles asked the same question that is on the mind of many Christians. The disciples said to Jesus, *"Tell us, when will these things be? And what will be the sign of Your coming, and the end of the age?"* (Matt. 24:3; Mark 13:3-10). Jesus told them about things that would happen in the world and to them. There would be wars and rumors of wars, nation against nation, earthquakes, famines, economic chaos at times, and persecution of Christians. But He told them not to be troubled by all these happenings, for they will be things that will continue until the end of this age. He also let them know that these things will not be the determining factors for how close we are to the end of the age of the mortal Church. He then revealed to them the thing that would be the greatest sign and determining factor for the end to come: *"And this gospel of the kingdom will be preached in all the world as a witness to all the nations, and then the end will come"* (Matt. 24:14).

It is the Gospel of the Kingdom of God being demonstrated in every nation as a witness to them of the sovereign Lordship of Jesus Christ that will determine how close we are to the end of this age. Jesus must be demonstrated with such supernatural power, wisdom, and miracles until heads of nations have to acknowledge that there is no true God and redeemer of mankind but Jesus Christ the Son of Almighty God (Dan. 4:24,34-35). They will have to acknowledge the sovereignty of Jehovah God as Pharaoh did when Moses manifested the mighty miracles of God against Egypt (Exod. 7–11).

GOD CAN MAKE HEATHEN KINGS ACKNOWLEDGE HIM!

During the Third Reformation, the Gospel of the Kingdom will include prophets giving prophecies to kings, presidents, and rulers of this world. God will confirm their prophecies with signs and wonders in men and to men. Prophets will make divine decrees that will cause mankind to bow their knee to Jehovah God and acknowledge that there is no God like Jesus. The prophesying of the two witnesses in the Book of Revelation is a good example of this. Record of this actually happening is found in the Bible in the Book of Daniel.

Prophet Daniel gave a prophetic word to Nebuchadnezzar, king of the whole Babylonian Empire, that made him bow his knee and acknowledge.

This is the interpretation, O king, and this is the decree of the Most High, which has come upon my lord the king: They [the heavenly watchers] *shall drive you from men, your dwelling shall be with the beasts of the field, and they shall make you eat grass like oxen. They shall wet you with the dew of heaven, and seven times shall pass over you, till*

*you know that the Most High rules in the kingdom of men,
and gives it to whomever He chooses* (Daniel 4:24-25).

After God implemented that word and fulfilled it as the prophet
Daniel had prophesied, King Nebuchadnezzar made this confession
and acknowledgment in a letter to all of the 120 nations under the
rule of his empire:

*And at the end of the time I, Nebuchadnezzar, lifted my
eyes to heaven, and my understanding returned to me; and
I blessed the Most High and praised and honored Him who
lives forever: For His dominion is an everlasting dominion,
and His kingdom is from generation to generation. All the
inhabitants of the earth are reputed as nothing; He does
according to His will in the army of heaven and among the
inhabitants of the earth. No one can restrain His hand or
say to Him, "What have You done?" At the same time my
reason returned to me, and for the glory of my kingdom,
my honor and splendor returned to me. My counselors and
nobles resorted to me, I was restored to my kingdom, and
excellent majesty was added to me* (Daniel 4:34-36).

SOME ARE GIVEN WILLING HEARTS TO SUPPORT

During the Third Reformation, all nations will be dealt with by God
Almighty. Some nations God will deal with as He did in His judgments on Egypt. Others He will humble and make willing like He
did Nebuchadnezzar the king of the Babylonian nations. Some God
will give a willing heart and desire to favor God's people and support them in building God's Kingdom. A living example of this is
found in the history of Cyrus, king of Persia. Isaiah prophesied hundreds of years before that God had predestined that a king by the

Trump

name of Cyrus would favor God's people in restoring their nation and even providing for the rebuilding of their holy temple. Proverbs 21:1 declares that the king's heart is in the hand of the Lord. God is still sovereign and able to deal with mankind to do according to His will, whether by force or willful persuasion of the heart. When God's timing arrives for prophecies to be fulfilled and purposes to be activated and accomplished, God will put it in the heart of national leaders to work with God's people to build God's Kingdom and fulfill His timely purpose.

KINGDOM OF LIGHT VS. KINGDOM OF DARKNESS

Jesus said in Matthew 24 that one of the intensified activities that would take place in the last days would be *"kingdom against kingdom."* This is warfare between the spirit worlds of good and evil. It is the spiritual saints of the Kingdom of God going against the evil principalities and powers of satan's kingdom. As the Third Reformation was activated on earth, there were things taking place in the middle heavens where satan has set up his domain since he was cast out of the third heaven where the throne of God is.

The character of satan and his host is selfishness and self-promotion. The kingdom of satan is ruled by the toughest, meanest, and most wicked angels. Every evil spirit wants to be the greatest in the highest position.

I believe there is a present application to Revelation 12:7-12 that does not contradict or take away from the description of what happened when lucifer was originally cast out of Heaven. Satan and his host are being pressed down to the first heavens, which is the immediate atmosphere around the earth. The prophetic statement in verse 12 is taking place as the saints are being launched into the Third

It feels like The Time is now!

Reformation: *"Woe to the inhabitants of the earth and the sea! For the devil has come down to you, having great wrath, because he knows that he has a short time"* (Rev. 12:12). The devil has intensified his activity of going about as a rogue lion seeking whom he may devour. The only safe and victorious place for the saints in this day is in that high position that God has prepared for them—the heavenly places in Christ Jesus at the right hand of God. This places the Kingdom saints far above all principalities and powers and every name that is named in the heavenlies and on earth with all enemies under their feet (Eph. 1:17; 2:6; 3:10). It will be a time of woe to those professing Christians who do not know their position in Christ or how to function from that heavenly place. While satan and his evil principalities are descending to earth, the overcomers in the Church are ascending to their heavenly place in Christ Jesus. This is not a physical place but a spiritual realm and reality for the saints. We will still be walking on earth in our bodies while in the spirit we are seated with Christ.

We are now facing top evil principalities and powers that we have not faced before. Satan is calling forth all of hell's highest and most powerful armed forces. We must now receive from God greater power, anointing, grace, wisdom, and faith than we have ever had before. Yesterday's blessings are not sufficient for today's challenges. The Second Reformation restored the truths and power needed to fulfill God's purpose in the Third Reformation. All restoration reformers must now become new wineskins capable of expanding sufficiently to receive the new wine of revelation and Kingdom demonstration being poured into the Church. The last generation of the mortal Church is arising to overcome and subdue the greatest enemies the Church has ever been challenged to conquer.

HEAVEN AND HELL WILL MEET FACE TO FACE IN THE HUMAN RACE

When I wrote the fifth division on the destiny of the Church in my book *The Eternal Church,* the following statements were made:

> Spirit-world activity will increase during the last days. Satan's demonic activity will be accelerated. As we enter the final years of this age, every person will either become more evil spirit possessed or more Holy Spirit possessed. The ministry of casting out devils will be accelerated.[9] The veil between the natural world and spirit world will be opened wider. This will allow the saints to have more angelic visitations.[10] The spirit beings from the evil world of satan's domain will be cast out of their self-appointed realms and forced into greater activity among humanity. The ministering spirits of God's angelic army shall descend to work more intimately with the Church army to establish God's Kingdom over all the earth (Heb. 11:14). The final battle of the ages will take place when all things are prepared for Heaven and hell to meet face to face in the human race (Rev. 19:17-21).[11]

NOTES

1. Rom. 8:4; John 3:7; Rom. 3:21-26; 4:11; 10:10; Phil. 1:11
2. Hamon, *Prophets and Personal Prophecy,* 6.
3. Ibid., 19.
4. Hamon, *Prophets and the Prophetic Movement,* 95.
5. Hamon, *The Eternal Church,* 305.
6. Rev. 2:7,11,17,26; 3:3,5,12,21; 12:11; 21:7
7. Johnny Enlow, *The Seven Mountain Prophecy* (Lake Mary, FL: Creation House, 2008).

8. Ibid; Cindy Jacobs, *The Reformation Manifesto* (Minneapolis, MN: Bethany House Publishers, 2008); Ed Silvoso, *Transformation* (Ventura, CA: Regal Books, 2007).

9. Mark 16:17-18; Matt. 10:7-8; 12:28; Luke 1:34; 9:1-6

10. Heb. 13:2; Matt. 1:20; 4:11; Acts 8:26; 10:3; 12:7; 27:23

11. Hamon, *The Eternal Church*, 324-325.

Chapter 12

stop QUALIFICATIONS
FOR KINGDOM
PARTICIPATION

Jesus said, *"Most assuredly, I say to you, unless one is born again, he cannot see the kingdom of God"* (John 3:3). Jesus then gave the two-fold requirement for entering the Kingdom: *"Most assuredly, I say to you, unless one is born of water and the Spirit, he cannot enter the kingdom of God"* (John 3:5).

Jesus declared that the Jews who rejected Christ Jesus as their Messiah were disqualified from entering the Kingdom of God, for those who rejected Him were thrust out, and the Kingdom was given to a nation (the Church) bearing the fruits of the Kingdom of God. One cannot participate in the Kingdom unless they receive the King of the Kingdom, Jesus Christ (Matt. 21:43; Luke 13:28).

Jesus said that it is hard for those who trust in the riches of this world to *enter* the *Kingdom* of God (Mark 10:24).

Whoever is not converted and does not receive the Kingdom as a little child shall by no means *enter* the *Kingdom* (Luke 18:17; Mark 10:15).

We must through many tribulations *enter* the *Kingdom* of God (Acts 14:22).

Jesus said, *"No one, having put his hand to the plow, and looking back* [longingly to the things behind], *is fit for the kingdom of God"* (Luke 9:62).

Not everyone who says Lord, Lord, and manifests mighty ministry shall *enter* the *Kingdom* but those who do the will of Father God (Matt. 7:21).

God has chosen *those who love Him* and are *rich in faith* to be the *heirs* of His *Kingdom* (James 2:5).

Practices That Will Stop One from Entering or Inheriting the Kingdom!

We need to realize that the following Scriptures were written to church members in Corinth and Galatia, not to sinners outside the church. Paul knew that the people he was writing to had been saved and filled with the Holy Spirit, but this did not guarantee them entrance into the Kingdom of God if they were practicing certain sins and things that were contrary to the righteousness of God. He was emphatic that if they were doing these things, they would have no part or inheritance in the Kingdom of God. Let us examine ourselves to determine if we have any of these unrighteous attitudes or practices:

> *Do you not know that the unrighteous* **will not** *inherit the kingdom of God? Do not be deceived. Neither fornicators, nor idolaters, nor adulterers, nor homosexuals, nor*

sodomites, nor thieves, nor covetous, nor drunkards, nor revilers, nor extortioners will inherit the kingdom of God (1 Corinthians 6:9-10).

*Now the works of the flesh are evident, which are: adultery, fornication, uncleanness, lewdness, idolatry, sorcery, hatred, contentions, jealousies, outbursts of wrath, selfish ambitions, dissensions, heresies, envy, murders, drunkenness, revelries, and the like; of which I tell you beforehand, just as I also told you in time past, that those who practice such things **will not inherit the kingdom of God*** (Galatians 5:19-21).

Let us read this same verse in a Bible written in contemporary language, *The Message*:

*It is obvious what kind of life develops out of trying to get your own way all the time; repetitive, loveless, cheap sex; a stinking accumulation of mental and emotional garbage; frenzied and joyless grabs for happiness; trinket gods; magic-show religion; paranoid loneliness; cutthroat competition; all-consuming-yet-never-satisfied wants; a brutal temper; an impotence to love or be loved; divided homes and divided lives; small-minded and lopsided pursuits; the vicious habit of depersonalizing everyone into a rival; uncontrolled and uncontrollable addictions; ugly parodies of community. I could go on. This isn't the first time I have warned you, you know. If you use your freedom this way, **you will not inherit God's kingdom*** (Galatians 5:19-21 MSG).

For God to have sufficient Kingdom workers He has to have the Holy Spirit do some major housecleaning. We have entered an intensified time declared by the apostles Peter and Paul and the prophet Malachi: *"For the time has come for judgment to begin at the house of God"* (1 Pet. 4:17). Every person's work shall be tested by fire, so think it not strange concerning the fiery trial that shall try you, as though some strange thing is happening to you, but rejoice that you are suffering with Christ by crucifying the works of the flesh so that you may participate when His glory is manifest on the earth (1 Pet. 4:12-13). For His glory shall cover the earth as the waters cover the sea, when He comes to be glorified in His saints (Hab. 2:14; Num. 14:21; 1 Thess. 1:10). Who can endure and make it through this day of His coming as a refiner's fire and a purifier of silver? He will purify the saints and purge them as gold and silver is purified in the fiery furnace (Mal. 3:1-3). Those who are called to be pioneers, propagators, and demonstrators of the Third Reformation have entered a baptism of fire that we may be fully purified and prepared to fulfill God's purpose for the Third and Final Reformation (1 Cor. 3:13).

THE KINGDOM AND THE SUPERNATURAL

Just about every time the preaching of the Kingdom of God is mentioned, it is accompanied by supernatural manifestations. The first time Jesus sent His 12 apostles out on their own, He told them, *"As you go, preach, saying, 'The kingdom of heaven is at hand.' Heal the sick, cleanse the lepers, raise the dead, cast out demons. Freely you have received, freely give"* (Matt. 10:7-8). Jesus said, *"If I cast out demons with the finger of God, surely the kingdom of God has come upon you"* (Luke 11:20). *"For the kingdom of God is not in word but in power"* (1 Cor. 4:20). The Kingdom does not come by natural observation, nor is it in religious ordinances of eating and drinking, but it is righteousness, peace, and joy in the Holy Spirit (Rom. 14:17). The Church is the spiritual Kingdom of God that will cause God's will to be done on earth as it is in Heaven. But the Church of this Third

Reformation must come to a new level of faith and power enabling them to demonstrate the Kingdom in a way that the world has never seen before. We must press into God until we are endued with greater power, wisdom, and grace that God has ordained to be released now to His Third Reformation reformers.

NEW POWER NEEDED TO MOVE INTO THE NEW AND UNKNOWN

When God was ready to birth the Church Age during the First Reformation, the apostles had very little comprehension of what was about to take place or what they would need to fulfill God's purpose. They were still asking questions about times and seasons and what Jesus was going to do for the nation of Israel (Acts 1:6). They did not realize Jesus was about to be crucified, buried, resurrected—and then birth the Church. They were about to be instrumental in bringing forth a new race of humanity. They were moving into a new realm, function, and responsibility they had never known or experienced before. They were about to fulfill a purpose of God that had been planned from the foundation of the world (Eph. 3:11). They were about to establish on earth that which had cost more than anything that had ever happened in eternity. It meant more to the Creator of Heaven and earth than life itself, for He gave His life in order to purchase the most precious thing to Him, the Church (Rom. 8:3-4; Acts 20:28; Eph. 5:25).

MOST IMPORTANT THING FIRST

Jesus told His disciples that the most important thing they needed to do was to go back to Jerusalem and wait until He sent the promise of the Father, which would endue them with power they had never known before (Acts 1:8-14). They would not be able to fulfill God's purpose unless they received a new endowment of grace and power. They would also receive the spirit of wisdom and revelation that would bring understanding of what God wanted to accomplish through them (Eph. 1:18-19).

During the first reformation and with each restoration movement, new revelation, anointing, and power was given to establish that truth back into the Church. Likewise, we who are entering the Third and Final Reformation of the Church do not fully realize all that we are going to need to fulfill our calling and commission. But Heaven has a new infusion of power, revelation, and grace for those who will be used of God to fulfill His Kingdom purpose in the Third Reformation.

PROPHETIC SCRIPTURES PROMISING INCREASED POWER

Most of the Scriptures that speak of *"that day"* in the books of the Old Testament prophets will find their fulfillment during the Third and Final Reformation. It is a biblical hermeneutics principle that the promises and prophecies concerning Israel and Jerusalem can be applied to the Church. Therefore, the following Scriptures have a present-day application to the Church, as they did in the past to natural Israel and the city of Jerusalem. Apostle Paul declared that all that was spoken and that happened to Israel was written to give examples and admonition to the Church at the end of this age. *"Now all these things happened to them as examples, and they were written for our admonition, upon whom the ends of the ages have come"* (1 Cor. 10:11).

> *In that day the Lord will defend the inhabitants of Jerusalem* [the Church]; *the one who is feeble among them in that day shall be like David, and the house of David shall be like God, like the Angel of the Lord before them. It*

shall be in that day that I will seek to destroy all the nations that come against Jerusalem [God's Kingdom people, the Church] (Zechariah 12:8-9).

The feeblest Kingdom saint in the day of the Third Reformation will be a mighty warrior like David. Those who are now functioning like the house of David will increase in power until they are doing the works of Christ and even greater works. This is the reason we must not base our future performance on our past abilities. All who become Kingdom demonstrators shall be given a great increase of new power and authority.

Church-Kingdom saints and networks are going to join together to accomplish the greater purposes of God. This unification of the Church and co-laboring together with Christ shall increase our power a thousandfold:

A little one shall become a thousand, and a small one a strong nation. I, the Lord, will hasten it in its time (Isaiah 60:22).

For the Lord has driven out from before you great and strong nations; but as for you, no one has been able to stand against you to this day. One man of you shall chase a thousand, for the Lord your God is He who fights for you, as He promised you (Joshua 23:9-10).

Five of you shall chase a hundred, and a hundred of you shall put ten thousand to flight (Leviticus 26:8).

How could one chase a thousand, and two put ten thousand to flight (Deuteronomy 32:30).

Please take note that when five are fighting together, they can put 20 of the enemy to flight per man, but when 100 warriors join together, they can put 100 of the enemy to flight per man. God can increase us to the power of ten when two join together and put 10,000 to flight when one by himself puts 1,000 to flight. All of these Scriptures were promises made to the Israelis for when they entered their promised Canaan Land to destroy the ruling kings and then to make their kingdoms the kingdom of Israel. These Scriptures are also promises to the Kingdom-Church-Saints who shall destroy the evil kings of the kingdoms of this world and make them the Kingdom of God. God has great things reserved for those who will co-labor with Him in fulfilling His purpose for His Church and planet Earth.

Jesus made a statement that is more profound and powerful than all these Scriptures: *"Assuredly, I say to you, among those born of women there has not risen one greater than John the Baptist; but he who is least in the kingdom of heaven is greater than he"* (Matt. 11:11). Jesus was saying that John the Baptist was greater than Abraham, Moses, or David, who were all born of women. But the most amazing thing is that He declared that he who is least in the Kingdom is even greater than John. This was as completely unacceptable to the Pharisees of that day as it is incomprehensible for us to fully grasp today. Are God's Kingdom enforcers going to be "greater" than any great man of God in the Old Testament? What does Jesus mean by "greater than" anyway? What made John the Baptist so great? John was a prophetic reformer who was preparing the way and making ready a people for the coming of the Messiah. Evidently, God puts great importance on those who fulfill His prophetic purposes. John neither worked miracles nor accomplished any great feats like Moses or David. He just prepared the way for the Messiah to be manifest upon the earth. Maybe that is one reason Jesus said that the least in the Kingdom would be greater than John the Baptist. The least who is making ready a people and preparing the way for God's Kingdom to come and His will to be done in earth as it is in Heaven will be counted great in God's sight.

Those who participate in pioneering the Third and Final Church Reformation will receive all of Heaven's resources to accomplish God's purpose. At the same time, all of hell's forces will seek to stop the Third Reformation reformers, for if they succeed it ends satan's freedom and reign on earth. He will be bound and cast into the bottomless pit for a period of time and then in the lake of fire for eternity. There is no greater reward for the saints than being an overcomer who is in the perfect will of God fulfilling His timely purpose.

Chapter 13

VOICE OF THE LORD

PROPHETS—KEY TO THE VOICE OF THE LORD

God walked and talked with Adam and Eve in the Garden. However, after they were cast out of the Garden, we do not find God personally speaking to groups of people. He always chose one man or woman to be His voice to mankind. The Bible reveals that it was 200 years *After Adam* (A.A.) before mankind prayed to God. It was more than 900 years A.A. before we have a record of God speaking to man through the prophet Enoch (Jude 1:14-15; Gen. 5:21-27). Enoch was very prophetic. He named his son *Methuselah*, which means, *"When he is gone judgment will come."* Methuselah was born in 687 A.A., lived 969 years, and died in the year of the flood, 1656 A.A. He probably died the week before Noah entered the ark and the flood destroyed the earth.

God spoke to one man out of the 20 million who were on the earth before the flood. He gave Noah instructions to build an ark to preserve the human race (Gen. 6:13-14). It was 400 years later that God spoke to another man on earth. He told Abraham to head up a special race of people who would be God's chosen people (Gen. 12:1-3). God spoke to Jacob and Joseph through dreams and interpretation of dreams (Gen. 37; 40–41). Around 400 years later, God spoke to Moses to take God's people out of Egypt by mighty miracles against Pharaoh (Exod. 3–4). In the wilderness on the top of Mt. Sinai, God gave Moses a video playback of the creation of Heaven and earth enabling him to write it in the Book of Genesis. At the same time, he was given the blueprint for a tabernacle and details of God's laws and commandments (Exod. 7–11; 33–40).

God spoke to Joshua to take His Israeli people into the Promised Land (Josh. 1:2). He then gave him instructions for taking the first city and a miracle of parting the Jordan for crossing on dry land to enter his destiny of possessing the promised Canaan Land. God gave him special instructions for conquering Jericho and how to conduct his military campaigns to dispossess all the "-ite" nations of Canaan (Josh. 1:6-9; 7–13). After a couple hundred years of judges ruling in Israel, God raised up the prophet Samuel. Prophet Samuel started schools of the prophets and trained hundreds of prophets. Prophets became the main method that God used to be the voice of God to kings, nations, and the people of Israel. Prophets continued to speak the "Thus saith the Lord" until God quit speaking to mankind for 400 years. After that time, He raised up John the Baptist to be the prophetic voice of God crying in the wilderness, "Repent, for the Messiah is here ready to be manifested on the earth."

Jesus was Prophet, Priest, and King, Israel's promised Messiah and Redeemer of mankind. After His resurrection, Jesus birthed the

Church by His Holy Spirit. He then put His ministry of prophet in the Church to be His prophetic voice. He even promised His Spirit-filled saints that they all could be a prophetic voice for the Lord (1 Cor. 14:3; Eph. 4:11). Now we have the Logos Word written into a Bible that is the foundation for all truth and ministry. But Jesus still needs His prophetic voices to speak His specific personal messages to individuals and nations.

PROPHETS SET OVER THE NATIONS AND KINGDOMS

God established a divine pattern and principle in His commission to Jeremiah. *"I ordained you a prophet to the nations. ...Behold, I have put My words in your mouth. See, I have this day set you over the nations and over the kingdoms"* (Jer. 1:5, 9-10). This also includes states and cities, for Jeremiah also gave God's prophetic word to cities and individuals. God speaks His warnings, promises, and purposes through the prophetic voice of mankind. God speaks His word and will through His prophets and how that nation responds to God's prophetic voice determines its destiny. Their response will in part determine whether that nation will be a sheep nation or goat nation (Matt. 25:31-33).

A VISION OF WORLD WAR III AND PERSONAL COMMISSION

In 1992, God gave me a vision and revelation of satan's plan to start World War III between 1996 and 2006. He revealed that China, an old communist nation, and two Islamic nations were in secret negotiations to make a trilateral agreement like Germany, Japan, and Italy made in World War II. The Lord stated that this was not something that He had decreed to happen, but rather was satan's plan to bring great destruction on the earth. He gave instruction through two major prophets that I was to go to all the Pacific Rim nations and bring together ministers and saints to do spiritual warfare against the plans of satan. He said that if the Church would arise and do warfare with their spiritual weapons, they could win the war in the Spirit, and our soldiers would not have to fight and die. If we only halfway won the battle, then 50 percent of the war would have to be fought in the natural.

I had to do research to discover the locations of the Pacific Rim nations. They were simply the nations whose shores touched the Pacific Ocean. I was instructed to go first to those nations that were closest to the nations seeking to make a trilateral agreement for World War III. In 1992, I started taking prophetic teams to South Korea, Japan, the Philippines, Singapore, Malaysia, Indonesia, Taiwan, Hong Kong, Australia, Hawaii, and some of the West Coast Pacific Rim states such as California and Alaska.

Our warfare in Singapore gives an example of what we did in each of these places. I preached on God's commission for us to stop satan's plans. I called all the ministers to the platform. There were approximately 100 who came. For 45 minutes we did spiritual warfare with the high praises of God, prophetic decrees, and the powerful shout of faith. It was like dropping atomic bombs on the enemy's camp and destroying their unity and plans. I kept going back to those nations every other year until after 2000. At that time, I felt the Lord showed me that we had won the war in the spirit, and it would not be fought in the natural. When the devil's plans for bringing an east-west war of nations against nations failed, he changed his tactics and began the terrorism attacks, hoping to cause a chain reaction that would result in World War III. The attack by the terrorists on the towers in New York was not just to kill a few thousand Americans and disrupt our economic system but to create an incident that would escalate into a world war. The prophetic proclamations of the prophets and warfare of the saints can change or stop the plans of satan and affect the destiny of nations.

PROPHETS AND APOSTLES: KEY TO TRANSFORMATION

Prophets and apostles have always been the key to anything new God has done on the earth and in His Church. God established prophets and apostles as those who receive the blueprint and lay the foundation of anything God builds on earth. Of all the ministries in the Body of Christ, they are the ones given the ability to receive revelation of the mysteries of Christ and God's time to make them known. *"To you it has been given to know the mysteries of the kingdom of God"* (Luke 8:10). *"The mystery...as it has now been revealed by the Spirit to His holy apostles and prophets"* (Eph. 3:3-5). *"The mystery of God would be finished, as He declared to His servants the prophets"* (Rev. 10:7). God does nothing on earth without first revealing His secrets to His servants the prophets (Amos 3:7).

There are prophets who function in the local church and in nonprofit organizations, but there are also those who function in the other kingdoms of culture. In my book *The Day of the Saints,* I stated that there are those called to be apostles and prophets who do not fulfill their calling behind a pulpit but in their professional position.[1] Daniel was a prophet, and he served as a top administrator in the Babylonian Empire (Dan. 2:46-49). David was a prophet, and he was a king of the nation of Israel (Acts 2:29-30). Moses and Abraham were prototypes of New Testament apostles. Ninety percent of the OT prophets did not function in the tabernacle and were not of the Levitical priesthood. God has ordained that the apostles and prophets will receive the revelations, creative ideas, and divine strategy for bringing transformation to this world as God has ordained from the foundation of the world.

NOTE

1. Hamon, *The Day of the Saints,* 252.

Chapter 14

GOD'S NEW WORLD ORDER VERSUS MAN'S NEW WORLD ORDER

VIEW OF MAN'S PLANS AND GOD'S PLANS

Lucifer failed in his attempt to become the one universal ruler of Heaven and earth (Ezek. 28:13-19). He was cast down to the domain of earth with his authority and rule removed. Satan's only rule now was over the fallen angels who followed him in his rebellion to overthrow God. His domain is a kingdom of wicked beings and demonic spirits (2 Cor. 10:4-5; Col. 2:15). Man was created to rule the earth under the authority of God (Gen. 1:26-28). Ever since man sinned and lost his authority and dominion over all the earth, satan has sought to arise within a man under his authority to rule the world. History has recorded many men who sought to conquer and rule the world. Mohammed and the spirit of Islam sought to take over the world in the year A.D. 600, and that spirit through terrorism is still seeking to conquer the world and be the one, supreme religion and dictator.[1] Communism during the 20th century had great ambitions to take over the world. Satan and his kingdom are anti-God and anti-Christ and all who are anti-Jesus Christ and His Kingdom are under the control and authority of satan. Antichrist is a spirit that is against God's only begotten Son, Jesus Christ (1 John 4). That spirit permeates most of the world order today.

MAN'S PLANS: ONE WORLD LEADER AND RELIGION

Dispensational theologians and preachers have been preaching about what is going to happen at the end of this age. Certain biblical prophecies indicate that there will be a world leader and government who seek to establish a one-world currency, governmental body, and conglomerate of all religions. These religions of the world will agree together to submit to the antichrist leader. But the true Christ believers will be excluded as an unacceptable religious group because they will not join the new world religion.

During the last hundred years, many things have been progressively preparing for this new world order, inspired by satan's desire to rule the world. He wants to possess, live, and rule in a man's body to become the one-world dictator. He is referred to as the Man of Sin (2 Thess. 2:3), the antichrist world dictator. The devil's desire is to be seen as the savior of the world, to bring peace to the world without the Prince of Peace.

Many things have happened to stir a desire in nations to unite under a one-world leader. World War I and World War II made mankind more world conscious. Jet travel makes it as easy to travel from nation to nation as we used to travel from state to state. The satellites in the sky make communication to the ends of the earth as easy as talking to your next-door neighbor. Satellite television and internet make it possible to view anything happening around the world. The current worldwide economic crisis is making the world want more universal unity and cooperation for their preservation and prosperity. Those ministers who have studied, written, and preached about this have seen the Illuminati Society, League of Nations, the United Nations, and the European Unification of Nations as progressive steps toward the establishment of a one-world leader and government.

Man's new world order will be according to the antichrist spirit and practices. The Bible states that the world will become darker and more wicked until their cup of iniquity is full. God told Abraham that He could not fulfill the prophecies that He had given him until the sin of the Amorites was full (Gen. 15:16). God came down to see for Himself if the sin of Sodom and Gomorrah was as full as had been reported to Him (Gen. 18:21). Their cup of iniquity was indeed full and running over, so God destroyed them off of the earth by raining down fire and brimstone (Gen. 19:13, 24-25). It was the same with the pre-flood generation (Gen. 5:11-13). Their cup of iniquity became so full of wickedness that God destroyed them off of the earth with a great flood. The present world's cup of iniquity is getting closer to the full status. The world's cup of iniquity must come to fullness, and the Church must come to full restoration and fulfillment before God can execute His judgments upon the world.

PRINCIPLE: IT GETS WORSE JUST BEFORE IT GETS BETTER

There is a principle revealed in the Bible and in nature that it becomes worse just before it gets better. In nature, it is the darkest just before dawn. A woman's labor pains are the worst just before the baby is born. A seed dies in the darkness of the ground before it sprouts with new life into the light of day.

A principle concerning a major prophecy is portrayed in God's prophecy to Moses to deliver God's people from Egypt. After Moses gave God's prophetic demand to Pharaoh to let God's people go, it got worse for the Israelites before it got better (Exod. 5). Also, the judgment became more and more severe upon Pharaoh and the Egyptians before it got better for them when they let the Israelis leave. But at the dark hour of midnight, the final judgment came, and the new day dawned as Israel left with the wealth of Egypt (Exod. 12:29-36).

In his book *The Coming Israel Awakening*,[2] Jim Goll gives a detailed account of the 100-year process of Israel's nationhood being restored in 1948. During one decade of the 1940s, they went from their darkest hour, when six million Jews were brutally murdered, to their most triumphant time, when they were given their own homeland nation. Jesus Christ went through His darkest hour of suffering, crucifixion, and death just before He arose victoriously and ushered in the New Church Age.

During the Third and Final Church Reformation, it will probably get worse just before it gets better. Prophet Daniel had a vision of the end times. He said, "I was watching and saw this horn of the wicked warring against God's people and winning, *until* the Ancient of Days came and opened His court and vindicated His people, giving them worldwide powers of government" (Dan. 7:21-22). Daniel also saw that this wicked one with the pride and ambition of lucifer would even dare to defy the Most High God. He would wear down the saints with persecution and try to change all laws, morals, and customs (Dan. 7:25-27). God's people seemed to be helpless for a period of time. But suddenly the Ancient of Days came and opened His court of justice and took all power from that vicious

king's kingdom to consume and destroy it until the end. Then every
nation under Heaven, and all their powers, was given to the people of
God; they shall rule all things forever, and all rulers shall serve and
obey them. For, in the end, the people of the Most High God shall
rule the governments of the world forever and forever. Even the event
that we are emphasizing in Revelation 11:15 is preceded with the two
prophet witnesses being martyred and great earthquakes and calamities taking place in the world.

DAY OF DARKNESS VERSUS DAWNING OF NEW DAY

The prophet Joel describes what I believe to be the day of the
Third Reformation:

> *For the day of the Lord is coming, for it is at hand: a day of
> darkness and gloominess, a day of clouds and thick darkness* [in the world], *like the morning clouds spread over
> the mountains* [dawning of a new day for the Church]
> (Joel 2:1-2).

Prophet Isaiah prophesies the same things concerning the Church
during the Third Reformation:

> *Arise, shine; for your light has come! And the glory of the
> Lord is risen upon you. For behold, the darkness shall cover
> the earth, and deep darkness the people; but the Lord will
> arise over you, and His glory will be seen upon you. The
> Gentiles shall come to your light, and kings to the bright-
> ness of your rising* (Isaiah 60:1-3).

*There are numerous prophetic Scriptures yet to be fulfilled in their
fullness.* They will all be fulfilled by the time the Third Reformation
has accomplished its purpose. There are prophetic Scriptures that

will be fulfilled yet in the Saints Movement. Then more will be fulfilled that relate to the Army of the Lord Movement, and most will be finalized in the Kingdom Establishment Movement.[3] The final climatic fulfillment will be when the prophetic Scripture is fulfilled that declares that Gabriel sounds his trumpet; Jesus gives a shout with such resurrection life that it causes the righteous dead to be resurrected and the bodies of the living saints to be immortalized in less time than a micro-second (1 Thess. 4:17-18). Jesus and His Church will then set up God's Kingdom over all the earth, causing the prophetic Scriptures to be fulfilled as the loud voices in Heaven declare that now the kingdoms of this world have literally become the kingdoms of Jesus and His Church. At last, all biblical prophecies from Genesis to Revelation are fulfilled and become historical reality. Then the saints will say, *"Even so, come, Lord Jesus!"* (Rev. 22:20).

And now Your Kingdom has come and Your will is being done on earth as it is in Heaven. Yours is the Kingdom, power, and glory, Lord Jesus, over the new earth forever and ever, which is now a new, righteous world without end (2 Pet. 3:13; Rev. 21:1). Amen and Amen.

NOTES

1. Hamon, *The Eternal Church*, 107-110.
2. James W. Goll, *The Coming Israel Awakening* (Grand Rapids, MI: Chosen Publishing, 2001), 55-56.
3. Hamon, Apostles, *Prophets, and the Coming Moves of God*, 269.

Chapter 15

TRANSITION TO THE NEW CHRISTIAN ERA

After reading this book, you should have a good understanding of the prophetic times and purposes of God. The following is a brief amplification of what has thus far been portrayed in detail within this book. A following chapter will give a listing and brief explanation of many of the prophetic Scriptures yet to be fulfilled during the Third and Final Church Reformation.

The Lord Jesus has revealed by His Spirit some insights and application concerning His timely purpose being activated in the year 2008. I had been prophesying for ten years that a "Saints Movement" was coming to the Body of Christ. The Saints Movement is a time when the saints—that is, believers in Jesus Christ—recognize and act on the understanding that Christ has empowered and commissioned each of them to be the Church 24/7, manifesting the Kingdom of God wherever they live and work. Every believer has the ability to manifest the supernatural in a miraculous way, and every saint is called to demonstrate the Gospel of the *Kingdom,* in addition to the Gospel of salvation, in their sphere of influence.

In my book *The Day of the Saints,* I predicted what would be many of the truths and ministries of the Saints Movement. Some of these include the following: every saint manifesting the supernatural; ministers appearing in the marketplace and in all arenas of society; saints becoming the Church 24/7—twenty-four hours a day, seven days a week, not just on Sunday; and Christians of all ages becoming activated as saintly ministers of Christ.[1] I started prophesying and preaching about these things in 1997 and started writing the book in 2000, with the first publication coming out in 2002. In the last several years, we have seen these things happening in the Body of Christ through the increased emphasis on signs, wonders, and miracles ministered in the marketplace. Some are using terms such as *saints in the workplace* and *ministers in the marketplace.*

A NEW ERA OF REFORMATION

In 2008, God brought new revelation and application: *the Saints Movement became the catalyst to launch the Church into the Third and Final Reformation.*

The *First Church Reformation* occurred in the first century with the coming of the Messiah and the launch of the era of the New Testament Church. The *Second Church Reformation,* which is known to historians as the Reformation, transitioned the Church out of the Dark Ages and into times of the restoration of the Church (Acts 3:21). *The Third and Final Apostolic Reformation* began with the Saints Movement. It is transitioning the Church into demonstrating and implementing the Gospel of the Kingdom for discipling the nations and bringing transformation to the seven world kingdoms, which are being illustrated as the "seven mountains" of business, education, government, media, family, religion, and entertainment.

This reformation is bringing about *a paradigm shift in the goal and purpose of the Church.* Most Evangelical and Pentecostal theologians see no purpose for the Church other than to win more souls to Christ so they are made ready for Heaven. Now we are receiving revolutionary, reformed thinking from the heart and mind of God. The expanded goal and vision of the Third Reformation Church is to co-labor with Christ in His passionate desire for the fulfillment of Revelation 11:15: *"There were loud voices in heaven, saying, 'The kingdoms of this world have become the kingdoms of our Lord and of His Christ, and He shall reign forever and ever!'"*

The First Church Reformation and purpose of God was for Jesus to shed His lifeblood for the salvation of sinners. God was in Christ Jesus reconciling the world unto Himself by purchasing them with His blood and making them members of His Body of Christ, the Church (2 Cor. 5:18; 1 Cor. 12:12,27).

God's Second Church Reformation and purpose was to restore and build His Church to the full maturity and ministry of Christ Jesus. This is being accomplished through Christ's fivefold ministers—of which the last two, prophets and apostles, were restored to recognition and began fully ministering during the Prophetic-Apostolic Movement, 1988 to the present. The fivefold ministers are for the purpose of equipping the saints to demonstrate Christ's Kingdom. The Saints Movement was brought forth for the purpose of activating, equipping, and commissioning the saints to be Kingdom enforcers in the seven-mountain kingdoms of this world.

Christ's Third Church Reformation and purpose is to use His restored Church to fulfill God's original mandate to mankind to subdue all things, to take dominion and fill the earth with a mankind race in God's own image and likeness, to bring more and more of God's Kingdom and will to earth, and to transform nations into sheep nations (those who do the works of Christ, see Matthew 25:31-46). This is the end result of the saints taking the Gospel of the Kingdom into every aspect of society until Revelation 11:15 becomes a literal reality on earth.

During the Third Reformation, more souls will be saved and the greatest harvest ever recorded in Church history will be reaped. There will be whole nations that become sheep nations, which means that the majority of those within that nation will have become born-again Christians. It is probable that more members will be added to Christ's Church during the last 100 years of the mortal Church than have been added to the Church during the last 1,900 years. Regardless of the time and effort required, God will make sure Christ has the total number and quality of members needed to fulfill the eternal purpose He predestined for the forever-functioning Body of Christ to fulfill. The Church, the Body of Christ, is as eternal as Jesus Christ, the head of the Body. Jesus and His Church are joint heirs of God with the same inheritance, purpose, and eternal destiny. There is nothing more important than being a member of Christ's eternal Church. This generation's destiny, overcomers' rewards, and positioning with Christ will be determined by how well we work with Christ in fulfilling His purpose for the Third Reformation.

THE TIMING

The year 2008 was the time of the official heavenly decree for the beginning on earth of the Third and Final Church Reformation. This Third Reformation will bring *as much transformation and fulfilling of God's purpose as the First and Second Reformation did, plus fulfill God's purpose for the last generation of the mortal Church.*

I have been prophesying this shift for many years, and many ministers and saints have been interceding for many years for this day of the Lord to come. It is with firm conviction that I believe this is now the time for it to fully be underway. Whenever a move of God occurs, there is much action and anticipation ahead of time, during the "birthing" process, and even greater activity afterward. In later years, historians pick a date that they consider to be the "official" start of that new move. Many currents were headed toward Reformation prior to the year 1517 to signal the beginning of the time of restoration of the Church. The Protestant Movement became the launching pad for the Second Church Reformation.

I believe and am declaring that 2008 was God's set time for launching the Third Reformation. At Christian International, we saw a birthing of the Saints Movement at our Watchman Intercessor Conference in April 2007, as prophesied by Cindy Jacobs, one of the speakers that week. I witnessed to that word and was glad that we had finally seen it officially launched. This time period makes an interesting correlation with a 490-year time period Daniel prophesied (70 weeks x 7 days per week = 490, with each day symbolizing a year). Daniel prophesied concerning the time period of the coming of the Messiah and the ushering in of the Church (Dan. 9:20-27). The end of that time period was the beginning of the First Reformation. The ending of the major restoration movements became the beginning of the Third Reformation. Many believe that this is also the period of time from the beginning of the restoration of the Church to the time when all restored truth and ministries will be activated into fulfilling God's end-time purposes. Church historians designated the year 1517 as the birth date of the Protestant Movement, which was the beginning of the period of Church restoration: A.D. 1517 + 490 years = A.D. 2007. This time period covers all the restoration movements from the Protestant Movement to the birthing of the Saints Movement in 2007. The Saints Movement launched the Third Church Reformation for the fulfilling and restoration of all things, which will be summarized later.

We do not know if Daniel's 490-year period had any prophetic applications to the 490-year period of Church restoration. Nevertheless, it does reveal a very similar and significant divinely orchestrated period of the times of Church restoration that the prophets and apostles had prophesied would take place. Maybe it is just a divine coincidence, but it is now a historical fact that these two time periods possess the same number of years.

A NEW ERA OF CHRISTIANITY

Many apostles and prophets from around the world are using similar and other terms to describe this new era of Christianity that we have entered into. But all are in agreement that we have moved into a new end-time purpose for the Church. From my prophetic revelation and knowledge of Church history, the best descriptive term for what is taking place is *the Third and Final Church Reformation.*

RECEIVE GOD'S GRACE TO PARTICIPATE

God is now releasing special supernatural grace and power to those who are willing and ready for Church reformation. They will be those who demonstrate the Kingdom of God for the transformation of nations. Expect to hear much preaching and see many books being written on the saints taking dominion, the Kingdom of God, transformation, wealth for Kingdom purposes, the Third and Final Apostolic Church Reformation, and God's purpose for His Church, His Kingdom, and planet Earth.

All the hundreds of apostles and prophets I know around the world are sensing and saying the same thing, although some may use different terminology to express these things. *I cannot emphasize enough the importance of understanding and participating in the major transition and new thrust of the Holy Spirit taking place in the Church today.*

A WORD OF WISDOM REGARDING THE END TIMES

I want to add a word of wisdom to all who read this book. Most of Christendom from Catholics to Charismatics believe in the second coming of Christ, when He will translate the bodies of the living saints and resurrect the bodies of those who have died.

The amillennialist and postmillennialist believe this all happens at one coming of Christ at the end of the Church Age. The dispensational premillennialist believes in two comings, one for the Church and one for the general resurrection, and then the great white throne judgment. Most see a seven-year period between Christ coming *for* the saints and Christ Jesus coming back *with* the saints. Some believe the Church will be resurrected and translated to Heaven at the beginning of those seven years, some believe it will happen three and a half years later, and some believe it will occur at the end. If I am still alive at that time, I would love to have a seven-year sabbatical in Heaven before we start working to establish God's kingdom over all the earth. I would take a three-and-a-half-year sabbatical or even five minutes. However, if that is not an option, then I will gladly be changed in a moment, in the twinkling of an eye, mount my white stallion, and join Jesus, the great Commander in Chief of the Army of the Lord (Rev. 19:11-16). We would sweep through the first and second heavens and bind lucifer and all his demonic host and shut them up in the bottomless pit (Rev. 20:1-6). We would then remove all humankind from the earth who have the antichrist spirit. Then we would inhabit *"new earth in which righteousness dwells"* (2 Pet. 3:13). If I am not privileged to be alive on earth at that time, then

I will be one of those Enoch prophesied about: *"Behold, the Lord comes with ten thousands of his saints* [Bill Hamon included], *to execute judgment on all...who are ungodly"* (Jude 1:14-15).

ALL CHRISTIANS ARE IN AGREEMENT

The wonderful and amazing thing is that whether the teaching says believers will be raptured to Heaven for seven years, for three and a half years, or for five minutes, all of them teach that the saints are coming back to join the reign of Christ's Kingdom over all the earth. *Regardless of the different eschatological beliefs, all Christians will end up on new earth where all the kingdoms of this world have become the kingdoms of our Lord and His Christ.*

PREPARE NOW TO MAKE THE TRANSITION

Those whom Jesus has made kings and priests unto God shall be the overcomers who reign with Christ on the earth (Rev. 1:5; 5:10). Please do not get stuck arguing and debating over what will happen during the seven years. Let us set our vision and goal beyond those seven years to Revelation 11:15. *Be an overcomer and make the transition.* Allow nothing to keep you from being a participant in this day of divine visitation and reformation. Begin now to earnestly pray, prepare, and work for God's Kingdom to come and His will to be done on earth as it is in Heaven. Participants must be established in Kingdom principles and all restored truths. They need to have a foundational understanding of God's progressive process for the First Reformation, Christ's purpose for Church restoration during the Second Reformation, and then become knowledgeable of God's purpose for the Third Reformation. Saints cannot fully participate unless revelation is received concerning the fact that there is a Third Reformation. Those who pioneer this reformation will understand its purpose and what must be received and believed in order to become the Kingdom enforcers who are co-laboring with Christ Jesus to fulfill His purpose as declared in Matthew 6:10 and Revelation 11:15: Thy kingdom come and Thy will be done on earth as it is in Heaven, until the kingdoms of this world become the kingdoms of our Lord Jesus and His anointed one, the Church.

NOTE

1. Hamon, *The Day of the Saints,* 357-358.

Chapter 16

PROPHETIC SCRIPTURES YET TO BE FULFILLED

PROPHETIC SCRIPTURES MUST BE FULFILLED REGARDLESS OF THE DOCTRINES OF MEN

There are many varying views on the future of mankind, earth, and the Church. Probably the two most opposite views are that of the extreme preterist and futurist. The futurist teaches that everything in the Book of Revelation from chapter 4 through chapter 22 is fulfilled after the Church is raptured to Heaven at the end of the Church Age. The preterist teaches that the Book of Revelation in its entirety was fulfilled during the first generation of the Church a short time after the fall of Jerusalem in A.D. 70.

67 YEARS OF PROPHETIC AND DOCTRINAL DEVELOPMENT AND EXPERIENCE

I have studied all of the different teachings during my years of ministry. When I taught eschatology in Bible college, we would have debates on all of the eschatological teachings. All have their strong points and weak points. The proponents of the opposite views have many Scriptures and logic to prove their points. A powerful, persuasive teacher could convince the average Christian that his eschatology is the right one; however, no named eschatological viewpoint is 100 percent accurate. The truth lies somewhere in the midst of all the extremes. This book does not seek to promote any particular viewpoint. It presents a portion of the postmillennial view of a restored, victorious Church at the end of the age of the mortal Church. It presents the portion of the "pre-mill" view that after the Church saints are resurrected/translated, they will rule and reign with Christ on earth for a thousand years. It also agrees with the amillennialist that the true believers are already seated in heavenly places in Christ Jesus and reign in life by Him; satan is a defeated foe, and believers triumph over him in Christ. It includes a portion of the futurist teaching that many prophetic Scriptures are yet to be fulfilled concerning the Church, Israel, mankind, earth, and all creation. It also presents a portion of the preterist view that some of the prophecies in Matthew 24 were fulfilled in the destruction of Jerusalem in A.D. 70.

As a prophet-apostle minister of God, I see several prophetic Scriptures that have not been fulfilled in their fullness. Those who dogmatically propagate one particular viewpoint declare that one must believe their way 100 percent. Nevertheless, I have not found that to be true to the context of the Bible or the Spirit of Christ. There are denominations such as the Church of Christ who have declared for years that they speak where the Bible speaks and they are silent where it is silent. They have offered money to anyone who can prove them wrong concerning their teaching—that there are no miracles today, no gift of the Holy Spirit with other tongues, or any supernatural manifestations for the Church in this day. Numerous Pentecostal ministers have debated them, showing many Scriptures that prove the miraculous. They have shown to them proven testimonies of saints who have been miraculously healed and of thousands who have received the gift of the Holy Spirit with a supernatural language. To this day, they have never admitted that anyone has proven to them by Scriptures that miracles are for today or that anyone has been healed of God in this present time. Those who are dogmatic on their beliefs have the same attitude and use the same terminology, but they always take Scripture proofs and interpret them in light of their own viewpoint that they have accepted as true doctrine.

MAJOR DOCTRINE NOT ESTABLISHED ON PROPHECY

Some try to prove their points by prophetic statements that Jesus made such as, *"This generation will by no means pass away till all these things take place"* (Matt. 24:34). *"Things which must shortly take place,"* and *"Come up here, and I will show you things which must take place after this"* ("after this" interpreted as after the rapture) (Rev. 1:1; 4:1). Functioning as a prophet and ministering in the prophetic during more than six decades, I have learned a few things about prophecy and prophetic statements. The Bible teaches a major truth that was demonstrated by the apostles at the Jerusalem Council—that major doctrine is never established on prophecy or visions without it being in agreement with and confirmed by the written Word of God.

CHARACTERISTICS OF PROPHECY

The Bible reveals that most prophecies are progressive, pluralistic, and parallel; there are general prophecies and personal prophecies. All personal prophecies have three major characteristics—they are partial, progressive, and conditional. There are some prophetic decrees in the Bible that are unconditional; however, most all prophecies have the same prophetic principles and guidelines for interpretation and application.[1] They can be fulfilled personally and then have a corporate fulfillment. They can have a spiritual and a natural fulfillment, yet do no injustice to hermeneutics or prophetic principles. An Old Testament prophecy can be progressive and pluralistic. It can have a natural fulfillment and application to Israel, also apply to Jesus being the Messiah, and then have a further application to the corporate Body of Christ, the Church.

For instance, examine the prophecy of Hosea 11:1: *"When Israel was a child, I loved him, and out of Egypt I called My son."* The context of the Scripture definitely shows that the prophet is speaking of the time when God led the Children of Israel out of Egypt. He showed His love by delivering them from their Egyptian bondage and slavery. However, Matthew, in his book, pulls one phrase from this Scripture, *"Out of Egypt I called My Son,"* to prove that it has a personal application to Jesus the Messiah (Matt. 2:15). The Pharisee and Sadducee theologians could have argued with Matthew that he was taking the Scripture out of context and was making application that God never intended. How could he use it to prove this Jesus (who they did not believe in) was the Messiah when it was clear that it was speaking of the nation of Israel? Regardless of seeming contradictions and the Pharisees' belief that the prophecy was limited to Israel, the Holy Spirit did inspire Hosea to prophesy concerning Israel and also inspired Matthew to apply it to Jesus.

In the same manner, Hosea 11:1 can be applied personally to a sinner whom Jesus loves and calls out of his personal Egyptian land of satanic bondage. It can also apply corporately to the Church, which consists of God's many sons. This would be very applicable and true, for at the beginning of the Second Reformation God called the Church out of its Egyptian land of religious slavery and dead works in which it had existed during the Dark Ages. His love for His Son/Church caused Him to call it forth from its religious Egypt and bring it into its land of full restoration. There are many more scriptural examples that prove the same prophetic principles.

PROPER PREPARATION MORE IMPORTANT THAN ESCHATOLOGICAL VIEWPOINTS

Regardless of our eschatological viewpoint and how strongly that doctrine is preached, it does not guarantee that we will participate in what is preached unless personal preparation is made. Our belief in God's purpose and ministry for the Church will make some difference in the preparation we make, however. It is better to prepare for more than needed than for less. As the saying goes, I had rather prepare a dollar's worth of preparation and then find out it only takes a quarter's worth than to only prepare a quarter's worth and then find at the last moment that it took a dollar's worth. This is demonstrated in Jesus' parable of the five wise and five foolish virgins. The wise prepared more than enough and were ready and were allowed to join the marriage party. The foolish virgins did not prepare enough and were not allowed in to the marriage of the Bridegroom and Bride (Matt. 25:1-13).

Jesus told the Pharisees that they had missed the mark because they had a head knowledge of the Scriptures without a proper understanding of them or an experience in the life and power of God (Matt. 22:29; Mark 12:24; John 5:39). Revelation must produce a greater relationship with Jesus Christ and commitment to His Church and Kingdom.

WHAT IS TO BE ACCOMPLISHED DURING THE THIRD CHURCH REFORMATION

Prophetic Scriptures Yet to Be Fulfilled

Matthew 24:14: Christ's Church saints must fully preach and demonstrate with the miraculous the Gospel of the Kingdom in all the world as a witness to all nations that Jesus is the one true God and only Savior for mankind. Jesus declared that the *end* could not come until this was accomplished in its fullness.

Acts 3:21: All biblical truths of the Church will be restored. All ministries must be activated within the Church, enabling the saints to arise in every kingdom of this world, being the light of the world and salt of the earth to bring world transformation and fulfill their seven-mountain mandate.

Hebrews 6:1-2: The Second Reformation restored and fulfilled the first four of the six doctrines of Christ. The Third Reformation brings revelation and activation in the Church to fulfill the fifth and sixth doctrines of Christ—resurrection life and eternal judgment. There are three phases of resurrection life: first, supernatural resurrection life to demonstrate the Kingdom of God; second, first resurrection-translation of the saints; third, general resurrection of all the rest of the dead. Eternal judgment refers to God's saints becoming the instruments whereby He executes judgments written (Ps. 149:6-9); then the final great white throne judgment will take place when all humanity will stand before the judgment seat of Christ. (For a full explanation, see pages 303-354 in *The Eternal Church*.[2])

Daniel 7:14,18,22,27: During this time, God will raise up Kingdom of God influencers such as Daniel, Joseph, Deborah, and

Esther. Plus, every Kingdom saint will be challenged to be Kingdom influencers in their sphere of influence. Jesus said we would receive power to *be* witnesses and influencers (Acts 1:8).

Matthew 28:18-19: The Third Reformation saints and five-fold ministers will accept and activate all the authority in Heaven and earth that Jesus has given to His Church to *disciple nations* to become *Kingdom of God nations.*

Revelation 6:11; Psalm 139:16; Ephesians 3:10-11,21: They will reap the great harvest of souls to make up the number of members Christ needs to complete His eternal corporate Body, the Church.

Revelation 10:7; Ephesians 3:3-5: Prophets and apostles receive the revelation of the final mysteries of God so that the Church can finalize its ministry of restoring all things that have been spoken of by the prophets since ancient times for the fulfillment of Christ's prophetic decree in Revelation 11:15.

Ephesians 4:11-16: Fivefold-ascension-gift ministers continue equipping the saints until the Church comes to the full maturity and ministry of Christ Jesus—personally conformed to Christ's image and doing the greater works of Christ Jesus.

Jeremiah 1:5,10; Revelation 11:3-6: God's true prophets will start ministering with their commission to be over the nations. They will begin to execute their authority to root out, pull down, throw down, and destroy all evil forces and kingdoms of this world. The two companies of prophets and apostles symbolized by the two witnesses will demonstrate the power and judgments of God like Apostle Moses and Prophet Elijah did. They will then lead the saints in planting and building the Kingdom of God on earth until the kingdoms of this world become the kingdoms of our Lord Jesus and His joint-heir Church.

Matthew 6:10: The Third Reformation saints will begin to pray the Lord's prayer to be fulfilled literally as well as spiritually—for the nations of the world as well as for our personal lives and ministries. We will pray, work, and expect God's Kingdom to come and His will to be done on earth as it is in Heaven—until God's will revealed in Revelation 11:15 is fulfilled!

Matthew 25:31-34: The Church will continue demonstrating the Kingdom, bringing transformation to the nations until every nation on earth becomes either a sheep or goat nation so that when Jesus returns He can fulfill His commission of separating the sheep nations from the goat nations.

Hebrews 1:13; Hebrews 10:13; Psalm 110:1: Jesus as joint heir with His Church sits at the right hand of the Father until God through Christ's corporate Body, the Church, makes all enemies His footstool.

Romans 8:18-23; Ephesians 1:13-14; Philippians 3:21: Jesus died on the Cross and rose again to redeem us body, soul, and spirit. I have been redeemed in my spirit, I am being redeemed from the self-life to the life of Christ, and I shall be bodily redeemed by the translation or the resurrection. The last act of redemption is the redemption of our bodies. The last act of redemption destroys the last enemy—death (1 Cor. 15:26). Apostle Paul declared that "[Christ Jesus] *will transform our lowly body that it may be conformed to His glorious body*" (Phil. 3:21). The body that Jesus is sitting in at the right hand of the Father is the same body that was born of the virgin Mary, ministered to mankind, and was crucified on the cross, only it has been resurrected into a glorious, immortal, eternal, flesh-and-bone body. Jesus said He would give all His saints a glorious body just like He has now. Jesus will resurrect the bodies of those who have lost their bodies through death, and the saints who are alive at His coming He will change in a moment, in the twinkling of an eye when He returns. Jesus has His mankind body transformed into an immortal mankind body. The saints living at Christ's return will have their mankind bodies changed to immortal bodies. The saints who have lost their bodies through death must have their mankind bodies resurrected so that they can be wholly redeemed mankind— spirit, soul, and body. Jesus and the translated saints have their earth bodies changed to immortal earth bodies, which are called heavenly bodies and glorified bodies. The saints who have lost their bodies must have them resurrected as immortal bodies so that they will be whole mankind beings like Jesus and the living translated saints. In the beginning, God created man as a spirit, soul, and body being. He has destined that at the end and throughout eternity His Church-Bride of Christ will be eternal spirit, soul, and body beings just like Himself. All that Adam lost by sin, Jesus restores to those who are His (1 Cor. 15:35-58).

When the saints receive their bodily redemption, it begins a chain reaction that brings about the redemption of all natural creation on earth (2 Pet. 3:13; Rom. 8:21). The Lord declared to Moses, *"Truly, as I live, all the earth shall be filled with the glory of the Lord"* (Num. 14:21). And the prophet declared, *"For the earth will be filled with the knowledge of the glory of the Lord, as the waters cover the sea"* (Hab. 2:14). The New Testament reveals that Jesus is the glory (expression) of God the Father and the Church is the glory (expression) of Christ Jesus (Heb. 1:1-3). His Church will be the glory that fills the earth with the knowledge of the glory of the Lord. Both planet Earth and the bodies of the saints are to be redeemed.

Revelation 5:10; 11:15, Daniel 7:14,18,22,27: These Scriptures reveal the climax of the Third Reformation—the saints of the Most High God possessing and establishing the Kingdom of God over all the earth until Revelation 11:15 is fulfilled. Then the saintly overcomers who have functioned as kings and priests unto God shall rule and reign with Christ on earth.

Psalm 149:6-9; 1 Corinthians 6:2-3; Revelation 2:26-27: These three Scriptures, plus many others, reveal that the saints of God have the honor and authority to execute the judgments written. Isaiah prophesied that the Church would be His weapon of indignation to destroy the wicked (Isa. 13:4-5). Jeremiah prophesied that the Lord of Hosts declares of His saints, *"You are my battle-ax and weapons of war"* (Jer. 51:20). Enoch's prophecy recorded in Jude 1:14-15 declares the Lord will come again with ten thousands of His saints to execute God's judgments upon all the ungodly. All the prophetic Scriptures that speak of the saints being the army of the Lord and God's instruments for executing His judgments must be fulfilled (Ps. 149:6-9; Rev. 19:11-21). Revelation 19:11-21 describes Jesus leading His great army of saints. We know they are redeemed saints and not angels because it says the warriors are clothed with fine linen, which is the righteousness of the saints (Rev. 19:8,14). Their great leader was King of kings and Lord of lords, and He wore a robe dipped in blood representing how He redeemed those who were with Him.

Ephesians 1:10; Acts 3:21-25: Finally, when all things are restored as spoken by the prophets, then all things will be consummated in Christ Jesus, who is the beginning and the ending of all that He has purposed in Himself:

> [God has] *made known to us the mystery of His will, according to His good pleasure which He purposed in Himself, that in the dispensation of the fullness of the times He might gather together in one all things in Christ, both which are in heaven and which are on earth—in Him. In [Christ] also we have obtained an inheritance, being predestined*

according to the purpose of [God] *who works all things according to the counsel of His will* (Ephesians 1:9-11).

The Third Church Reformation will not cease until all prophetic Scriptures are fulfilled. We know they are not all fulfilled yet, for Acts 3:21 reveals that when the last prophetic Scripture is fulfilled, then Jesus will be released from Heaven to return to receive His Church-Bride to join Him in an eternal reign over all the earth and eternity.

NOTES

1.   Hamon, *Prophets and Personal Prophecy*, 145-159.
2.   Hamon, *The Eternal Church*, 303-354.

Chapter 17

THE THIRD UNVEILING OF THE PRESENT AND END-TIME EVENTS

God does everything in threes. Even the Godhead is three in one. God the Father was Jehovah God of the Old Testament. Jesus the Son was the second to dominate the scene by being the manifest Son of God who was Israel's Messiah and Redeemer of mankind. Jesus then sent the third ministry of the Godhead, the Holy Spirit, to birth His Church and grow it to maturity.

God had Moses build a tabernacle in three areas. An Outer Court, which was the first place man would meet with God; then a second place called the Holy Place; then a third place called the Holy of Holies. Each place revealed more of God and His Presence. The third brings the greatest revelation of God and the fullness of His purpose and presence (Exod. 26:33-34; 25:40).

Zechariah prophesied what God had to say about this third group: *"I will bring the one-third through the fire, will refine them as silver is refined, and test them as gold is tested. They will call on My name, and I will answer them. I will say, 'This is My people'; and each one will say, 'The Lord is my God'"* (Zech. 13:9). Those being prepared to be the Third Reformation participants are going through this testing, refining, and purifying process now. Those who participate and demonstrate must be conformed to the pure gold nature and righteousness of Christ Jesus.

There was first the tabernacle of Moses; second, there was the tabernacle of David; and third is the tabernacle of God with man. The fulfillment and end result of the Third Reformation will be the tabernacle of God with man (Rev. 21:3).

The first 2,000 years of humanity was the fallen human race. The second 2,000 years was the Abrahamic race of God's specially chosen Israeli people. The third 2,000 years is Jesus and His Church race. The third is the one that fulfills the will and purpose of God that has been planned since the foundation of the world (Eph. 3:3-5; 9-11).

The first millennial Church began victorious and glorious but ended in the middle of the Dark Ages. The second millennial Church began in the middle of the Dark Ages and ended in the restoration of the Church. The third millennial Church began with the restoration of the Church and is destined to subdue all things under the feet of Christ Jesus and rule and reign with Him on new earth, where the kingdoms of this world have become the kingdoms of the Lord Jesus and His Church (Rev. 11:15).

BLESSINGS AND POWER OF THE THIRD

God is bringing forth the blessings of the "third." God's third purpose will be fulfilled during the Third Reformation, establishing the third tabernacle of God. He is bringing forth Gideon's third group, the mighty 300 warriors. The first group was the 22,000 who went home from the battle; the second was the 9,700 who were rejected at the river; the third group was the 300 mighty warriors who came to the third level of overcoming. The first level is overcoming by the blood of the Lamb, the second is overcoming by the word of one's testimony, and the third overcoming is by loving not one's lives unto death (Rev. 12:11). This is a generation who has died completely to self (Rev. 6:11). They are dead to everything except Christ, and they live with their life hid with Christ in God (Col. 3:1-3). The Third Reformation saints will be the most radically committed and dedicated to God ever to live. Fearlessly bold, they will be the most Jesus-loving, God-fearing, and devil-hating saints who have ever lived on earth—overcoming and subduing all things under the dominion of God's Kingdom. Their passion will be for God's Kingdom to come and His will to be done on earth as it is in Heaven.

A LAST DAYS GENERATION WITH CALEB AND JOSHUA FAITH

God delivered the Israelis out of Egypt with ten miraculous acts. He promised them that He was taking them to a land flowing with milk and honey. They would have their own land and nation with the right to govern themselves. As we revealed in previous chapters, God told His people that they were not going to an uninhabited land, for there were seven nations occupying their promised land. God said these nations were greater and mightier than Israel, but that He would be the equalizer by fighting for them against their opposition.

The people wanted Moses to send Israeli spies in to check out the land to see what it was like. Moses commissioned a leader from each of the 12 tribes to go spy out the land (Num. 13:1-2). Joshua was of the tribe of Ephraim and Caleb was of the tribe of Judah. The twelve spied out the land for 40 days and came back with their report and samples of the fruit of the land.

WE ARE "WELL ABLE" REFORMERS

Ten of the spies gave a negative presentation, which God called an evil report (Num. 13:27-29). But Joshua and Caleb gave a positive and victorious report. Joshua and Caleb saw the giants, the walled cities, and well-equipped fierce warriors just as the others did. The ten conveyed to the Israelis that it was impossible to overcome and possess the land against such formidable occupants of the land. Nevertheless, Joshua and Caleb said, *"Let us go up at once and take possession, for we are well able to overcome it"* (Num. 13:30). The ten spies rose up and said, *"We are not able to go up against the people, for they are stronger than we"* (Num. 13:31). This was no new revelation, for God had already told them that the nations of their promised land were stronger than they, but God was going to make up the difference by fighting for them.

The same situation faces the Third Reformation Church. The challenge for the Church to demonstrate the Kingdom of God and bring transformation to the nations of this world is no greater than Israel's challenge to take possession of the nations of Canaan and make them the nation of Israel. Both are impossible in the natural. Both require the supernatural help of God and His holy war angels. Both require that God personally fight for us. A prophetic Scripture gives us this assurance, *"Then the Lord will go forth and fight against those nations, as He fights in the day of battle"* (Zech. 14:3).

This story of God challenging Israel to do the impossible was written not just to give an historical account for Israel. The happenings were written to give an example of what we, who are now living at the end of the ages, would be challenged with: *"Now all these things happened to them as examples, and they were written for our admonition, upon whom the ends of the ages have come"* (1 Cor. 10:11). *"For whatever things were written before were written for our learning, that we through the patience and comfort of the Scriptures might have hope*" (Rom. 15:4). Based on this scriptural example, we can expect for every two ministers saying we can bring transformation to the nations, there will be ten saying it cannot be done. There are usually only a few major leaders who pioneer the new; then the multitudes follow after the reformers have prepared the way.

WHAT IS GOD SAYING TODAY?

God is saying to us today, "I had the Children of Israel go through that experience so that you can learn from their mistakes and successes. You will succeed by taking the Joshua and Caleb attitude." From these Scriptures, we can gain hope and confidence that the Church can fully demonstrate the Kingdom and bring transformation to the nations. The "last days" started with the first coming of Christ to the earth and the first-century Church (Heb. 1:2). Now the twenty-first century Church and Third Reformation people are the ones to whom "the ends of the ages have come." Mankind started out in the Garden of Eden eating of the tree of life with the potential to live forever. But man sinned, and mortality began in mankind. There was a time when mortality began in man, and there will be a time when mortality will end. When the time for the end of the age of mortal man comes, all will be resurrected and become immortal beings to spend eternity with the devil or with Jesus Christ. The Third Reformation is to progress the Church and mankind to the end of the time of mortal man.

CONCLUDING ENCOURAGEMENT AND EXHORTATION

I will conclude this by encouraging everyone who reads this book to take the Caleb attitude that we are well able to fulfill everything God has prophetically promised and challenged us to do. I am taking the attitude that Caleb expressed when he came to his promised land. He reminded Joshua that Moses had promised that the land that he had spied out would be his promised-land inheritance. He declared, "Give me my mountain." He acknowledged that the biggest giants and in fact the head of all the giants headquartered in his territory. But he still had the overcomers' attitude. He declared, "Though I am now 85 years old, I am still as strong a warrior as I was at 40 years of age when Moses gave me this promise" (Josh. 14:6-15).

REFORMERS LIKE JOSHUA AND CALEB

God is bringing forth some Joshua and Caleb senior leaders who have the revelation, faith, vision, and commitment to pioneer and fulfill our part in fulfilling God's purpose for the Third and Final Church Reformation. Personally, I am taking the attitude of Caleb. I turned 85 July 29th, 2019 so I am one year older than Caleb was when he came to his inheritance and made his declaration, "give me my mountain." I have received prophecies from major prophets that I would be like Caleb, and as my days were, so would my strength be. And like David, who wanted to build the temple, I want to build the Third Reformation. However, if it extends beyond my years, then I will be like David, who received the blueprint-architectural drawing for the temple and provided most of the resources needed in building the temple. I want to provide the revelation, wisdom, and ministries for fulfilling God's purpose for the Third Reformation, just as David prepared the things necessary for the Solomon generation to fulfill the commission of building God's temple in Jerusalem. Jesus has been building His Church for almost 2,000 years in order for a matured Church to demonstrate and build His kingdom on Earth for His 1,000-year millennial reign on Earth.

THE PURPOSE OF THIS BOOK!

This book is mainly the blueprint or revelation that there is a Third Reformation that has been activated to fulfill God's third purpose through, in, and with His Church. I am trusting that I will receive further revelation for the strategy and how to empower the Church to fulfill this commission, which will be written in book form for the generations. Other apostles and prophets are writing books covering it from other areas. Together with Christ leading, revealing, and imparting, we will fulfill God's third purpose for His Church. To me, it is not relevant how long it will take or how much of the work we will do as mortal saints or how much as immortal saints. I am a joint heir with Christ and will forever be a co-laborer with Jesus while mortal and immortal, whether in this mortal body or out of this body as a spirit being in Heaven; none of these things change my relationship with Jesus Christ or my continuous, eternal ministry with Him (Rom. 8:17, 35-39).

THE NEW JOSHUA GENERATION

For you who are the younger generation—you have been and are being prepared to be Kingdom demonstrators with the commission to bring transformation to the seven-mountain kingdoms of this world until God's prophetic decree in Revelation 11:15 is fulfilled. Be encouraged and assured that God is raising up a new Joshua generation who is willing and ready to demonstrate the Kingdom of God, bringing transformation to the nations until every nation is established either as a goat nation or a sheep nation (Matt. 25:31-33).

This earth belongs to God and everything on it (Ps. 24:1; 1 Cor. 10:26-28). God so loved the world that He gave His only begotten Son that every human being who would accept Jesus could be saved and restored, and planet Earth was also included in that redemptive process

(Rom. 8:19-23; Rev. 5:10). Let us all develop the faith and passion to fulfill the prayer that Jesus told us to pray (Matt. 6:9-11; Luke 1:38):

Thy kingdom come, and Thy will be done on earth as it is in Heaven! And so be it unto me according to Your Word. Yes, Lord, Amen!

2/5/22

BIBLIOGRAPHY

A few of the books that are declaring the new era of Christianity in the Third and Final Reformation.

- Rebecca ("Becca") Greenwood, *Destined to Rule* (Chosen Books, 2007)
- Ed Silvoso, *Transformation* (Regal Books, 2007)
- C. Peter Wagner, *Dominion!* (Chosen Books, 2008)
- Sunday Adelaja, *Churchshift* (Creation House, 2008)
- Johnny Enlow, *The Seven Mountain Prophecy* (Creation House, 2008)
- Cindy Jacobs, *The Reformation Manifesto* (Bethany House, 2009)
- Joe Mattera, *Kingdom Revolution* (Destiny Image, 2009)

Books by the Hamon Family

DR. BILL HAMON

The Eternal Church

Prophets and Personal Prophecy

The Prophetic and the Movement

Prophets: Principles to Practice Pitfalls to Avoid

Apostles, Prophets and the Coming Moves of God

Day of the Saints

Who Am I & Why Am I Here?

70 Reasons for Speaking in Tongues

Prophetic Scriptures Yet to Be Fulfilled

How Can These Things Be?

God's Weapons of War

Your Highest Calling

The Third and Final Reformation

Fulfilling Your Personal Prophecy

Birthing God's Purpose

Prophetic Destiny and Apostolic Movement

DR. EVELYN HAMON

The Spiritual Seasons of Life

Divine Flexibility

God's Tests Are Positive

DR. JANE HAMON

Dreams and Visions

The Debra Company

The Cyrus Decree

Discernment

Declarations for Breakthrough

DR. TIM HAMON

Upon This Rock

DR. TOM HAMON

The 7 Anointings for Kingdom Transformation

The Apostolic Mantle

SHERILYN HAMON-MILLER

Stewarding Your Best Life

TO ORDER THESE OR OTHER PRODUCTS:

Online Orders: www.Christianinternational.com

Or write:

Christian International Ministries Network

P.O. Box 9000

Santa Rosa Beach, FL 32459

Call: 850-231-2600 or 1-800-388-5308

Fax: 1-877-310-2763

Email: Products@bishophamon.org

BOOKS COVERING RESTORATION MOVEMENTS

by

Dr. Bill Hamon

The Eternal Church: Covers the birthing of the Church, 1,000-year Dark Age, the 500-year Restoration of Church from Protestant to Charismatic and destiny of the Church. The most complete book on Church restoration in existence.

The Prophetic/Apostolic Movement

Prophets and Personal Prophecy

Prophets and the Prophetic Movement

Prophets: Principles to Practice and Pitfalls to Avoid

Apostles and Prophets and the Coming Move of God

Fulfilling Your Personal Prophecies

The Saints Movement

The Day of the Saints

The Army of the Lord Movement

God's Weapons of War (For God's WWIII)

The Third and Final Reformation

The Final Reformation and Great Awakening

Books Covering God's Purposes for Mankind, Church, and Individuals

Birthing God's Purposes

Who Am I and Why Am I Here?

70 Reasons for Speaking in Tongues

How Can These Things Be?

Your Highest Calling

ABOUT BILL HAMON

Dr. Bill Hamon is the founder of Christian International Ministries. A prophet for over 60 years, he has prophesied to more than 75,000 people and provided training for over 500,000 in prophetic ministry. He has authored seven major books, specializing in the restoration of the Church and what to expect next on God's agenda.

Dr. Bill Hamon is respected by church leaders around the world as the senior leader of the prophetic/apostolic company God is raising up in these last days. Dr. Hamon was recently featured by Charisma Magazine as one of the 40 people who radically changed the Church.

He serves as bishop to over 900 ministers and churches in the United States as well as over 3,000 ministries overseas via Christian International's headquarters around the world. Dr. Hamon resides in Santa Rosa Beach, Florida. He has three children, eleven grandchildren and twenty great-grandchildren.

Connect with Christian International

APOSTOLIC NETWORK CI Apostolic Network is a network of over 900 ministers and churches in the US and over 3000 around the world in our Global Network, with ministries on every continent. CIAN provides relationships to ministers and churches as they grow in hearing God's voice and impacting their world.

PROPHETIC TRAINING CI provides intensified prophetic training in person & on-line through seminars, e-courses, and our many local churches and schools. CI has trained over 500,000 in hearing God's voice with our prophetic training courses during the last 40 years.

ADDITIONAL NETWORKS CI also has an Equipping Network of schools and training centers around the world; a Culture Influencers network of believers bringing transformation to their workplace; a Spanish network producing CI resources & relationships for Spanish speakers in the American community, and more. CI is a network of networks, resourcing believers to bring the voice of God to every sphere of society.

INTERNATIONAL GATHERING OF APOSTLES & PROPHETS (IGAP) IGAP is the first prophetic global gathering that began in 1985. Every October IGAP brings together prophetic and apostolic people from all over the world to be equipped and find community. We've had people from as many as 33 nations join us at one time in this gathering!

ANNUAL WORD OF THE LORD CI releases a prophetic word for the coming season each year from CI ministers and beyond, in a variety of outlets including events, print publications, digital audio and reader downloads, social media and more.

CALL OR VISIT US ON-LINE FOR MORE INFO

800-388-5308 | christianinternational.com

5200 HWY 98 E, Unit CI, Santa Rosa Beach, FL 32459

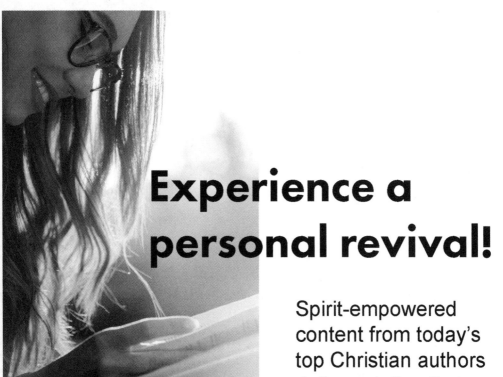